GLORIA

by

Emmaline Severn

© Emmaline Severn 2021
Lost Voices Publishing

ISBN 978-1-7385568-2-3

Front Cover Illustration © Steve Wells 2021

I dedicate this story to Alan, my dear departed friend and mentor, without whom this would never have been possible. I miss you and thank you for all the fun we had and for everything you taught me xxx

CHAPTER 1

It was a bitterly cold, early January afternoon in the year of 1903. Snow lay on the steps outside the Durham Register Office, where eighteen-year-old Gloria Armstrong held on to the arm of her fiancé. He had purchased their marriage licence the day before, but it was certainly not the wedding Gloria had always dreamt of as no one from either side of their families were present. She was pregnant.

Gerald was in the final year of his medical degree when Gloria realised her condition, and it seemed the only solution for them to marry quietly without causing too much of a scandal. Being the gentleman he had been brought up to be, Gerald knew he would have to do the honourable thing, despite his misgivings and the disappointment it would cause his father when he learned of his irresponsibility. He could hear his words.

'How could you jeopardise your career in this way? All you had to do was study well and return to London, start your career and then marry.'

In turn, Gloria imagined her mother chastising her for how reckless she had been.

'The scandal if people were to find out! Ever since your sister married Filkes, you have been determined to find a doctor of your own, whatever the cost. Well, my dear, you will pay a high price for this, mark my words. A hasty marriage never has the foundation

required to build a strong relationship. One way or another, it will flounder!'

As for what her domineering father would say, Gloria dreaded the thought…..

The fiery relationship Gloria endured with her father frequently led to arguments, however, with a flick of her head and a flash of her exquisite emerald green eyes, more often than not, she won the better side of him. A few months before Fleur's wedding, a Christmas trip to London was arranged, and Gloria was beside herself with excitement, as an evening at the theatre had been planned. She loved the theatre and frequented the local one in her hometown as often as possible, despite her father's disapproval. He considered it frivolous and thought the actresses were of dubious reputation. Somehow though, Gloria always managed to manipulate him into letting her see the latest production when it opened, she would either pout and sulk or smile and plead with him relentlessly until he surrendered. Much the same scene played out before the family travelled to London when Gloria had pleaded with him to let her go to the Gaiety Theatre to see a new musical play, *The Toreador.*

'Musicals are the worst scourge of all as far as the theatre is concerned,' James said sternly, 'how ridiculous, everyone bursting into song at the drop of a hat and dancing around, I do not know where you get it from, it is certainly not from your mother.'

In his head he thought to himself, 'Why I spend a small fortune on that girl's deportment class I do not know, a good wife she is never going to be.'

Eventually, the drama quietened down in the Armstrong household, and James decided that Frances's sister would be invited to chaperone his two daughters and attempt to keep the beautiful and headstrong Gloria under control.

That is how it came to pass that Gloria and Fleur were seated with Aunt Esther in the grand tier of The Gaiety, impatiently waiting for the curtain to go up, well at least the sisters were, Aunt Esther had a similar opinion of musicals as her brother-in-law.

The conductor tapped his baton on the podium, and the orchestra gradually quietened from those dissonant minutes when the musicians warmed up. There was a short silence before the strains of the overture began, and the enormous red and gold curtain went up.

Gloria was immediately entranced by the songs, the lights, the costumes, everything about the show was magical to her, and she longed to be on the stage with them. However, she knew Papa would have a fit of apoplexy if the idea of her becoming an actress were even mentioned.

The first act was over far too soon for Gloria, making it time for them to venture their way through the bustle of people to the refreshment area for a lemonade. Everyone was talking excitedly about how much they were enjoying the show.

'Gertie Millar is so marvellous,' Gloria gushed to her sister, at which Aunt Esther made a sort of "humph" sound with a scornful look on her face. 'Aunt, you are just like Papa, you must learn to have fun.'

'Life is not all about fun, dearie, especially if you cannot find a suitable husband to support you,' Esther replied.

'Well, I intend to find myself a most suitable husband as soon as possible and preferably a doctor as Fleur has done,' Gloria said. 'Anyway, I need to visit the powder room.' She flicked her head, turned and walked down the corridor towards the ladies' room.

'That girl, she is quite a handful, I cannot imagine any man having a desire to marry her unless she gains some self-discipline,' Esther declared.

'Worry not, Aunt, she is still young, I am sure she will settle down soon.'

Aunt Esther made the same "humph" sound and changed the subject of conversation to how well the last Temperance Society meeting had been attended, just before they travelled to London.

Meanwhile, Gloria had powdered her nose and re-applied some rouge to her lips, looked at herself in the mirror and imagined she was "making up" ready for the next scene of the musical she was starring in. Humming a song quietly to herself with her mind elsewhere, she walked out of the powder room, and just at that moment, collided with someone in the walkway.

'I say, please forgive me, Miss, how utterly clumsy of me.' A well-mannered and extraordinarily handsome young man of about twenty-one years of age spoke with concern as Gloria regained her composure and checked that her dress was not crumpled or damaged. When she looked up, her eyes met his, and she noticed they were two different colours, one dark brown the other green, with specks of amber. Then she saw his beautiful face, Gloria felt colour flush in her cheeks as the gentleman before her apologised once more and led her to a chair in order that she could sit for a moment and recover from the unfortunate incident.

'Are you unharmed?' the young man asked.

'Quite well, sir, thank you, just a little flustered.'

'May I introduce myself, Gerald Phelps, at your service. To whom do I have the pleasure?

'Miss Gloria Armstrong,' she said and held out her arm for him to help her up from the chair. He gently took her gloved hand as she rose, and they stood face to face, never had she seen anyone so handsome, it was one of those fated moments in time, and Gloria's heart was beating fast.

'I feel it my duty to return you safely to your friends. With whom have you attended the theatre this evening?'

'I, I am here with my sister and aunt,' Gloria answered with a slight stutter, thinking to herself that Aunt Esther would not be too impressed when she saw her returning on the arm of a man. On the other hand, Gloria did not want to lose the company of this debonair stranger before having the opportunity of learning more about him. Therefore, she took his arm and steered him back towards the refreshment room where Fleur and Esther were just beginning to wonder where Gloria had disappeared to.

Aunt Esther spotted her first. 'In heaven's name, who is that with Gloria?' she exclaimed. 'Look at her, she cannot be trusted for a moment, what does she think she is doing walking arm in arm with a strange man.'

'He is a fine-looking stranger though, is he not?'

'Good grief, Fleur! You are as bad as your sister, and you are spoken for, what is it with young ladies these days? Your mother and I were not allowed out alone, even when we were betrothed.'

Gloria had witnessed the expression on her aunt's face from a distance and could imagine what she had said.

'I am indeed in trouble now,' Gloria told Gerald, 'we have been spied by my aunt.'

At this, he speeded up their pace a little, and with a dashing smile, greeted Aunt Esther, saying, 'May I return Miss Armstrong to you in good health, it was entirely my fault that we had a small collision outside the ladies' room a few minutes ago. I assure you she is undamaged and quite well. Gerald Phelps is the name madam, and I apologise for causing your niece any distress.'

He gave a small bow to Aunt Esther, who for once was momentarily speechless. Suddenly, the bell rang to announce that Act II was about to begin, which gave Aunt Esther very little chance to challenge the young man before her in regard to man-handling her niece.

'May I escort you ladies back to your seats. Whereabouts are you?' Gerald enquired.

'We are on the front row of the grand tier,' Gloria said quickly before her aunt could say anything, she did not want the last few minutes of her life to end quite so abruptly and wished to delay his departure for as long as possible, therefore, she clung on to his arm.

Aunt Esther had no choice than to allow Gerald to accompany them back to their seats, it would be rude and improper, after all, the young man had done the gentlemanly thing and returned Gloria safely.

'May I ask where you are seated, Mr Phelps?' Gloria asked.

'I am in the box over there,' he gestured to his left, 'with two of my university chums, we are studying medicine at Durham.'

His words made Gloria's insides flutter, and her immediate thought was, 'He is going to be a doctor. This must be fate, but how am I ever to see him again?'

The first number of Act II passed by with Gloria hardly hearing any of it, she was too busy glancing over towards the box where Gerald was sitting with his friends, he was by far the most handsome of the trio. She turned her head slightly once more to discover that Gerald was looking intently at her, she blushed as he smiled and then felt an elbow dig into her arm. It was Aunt Esther.

'Stop making a fool of yourself, Gloria, giving that young man the eye, it is not appropriate.' Hissing the words into Gloria's ear and making her wince.

Gloria turned her attention towards the stage again, Harry Grattan had begun to sing, and once more, she found herself engrossed in the musical. Occasionally, she took a peek at Gerald, he was talking with his friends and enjoying the performance, and their eyes did not meet again until the finale. The show ended to rapturous applause, and as they gazed at each other, Gloria willed him to engineer a chance meeting as they left the theatre, but the throng of people made it nigh on impossible to alter one's course, especially as Aunt Esther seemed resolute on keeping their exit path directly towards the front doors where the hansom cabs would be waiting for fares.

It was not to be, Gloria felt as if she were being pulled away from something that was meant to happen in her life. Aunt Esther was hurrying her into the cab, and Gloria searched frantically for Gerald amongst the crowds. 'Where are you, where are you?' but alas, he was nowhere to be seen. She sat down heavily in the seat of the cab and felt her heart sink, wondering if she would ever see him again. He was the first man she had ever encountered that had aroused such emotions inside her, and at that moment, as the horse's hooves clip-clopped across the cobbled streets carrying her away from the theatre, she felt exceedingly downhearted.

The cab drew up outside the Hotel Cecil, where the Prudential dinner was in full swing. Gloria and Fleur were sharing a large room with Aunt Esther next door. Although the evening was not yet late, Gloria was in a melancholy mood, and feigning a headache retired to bed. Aunt Esther and Fleur decided to take a light supper in the hotel lounge before turning in.

'I do hope Gloria is not pining for that young man,' Aunt Esther said derisively, 'he seemed far too familiar if you ask me.'

'Times are changing, Aunt, we need to stand up for ourselves and become women in our own right, not the appendage of some man who owns us. It does not mean we cannot marry and have families, but we do need respect,' Fleur replied.

She was a member of the suffrage group at home and felt very strongly on these matters, and even though her mother had more or less thrown her and Filkes together, she had grown to love him and was very much looking forward to their wedding in April.

'I admit Gloria is wilful, but Mr Phelps was a gentleman and behaved as such, and I feel a little sorry for her in that she did not see him again after the show had finished, it would not have done any harm.'

'Well, let us hope she does not pine for days, swooning around the house like those actresses she is so fond of.'

Fleur sighed. 'Aunt Esther, can we go to bed? I am tired, and I would like to be sure that my sister is well.'

With that, the two women walked to the hotel lobby and took the lift to their rooms. They found Gloria in one of the luxurious beds, she had cried herself to sleep, not able to understand the strength of her emotions for a man she had barely met and cursing Aunt Esther for practically dragging her away from the theatre. When she awoke the next morning, she felt exceedingly morose.

Gloria remained very quiet on the train journey home, her mother repeatedly asked if she was feeling unwell, and each time her reply was, 'No, Mama, I am fine. Just a headache.'

Fortunately, Aunt Esther was catching a different train, so there had been no opportunity to reveal any of the events at the theatre.

The family returned to Cambridgeshire, and over the coming weeks, all focus was on preparations for Fleur's wedding. The sisters had spoken briefly about the evening at the theatre, Gloria admitted that she was confused as to why she felt so upset at not seeing Gerald again, and her wiser older sister tried her utmost to cheer her up, even suggesting that fate might intervene and perhaps they would meet again.

'What we really needed at times like this would have been Grandmama Huxley to read your tea-leaves,' Fleur said, and they both laughed. As young girls, they had spent hours listening to their grandmama's stories, she read palms and the tea leaves of anyone who took tea with her, and it was even said she was a medium. Lizzie Huxley lived to the grand old age of ninety-three, and both had loved her dearly.

Since Filkes now worked at the Children's Hospital in London, the wedding was to be held in Kensington, as Fleur and Filkes were to live there once they were married. With all the excitement of the wedding, Gloria's mood soon lightened, and she returned to her usual self.

There had been a further announcement in the Armstrong household earlier in the year, one that pleased Gloria immensely. Her father had been promoted to chief insurance manager which required the family to take a flat in London, and it meant that Gloria would be close to her sister after the wedding, it was terribly exciting. She had loved London when she visited at Christmas, it bustled with energy, and there was so much to see and do, far more exciting than the dull countryside of Cambridgeshire. Gloria was beside herself when Papa had broken the news and immediately pored over a map of London to find the best area to live.

'Do not even think of looking anywhere near where Fleur will be living, Gloria, I may be the area manager now, but Kensington is quite off-limits,' her father warned.

'Papa, you are always such a spoilsport, why can we not live near Fleur, it is so unfair.'

This conversation had ignited yet another sparring match between father and daughter, which ended in Gloria performing one of her most superior head flicks, almost setting her off balance as she flounced up the stairs to her room. Eventually, James decided upon the Fitzrovia district, affordable and well within walking distance from Draycott Place where Fleur and Filkes were to live. Thus, Gloria was pacified once more.

CHAPTER 2

The Allen-Armstrong wedding was quite the society event, with the guest list being made up of a significant number of doctors from the various London hospitals. Gloria had attended her sister as bridesmaid and looked almost as becoming as the bride on the day in her gown of pale blue satin and lace.

The room was crowded with dancing guests, Gloria was extremely popular, she barely had the opportunity to sit down, and as she polkaed around the room with a perspiring and rather portly surgeon, her eyes fixed upon a face that made her heart stop. 'It cannot be, after all these weeks, it is not possible.'

As she twirled, she saw him again, he was watching her, and this time Gloria was convinced that the man she had seen was Gerald. He seemed to be scouring the room looking for someone, then on the next spin of the polka, Gloria looked once more, but he was gone. 'No, no....' Her heart was racing, fate had played its hand, she could not, would not lose sight of this man again.

At last, her dance with the portly surgeon, Gloria could not remember his name, came to an end. Then, and as far as etiquette would allow, she made her way towards her newly married sister, who was glowing amidst the attention of just about every man not already engaged on the dance floor. Gloria desperately wanted to speak to Fleur to ask if she had seen Gerald amongst the guests. She hovered in the background waiting for Fleur to excuse herself from the group of gentlemen around her. Finally, Fleur spotted Gloria trying her utmost not to look too excited but not being entirely successful.

'Excuse me, gentlemen, but I think my sister requires my attention,' she announced and walked over to Gloria.

'Fleur, Fleur,' she gasped. 'I have seen him, he is here.'

Her sister looked quizzingly at her. 'Who, where?'

'That is just it, I do not know where he has gone, he was over there while I was dancing, I spotted him, and then he disappeared. Please, Fleur, you must ask Filkes, he knows everyone.'

She looked at her younger sister, they were very close, and she was quite aware of Gloria's romantic notions, though she had never seen her quite like this before. Who could possibly have stirred her up into such a frenzy?

'Who are you talking about, for heaven's sake?' she asked.

'Gerald Phelps, you know, the man from the theatre last Christmas, the one I collided with, you must remember, he is the most handsome man you have ever seen.' Gloria was flushed and breathless.

'Yes, of course, I remember, Aunt Esther nearly had a fit when she saw you with him. Look, Filkes is over there, we will mention his name and see what he has to say.'

It took the sisters at least five minutes to glide their way around the outside of the dance floor, smiling at the wedding guests as they congratulated Fleur on her marriage. Finally, they reached Filkes, who was engaged in conversation with a gentleman who had his back towards them, but as soon as he saw his beautiful young bride, Filkes stopped talking and took his wife's hand.

'Darling, I would like to introduce you to Gerald Phelps, he is Marcus's son home from Durham for the Easter holidays, here to gather some valuable experience at the hospital.'

The gentleman in question turned around, and Gloria gasped under her breath, it was him. Her heart was pounding, and at that same moment, Gerald immediately recognised Gloria as the enticing young lady he had searched for in vain when the curtain had gone down after *The Toreador* finished that night.

Fleur spoke. 'I am pleased to make your acquaintance once more, Mr Phelps. You have already met my sister, Miss Gloria Armstrong.'

Filkes looked slightly bemused that his wife and sister-in-law knew Gerald, whilst Fleur looked at her sister, whose beautiful emerald green eyes were wide and sparkling.

'Enchanted, Miss Armstrong.'

Gloria could barely hear Gerald's voice above the frantic beating of her heart, but she stammered a reply and held out her white-gloved hand, which he pressed to his lips.

The orchestra struck up a Viennese Waltz, and Gerald politely asked Gloria if she would care to dance. He led her to the floor and grasped her waist, pulling her towards him, perhaps just a little too closely. As he circled her round and round, Gloria felt as though they were the only two in the room. As they danced, she looked into his bewitching eyes, beyond this, everything and everyone else was a blur, and she believed herself at this moment in time to be the luckiest girl in the world.

They danced together for the next two dances, but when the music stopped, just as Gloria was catching her breath from emotion and the exertion of dancing, Gerald pressed his lips to her hand once more. 'Please, forgive me, Miss Armstrong, but I must return to the hospital.'

Gloria stopped in her tracks. 'But you have only just arrived, must you leave so soon?'

'Unfortunately, I am not actually on the guest list, I was sent from the hospital to seek out Dr Allen as he only could provide some information required for one of the patients. I really must return immediately.'

Gloria was desperate, young ladies were not supposed to chase after men, but she could not, would not lose Gerald a second time and blurted out, 'We are staying at The Regal Hotel, perhaps you could call on us in the morning?'

'I believe I will, Miss Armstrong, but now I must bid you adieu.'

He returned her to Fleur, who was just finishing explaining to her new husband how they first became acquainted with Gerald. He spoke briefly to Filkes and then excused himself, he looked at Gloria affectionately as he turned and left the room. She watched him walk away and felt exceedingly dizzy, Fleur caught the expression on her sister's face, swiftly took her arm and led her to the ladies' room.

'Darling, you looked like you were about to faint, what did Mr Phelps say to you?'

Gloria's eyes were brimming with tears. 'Nothing to upset me, quite the contrary, he promised he would call on me tomorrow at the hotel, I just did not want him to leave so soon. It must be fate, please say you agree, I feel as if we are destined to be together.'

'Dear, darling, Gloria, you are such a romantic, maybe you are destined, but we do not know the man, Filkes has never mentioned him before, only his father, Marcus, and Papa will not be best pleased that you told him where you are staying.' To this, Gloria replied by saying that perhaps it would be best he did not know.

Eventually, as the wedding reception came to a close, Gloria had composed herself enough to face her parents, enough guests were present to mingle with for her not to have seen them throughout almost the entire evening. Fleur had changed into a most becoming dove grey wool travelling dress and coat embellished with black tassels and velvet appliqués, it suited her perfectly. James had arranged for one of those new-fangled motor cars to take them to the train station, Fleur was very excited to be carried in such style, and as the motor car set off with a back-fire, she held on to her hat as the happy couple waved to their family and friends.

Gloria slept fitfully that night, her mother and father were in the adjoining room knowing nothing of the evening's events, and when she finally awoke, she had tossed and turned so much the quilted eiderdown on her bed had fallen to the floor, and despite the coolness of the room, Gloria felt quite feverish. In her head, she was imploring Gerald to come to the hotel that morning, but also dreading what Mama and Papa would say if he did.

By now, it was ten o'clock, and Gloria could hear her mother and father stirring next door, she hastened to tidy her hair and make herself presentable after her restless night. Fleur and Filkes would be on their way to the French Riviera for their honeymoon by now, having caught the late-night train to Dover in time to board the morning ferry to Calais, leaving Gloria, James and Frances to return to their new flat on Gosfield Street.

Just as Gloria's head was filling once more with thoughts of Gerald Phelps, her mother tapped on the connecting door of their room and asked if she was ready for breakfast.

'Yes, Mama, I am almost ready, give me a moment.' She looked at the girl in the mirror, saw the dark circles under her eyes and wondered what the morning would bring.

They made their way downstairs to the hotel reception. James walked over to the mahogany desk and asked the clerk if there were any messages for him. He was handed a note which he read and promptly returned to his wife and daughter, who were waiting impatiently.

'I am afraid I have been summoned to the office post-haste, the price of promotion, unfortunately. You ladies have breakfast as planned, I will just have to go hungry this morning, I may be home for tea,' James said with disappointment in his voice. The family had planned to do some sight-seeing around London that day and for James to return to work the next.

'What a shame, dear, we had such a lovely day planned,' Frances replied.

'Nonetheless, I am quite sure you two will have a splendid time without me. Now hurry along and enjoy your breakfast, and this evening you can tell me all about the day's adventures.' James kissed his wife and daughter, and hurriedly left the hotel to hail a cab.

'Never mind, Mama, at least we can go shopping without Papa complaining about how much money we are spending,' Gloria teased.

'Daughter dear, you are incorrigible,' Frances scolded with a smile.

The breakfast room at the Regal Hotel was sunny and bright, decorated with a fresh floral wallpaper of lilac and wisteria. The two ladies were shown to a table by the window with a view of the courtyard garden.

'I suppose Fleur and Filkes will be on the boat already, I am so happy for her but a little jealous also,' Gloria said to her mother. 'Maybe one day some rich and handsome doctor will sweep me off my feet and -'

Frances interrupted. 'Now, Gloria, what have I told you about that sort of nonsense? Those sorts of things only happen in novels, and Filkes hardly swept Fleur off her feet. He asked for her hand twice before she accepted him, and that was only after I persuaded her that eligible bachelors of his standing in society do not come along very often, and she would be a fool not to marry him, love grows, I told her.'

Breakfast arrived at the table, and both tucked into bacon and fried potatoes served with hot rolls and buttered eggs, tea was poured from a silver-plated teapot, and no more was said on the subject of love and marriage.

An hour later, Gloria and Frances were waiting in the lobby for a hansom cab to take them to Madame Tussauds. They sat in a pair of wing chairs upholstered in cream damask, facing the staircase that led directly to the reception desk where the clerk was busy with a guest. Gloria was chattering about how different life would be at home without her sister for company when she suddenly stopped mid-sentence, the colour draining from her face.

'What on earth is the matter?' Frances asked, 'you look like you have just seen a ghost.'

With that, a man strode towards them, bowed and said, 'We meet again, Miss Armstrong, how are you this fine morning?'

Then speaking directly to Frances. 'Mrs Armstrong, may I introduce myself? My name is Gerald Phelps, and I am very pleased to make your acquaintance.'

Frances raised an eyebrow and looked into his unusual eyes. 'Good morning, sir, may I ask how you are acquainted with my daughter?'

'Ah, it would seem that Miss Armstrong did not inform you of our dances together last night, it was a most enchanting experience.'

Frances was curious, this man was indeed a charmer, and Gloria would usually tell her everything. Why had she conveniently failed to mention dancing with this incredibly good-looking man, and moreover, how had Frances missed it?

Before she could utter another word, Gerald said, 'I can see that you are about to depart, but may I beg that you postpone your journey and take coffee with me in the lounge, I promised Miss Armstrong I would call on her this morning, and I can see that I was very nearly too late.'

Gloria was in an absolute turmoil, she looked at her mother, trying to gauge her feelings, and her mother returned the look to her daughter with the same intent.

It felt like time had stopped until Gloria heard her mother reply, 'Well, Mr Phelps, our engagements today have already been altered once, I am sure we can accommodate another, we would be delighted to accept your invitation.'

Frances gave Gloria a look as if to say she would find out herself about this young man if her daughter were not going to tell her, and she politely took Gerald's outstretched arm as he escorted the ladies to the lounge.

Gloria's mind was racing, what had she done? She had been foolhardy for certain, what was her mother going to say? What was Gerald going to say? She wished that the ground would open up and swallow her to save her from hearing any of the conversations that were about to take place.

'So, Mr Phelps, I do not recall your name on the guestlist at Fleur's wedding, so how was it that you came to dance with my youngest daughter?' Frances questioned Gerald.

Glancing over at Gloria with a mischievous look in his eye, he said, 'Perhaps Miss Armstrong did not remember the moment so well, it must have slipped her mind for her not to tell you.'

'Mama, it was only one or two dances, and I danced with a lot of gentlemen yesterday,' Gloria replied, trying her best to stay calm. Inside, she was melting, Gerald's eyes were fixed on hers, and she wished so much that her mother was elsewhere.

In a daze, she heard Gerald explain that he had been at the hospital that afternoon, and the physician on duty required some advice regarding a patient, and even though he was aware it was Filkes's wedding day, he was the only doctor who could supply the information required. He had come to the reception to speak to him, only to be captivated by a young lady doing a fine job of a polka with a not so nimble partner. He only had time to dance for a short while before having to return to the patient for whom he required Filkes's advice. Gerald went on to inform Frances of his studies at Durham University and his ambition of becoming a consultant like his father. Before long, Frances was quite captivated by this handsome, intelligent and charming young man.

Gloria had hardly said a word during the conversation, she sipped her coffee in awe of the man talking to her mother, desperately hoping he would not disappear again without wishing to see her once more. Holding this thought in her head, it was suddenly broken by the sound of her mother's voice.

'Gloria, Gloria, what is the matter with you? Mr Phelps is asking us a question.'

Startled, she flushed and apologised, Gerald repeated his request, Gloria then could not believe the words she was hearing.

'Miss Armstrong, I have tickets for the Saturday evening performance of *Merrie England* at the Savoy, I hear it is particularly amusing, would you care to join me, with your mother as chaperone, of course?'

She glanced at her mother, who nodded her head slightly, showing her approval, therefore, with a racing heart, Gloria replied, 'Thank you, Mr Phelps, I would be delighted to accept your invitation.'

'Shall we say seven o'clock?' he said, 'I will call on you at your home, and we can take a hansom to the theatre.'

He took a calling card from Frances, then stood up and said his farewell. As she watched him walk away and pass through the revolving doorway of the hotel entrance, Gloria could scarcely believe the events of the last half an hour. The man of her dreams had just asked her to the theatre, and Mama had granted her permission, what more could seventeen-year-old Gloria Armstrong require? Ah, yes, a new dress for the occasion and her sister to hurry home so she could tell her everything. Once more, her mother's voice broke Gloria's thoughts.

'Well, my dear, you are a dark horse, I must say, what a charming and forward young man Mr Phelps appears to be. How on earth did you manage to attract his attentions, may I ask?' Gloria remained silent, trying to decide whether or not to tell her mother the whole story about meeting him at the theatre last Christmas. 'Well, come on, girl, speak up.'

'I am not sure whether you will believe me or not,' Gloria said.

Of course, that made her mother even more suspicious, and so Gloria felt obliged to relate the whole account from their collision outside the powder room. Frances made a very similar sort of "humph" sound as her sister at the rather unconventional meeting of a couple. She was also acutely aware that Gloria's wayward ways had not attracted any other suitable suitors to date, and Mr Phelps would be a good catch in a couple of years once he qualified. Better not let this one slip away if indeed he was genuinely interested in her daughter.

'Well, come on, dear, let us not waste the day, I would still like to see the latest creations at Madame Tussauds and do a little shopping. We must also make a plan as to how I am going to inform your father of the morning's events and soothe him into agreeing for you to see Mr Phelps. Let me do the talking, dear, you will only say something to inflame your father, and then he will never allow you out.'

That evening, once Frances had persuaded James that the young man in question was from a respectable family with excellent prospects, he continued to express his reservations over Gloria being not eighteen years of age.

'What do a few months matter when an opportunity like Mr Phelps comes along. Times are changing, and the youngsters do appear to be very taken with each other. Besides, I will be there to chaperone unless you would like to see the play with us,' Frances said.

'Good heavens, woman, why in God's name would I want to see a musical play? You know how I feel about them. You are more than welcome to sit through the torture and make certain Gloria behaves herself,' James replied.

Saturday was in two days, enough time for Gloria to wind herself up into quite an emotional state, where was Fleur when she needed her? No doubt having the time of her life on the French Riviera. She actually "humphed" like Aunt Esther and burst out laughing when she realised what she had done.

'Come on Saturday, hurry up.' She sat on the bed, hugging her knees, closed her eyes and began to imagine how the evening would unfold.

Finally, Saturday evening arrived, and Gloria dressed carefully, wanting to look her absolute best. She chose a mauve silk gown embellished with black beads and sequins and wore the beautiful Whitby jet necklace that had belonged to her grandmother. Her long, thick dark brown hair had been styled in a pretty chignon into which she had pinned a diamante hair decoration.

She looked in the dressing table mirror, her emerald green eyes shone between her long dark lashes as she blinked. She smiled at herself, took up a small pot of rouge and applied a little to her cheeks and lips. It would not do to look too fresh, a pale complexion was the fashion, one which Gloria found difficult to achieve as her skin tanned very easily in the sun. Her grandmother had once told tales of an ancestor being an Indian princess, which accounted for the dark hair and complexions of the Huxley women of the family.

This had never been confounded with any evidence, but Grandmama Huxley was not a woman to be trifled with.

Eventually, Gloria was satisfied with her appearance, she picked up her paisley wrap as it was still cool in the evening despite being spring and went to the sitting-room where her parents were having sherry.

Frances gasped, 'You look beautiful, Gloria.'

James looked at his youngest daughter and suddenly felt his middle age. Where had his little girl disappeared to? Who was this dazzling creature standing before him?

'Yes, indeed Gloria, you look quite charming,' he admitted.

'A compliment from Papa,' Gloria thought to herself, 'I must look astounding.'

The doorbell rang, and the maid went to welcome their visitor, 'Good evening, Gerald Phelps.'

Gloria heard his voice from the hallway, and her heart skipped a beat. The maid led Gerald through to the sitting-room, and he presented Frances with a box of Fry's Chocolate Creams which she accepted graciously, they were her favourites, he then walked over to James and shook his hand. 'Good evening, Mr Armstrong, I am very pleased to make your acquaintance. Are you sure you would not like to join us this evening?'

Gloria flinched when she heard Gerald's words and gave her father a pleading look, begging him not to express his strong feelings on the subject of musical theatre.

'Ah, musicals…' James saw the look and bit his tongue. 'Thank you, but no, I will let you escort the ladies, I shall be quite content with my book and cigars.'

The hansom cab had waited outside their flat, which was actually the ground floor of a large three-storey townhouse and quite spacious, Gloria loved it. Gerald helped her and Frances into the cab, the driver flicked his whip by the horse's ear, signalling it to trot on, carrying the small party to The Savoy.

They had wonderful seats on the front row of the circle, which afforded them an excellent view, although it is said that there was a perfect view from any seat in the theatre. The evening passed effortlessly, Gerald was the perfect gentleman, amusing and charming. He was very easy to like, and Gloria found that she liked him very much, even Frances felt comfortable in his company.

All too soon, the finale was over, and the company were taking their bows, Gloria had enjoyed a magical evening and was quite overwhelmed with happiness. Gerald hailed a cab to take the ladies home, and the three chatted animatedly about the play and the actors, before long, they pulled up outside the house. Gerald helped Frances from the cab and then took Gloria's hand as she stepped down. He looked into her eyes as he kissed her gloved hand.

'May I call on you tomorrow, Miss Armstrong?' he asked, rather formally.

'Why, yes, you may, it would please me very much,' she replied with just a hint of coyness.

'Then I bid you both good-night and thank you for a most pleasurable evening.' He stepped back into the cab and instructed the driver to take him to his home in Finsbury.

'Well, I must say that Mr Phelps is indeed the most pleasant young man you have managed to encounter, let us inform your father as such,' Frances proclaimed.

Gloria slept in blissful happiness that night, dreaming vivid multi-colour dreams that woke her just at the moment when Gerald was about to kiss her. Sunlight was peeking through the crack between her bedroom curtains as she stretched and smiled to herself.

True to his word Gerald called at about half past-eleven and took coffee with Gloria and Frances in the sitting-room. After a short while, Frances left the young couple to talk between themselves. Unbeknown to them, she could keep a watchful eye out through the etched glass in the dividing doors between the sitting-room and dining room.

Gerald asked Gloria about her family and laughed when she told him about her favourite Grandmama Huxley. He also spoke of his father with extreme fondness and respect.

Everything was progressing very well until Gerald informed her that he would be returning to Durham at the weekend, as the Easter break was nearly over. Gloria felt a small thump in her chest and could not help expressing her disappointment. 'You are going away so soon? But we have only just found each other again.'

'I know, Gloria, I am terribly sorry, it does rather feel like fate has played a part in our meeting again, but I will write if that is acceptable to you. I usually try to come home for the weekend once a month to visit Mama and Papa, so I will be able to see you then.' He took her hands in his and smiled. 'Do not look so glum, my sweet Gloria, I promise that the next time I am home, we will go to the theatre again, and perhaps this time your mother might allow us to go alone.'

'Mama might, but I will have to work on Papa.' Gloria flashed a smile, and the two gazed longingly at each other. Gerald leaned forward and kissed her gently on the lips, it made her blush, and he stroked her cheek.

'I shall not let you go again,' he said quietly.

By now, it was nearly lunchtime, and Gerald knew he must return to the hospital, he bade Gloria farewell. Although her eyes were glistening with tears, she managed to hold them back as she watched him walk out of the front door.

CHAPTER 3

Gerald did keep his promise and wrote to Gloria twice a week, she waited in every morning for the post to be delivered and rushed to her room, clutching his letter to her chest. She draped herself over the walnut chaise longue, opening the envelope carefully with a small silver paper-knife so as not to rip the paper. Gloria kept every letter in a lockable mahogany box, closeted away in her wardrobe. While his letters were not written in the most romantic fashion, Gerald did express his fondness for Gloria and how much he missed her company. His enthusiasm for medicine was plain to see, and his determination to pass with a 1st class honours was second to none. It was apparent he did not want to disappoint his father, who had invested heavily in Gerald's education.

Gloria would write back with tales of the latest play or musical she had seen with her mother and tell Gerald her opinion, in no uncertain terms, if any of the actresses had not met up to her exacting standards. As he read the words, he could hear Gloria chastising some poor woman because she forgot her lines or missed a cue. But more than anything, her letters expressed how much she wished he had been there with her, and Gloria tried hard not to dwell upon how much she missed him.

She was desperate for Fleur to return from her honeymoon so she could tell her everything, and of course, squeeze out every detail of the French Riviera and marriage from her.

Gloria loved London, and for the first time in her life, felt more in control of her feelings and emotions, and surprisingly, she had not argued with her father once since Gerald had come into her life, could this be a sign? She sincerely hoped so.

In his last letter, Gerald had written he would be home that weekend and would call on her as soon as possible. True to his word, he arrived carrying a beautiful bunch of dark pink roses for Gloria, a box of Frances's favourite Fry's chocolates and a box of cigars for James, all of which were gratefully received.

Gloria was beside herself with excitement at seeing Gerald again, and the young couple sat together in the Armstrong's sitting-room holding hands and talking animatedly.

'You look so pretty, I have missed those dazzling green eyes of yours very much,' Gerald said.

'I have missed you too, and since not a cross word has passed between Papa and I these last few weeks, he has agreed that we may go for dinner together, on our own.' Gloria smiled triumphantly.

'Then dine we will, sweet Gloria, tonight at The Carlton at seven-thirty, I will call for you in a hansom,' he replied.

And so, their courtship began. During the weeks that Gerald was in Durham, they continued to write to each other, and when he came home, the theatre became their favourite venue. Very quickly, Gloria felt herself falling in love. Then, at last, the summer break arrived, and Gerald came home for two months, already the weather was warm and sunny, much to Gloria's delight as summer was her favourite season. They had already been planning long walks and picnics in the London parks, and Gerald had promised to take her rowing along the river Thames.

It was August when Gerald took her by surprise, saying that his parents wished to meet her, and an invitation was sent out for

Gloria and her parents to have dinner at his home in Finsbury. On the evening of the dinner in question, Gloria was terribly nervous. Gerald had spoken about his father a great deal, telling her how he had come from a relatively modest background, his own father being a school-teacher. Nevertheless, he had studied extremely hard, and with the help of his grandfather, his parents were just able to afford to pay for him to study medicine at University College Hospital. He was now in private practice and a consultant at the Children's Hospital. Gerald was an only child, and it was always expected he follow in his father's footsteps and take up medicine, Gerald had been only too happy to oblige, he had never imagined being anything other than a doctor.

Fleur and Filkes would also be at dinner, which was a relief, Filkes and Marcus were acquainted in the medical worlds, and the other guests were made up from the Phelps family and friends.

Gloria had grown in confidence over the last few months, and dressing for the dinner engagement was not as daunting as on previous occasions. She decided to wear the mauve silk gown that she wore on the night they had watched *Merrie England*, knowing that it suited her perfectly and enhanced her slender figure.

It was a little after seven o'clock when the hansom arrived to whisk Gloria and her parents to Gerald's family home. Gloria pulled her wrap around her shoulders. 'Mama, I am so nervous about meeting Dr and Mrs Phelps, do you think they will like me?'

'I am certain they will, just remember your manners and try not to swoon too much every time Gerald looks at you,' her mother teased.

Frances had to admit that they did make a very attractive couple, James, on the other hand, was holding his judgment in reserve until he met the Phelpses. Although their occupations aligned them to the same social class, Marcus Phelps was a far wealthier man, and

James needed to be reassured that Gloria was not just a passing fancy. He wanted to be certain that Gerald would not lose interest in her if a more suitable, more affluent young lady appeared on the scene.

They arrived at the Phelps's house in Granville Square, it was actually two townhouses converted into one large house, one part of which Marcus ran his practice from and the other their home. They were greeted at the door by the maid and entered the hall, it had a beautiful curved wooden staircase leading to the upstairs rooms. The maid showed them through to the spacious sitting-room, decorated in the latest Art Nouveau style, light and airy with electric lighting. Gerald was on the far side of the room sipping a glass of champagne, and as soon as he saw Gloria, he set it down and moved towards her, smiling that charismatic smile she loved so dearly.

'Good evening, Gloria.' He kissed her hand. 'It is a pleasure to see you again, Mr and Mrs Armstrong, I hope you are both well. Come, I would like to introduce you to my mother and father.'

With Gloria attached to his arm, he led them towards a man in his mid-fifties, tall and straight with a thick shock of silver hair and exceedingly handsome for his age.

'Pater, may I introduce Mr and Mrs Armstrong and their daughter, Gloria.'

'At last, my son has talked for weeks of nothing else other than the beauty with the green eyes.' Marcus Phelps spoke with a soft, kind voice and a vague hint of a west country accent. 'It is a pleasure to make your acquaintance and your parents also.'

He took each of the ladies' hands and lightly touched them to his lips, then shook James's hand firmly. He beckoned towards an older woman who excused herself from the two women she was talking to and walked towards the small group.

'My dear,' Marcus said, 'this is the delightful, Miss Gloria Armstrong, her mother, Mrs Frances Armstrong and her father, Mr James Armstrong, may I introduce my wife, Edith.'

'Charming, most charming,' Edith said, looking directly at Gloria, she took her chin in her hand, moving her head from side to side, peering at her. 'What a beauty, my congratulations to you, Mrs Armstrong, for producing two fine daughters.' Edith spoke with even more of a west country accent, inadvertently revealing their origin before moving to London.

Gloria was a little taken aback by Mrs Phelps's way of assessing her looks, she rather felt like a horse being examined for its breeding characteristics. However, she remembered her manners and smiled sweetly with a slight flutter of her eyelashes. Gerald caught her eye and smiled, silently mouthing, 'She likes you.'

Just at this moment, Fleur and Filkes came into the room and made their way towards them.

'Good evening, Mrs Phelps, Dr Phelps, a pleasure to meet you again,' Fleur said.

Filkes shook Marcus by the hand, greeting him warmly. Gloria was extremely relieved to see her sister, she suddenly felt much braver, knowing Fleur could come to her rescue if any part of the evening began to falter. Dressed in a gown made of gold-coloured lace with dark blue and gold embroidered silk, Fleur looked exquisite, married life agreed with her very well indeed.

'Now, Miss Armstrong, come with me, I want you to meet my sisters.' Edith Phelps took her by the arm firmly and led her to the other side of the room, leaving her mother and father to get better acquainted with Marcus. Away from the safety of Gerald and Fleur, Gloria felt quite apprehensive, this aside, she actually thought the sisters looked intriguing. One was of a similar age to Edith, both in their late fifties, but the second woman appeared much younger, only in her mid-thirties.

'Miss Armstrong, may I introduce my sisters, Miss Clara Napier and Miss Lilian Jessop.' Slightly confused, Gloria greeted them, then Edith added, 'Lilian is my step-sister, she and her sister Mabel came to live with Clara and I when they were very young, and Lilian especially has stayed close to our family.'

'Yes, I am eternally grateful to Mr and Mrs Napier for their great kindness to us. Mabel now lives in Montreal, we write regularly to each other though, she is Matron of the Protestant Orphan Asylum and does sterling work with the poor orphans there,' Lilian said.

She also spoke with the same soft accent as Edith, and Gloria thought the sisters seemed like lovely people. Indeed, her first impressions of Gerald's family were very pleasing, she dearly hoped they would feel the same of her as the evening progressed. Gloria glanced across the room where Gerald was talking to her mother, she looked comfortable and as usual, totally in control of herself. Grandmama Huxley's training had prepared Frances for every eventuality, a small dinner at the Phelps's house was nothing to her, but to Gloria, it felt like everything, she would much rather be having dinner with Gerald all to herself.

There was a final guest to arrive, she was told by Edith, a friend and colleague of her husband and quite a character by all accounts, Dr Antony Stevenson, the hospital pathologist. Within five minutes, there was the sound of voices in the hallway, and Dr Stevenson appeared at the door of the sitting-room. He was of a similar age to Marcus but of shorter stature and sported a well-groomed silver handlebar and chin puff.

He strode across the room. 'Marcus, old chap, sorry to be a little late had a most unusual case to write up, poisoning by wolfsbane, will reveal all over brandy. Now,' he whispered, 'where is this beauty we have all been invited to see?'

Marcus subtly steered his dear friend around slightly, so he was facing in Gloria's direction.

'Over there, she is like a breath of fresh air compared to the other young women that fawn around Gerald, an engagement announcement to Miss Armstrong would more than quell the gossip around his indiscretion with Mrs Durrant,' he said.

'Let us hope so, old chap, she is indeed a beauty alright,' replied Antony.

The maid entered quietly, informing Mrs Phelps that dinner was served, and the guests made their way through to the dining room. They were seated so that Gloria and Frances were next to Marcus at the head of the table. Gerald sat next to Frances and Antony next to Gloria. At the other end, Edith sat with James, her sisters, Filkes and Fleur, it was a pleasant and informal arrangement that made Gloria feel a little more relaxed.

The Phelps's dining room was tastefully decorated in gold damask and white, with red and gold patterned curtains at the windows, and hanging from the ceiling was a splendid crystal chandelier. Gloria was very impressed, whilst their new flat had electricity, their home in Cambridgeshire only had gas-lighting, and the electric light made the crystals sparkle brightly so that she could see tiny rainbow colours amongst them. The dining room furniture was Baroque style mahogany, set upon a luxurious carpet, and the whole effect of the room made Gloria hope that maybe one day she too may host a dinner party in such elegance, with Gerald at the head of the table.

The five-course dinner was delicious, and the conversation light and jovial. Dr Stevenson kept Gloria thoroughly entertained with stories from his laboratory, perhaps not the most appropriate conversation for the dinner table. Nonetheless, Gloria was fascinated even when he described the latest additions to the pathological museum, which included a lardaceous thyroid, a necrosed coccyx amongst various other diseased organs, and the heart of a bird that had caused the complete obstruction of some poor chap's oesophagus for eight hours.

'The patient had to be given an injection of antimony to induce vomiting to expel the wretched thing. All ended well, thankfully,' Antony explained.

Whenever she glanced at Gerald, he returned her look with an expression that melted her heart, the evening was going well, much better than Gloria had first anticipated.

The Charlotte Russe served for dessert ended the dinner perfectly, and although only a few years ago it was customary for the ladies to withdraw to allow the gentlemen to smoke cigars and drink brandy, times were changing now Edward was king, and the Phelps household embraced these changes. Thus, both ladies and gentlemen withdrew to the sitting-room to have drinks and for the men to smoke the more fashionable cigarettes.

Fleur sat beside her sister on one of the pretty chintz sofas, and they spoke together about how they thought the evening was progressing.

'They seem to be a lovely family, but then Gerald is even more than lovely, so one would expect his family to be,' Gloria gushed. 'I love him, Fleur, I do so want him to propose to me, do you think that he might?'

'I do not know, darling, you have not known each other that long, but I can see by the way he looks at you that he appears to like you very much. But you must realise that being the wife of a newly qualified doctor is not for the faint-hearted, he will hardly ever be at home, and when he is, he will be exhausted from long hours at the hospital. Filkes told me that it is only since becoming a consultant that he has any time for a life outside of being a doctor, hence not marrying when he was younger,' Fleur replied.

'Surely it cannot be as bad as all that, living with Mama and Papa since you married is no fun either, I miss you, Fleur. If Gerald and I were married, we could all socialise together, it would be so wonderful.'

Her sister continued to tell her that medical students have no means of supporting a wife, and at best, if Gerald were even thinking of proposing to her, she would have to wait until he had finished his degree and taken up his first house position.

Gloria half-closed her ears to the sensible talk Fleur was delivering and gazed towards Gerald with aching thoughts of love, only to see his mother coming over to sit with her.

'So, Gloria, tell me what you do with yourself when you are not out with my son.' Gloria tried to think of something she imagined might impress Mrs Phelps.

'Fleur and I enjoy a game of tennis, and since she married Filkes, I have bought a bicycle, so I can ride over to visit her more often, it is very invigorating.'

She chattered on about how she loved to read The Tatler every week to catch up on fashions and all the latest society news, as going to the theatre was her favourite past time. And so as not to appear too frivolous, hastily added that she also read novels, especially the gothic novels such as Dracula and Frankenstein as she found those most thought-provoking. 'Science is so mysterious, who knows what could be possible,' Gloria stated.

Edith smiled and nodded as Gloria spoke with honesty about herself. The older woman concluded that she had just the right combination of innocence but not so naive of the ways of the world that too much would surprise her. Frances had kept both of her daughters level-headed.

'I think the time is right, she will do very nicely for my Gerald,'

Edith thought, and with that excused herself to seek out her husband, leaving Gloria and Fleur with Dr Stevenson, who was entertaining the sisters with tales of the morgue, quite fitting for Gloria's taste in novels.

'Marcus, I wish to speak to you in private for a moment.' Edith spoke quietly, and Marcus excused himself from his conversation with Filkes on the subject of childhood epilepsy and went with Edith back into the dining room, so they could not be overheard by their guests.

'Well, Marcus, your honest opinion, please. I know she is still young, but do you think the lovely Miss Armstrong will make a suitable wife for our Gerald?'

'Yes, I do honestly think she might,' he replied.

Edith was a few years older than Marcus, they had married later in life which meant Gerald had been their only child. He was a beautiful child and rather indulged as he grew up, being adored by everyone. Consequently, as he matured, his attraction to women had recently resulted in a dalliance with one of the lecturer's wives. Therefore, when Gerald told them of the exquisite young lady he had chanced upon, they encouraged him to pursue his attentions. Though Gloria did not come from a vastly wealthy background, her father was well respected in society, and both his father and grandfather had been officers in the British Army, serving in India. Marcus and Edith had watched how Filkes and Fleur were accepted when they married and decided that on meeting Gloria this evening, she was just what Gerald needed to settle him down on his return from Durham, now to tell their son.

Gerald was in the sitting-room winding up the new gramophone his father had just purchased, and it began to play *Sweet Adeline* by the Haydn quartet. Gloria and Frances were enthralled.

'Papa, we really must have one of these, they are so much fun,'

Gloria said excitedly.

'So you can play those dreadful musical songs all day long? I think not,' her father replied.

Gloria thought how stuffy he was compared to Marcus and wondered if he would ever change and embrace the new world emerging out of the Victorian era.

The small gathering stood or sat listening to the music coming out of the brass horn, it was a truly marvellous invention. Gerald changed the gramophone record, and as the next tune started up, Marcus walked over and quietly spoke to his son. He immediately excused himself from the party and went with his father to the dining-room where his mother was waiting.

'Why all the cloak and dagger, why do you both wish to speak to me in private? The party has just begun.' Gerald said.

Marcus offered Gerald a cigarette and lit it for him, then lighting one for himself, he said to his son, 'Your mother and I are most enchanted with Miss Armstrong and feel very strongly that she will make a most suitable wife for you in a year or so when you qualify. I think this evening would be a most fitting time for you to propose to her.'

Gerald was very taken aback. 'But I am not ready for "settling down" yet, Gloria and I are enjoying our outings and evenings out, but I had no intention of proposing to her,' he said.

'Well, son, there is no time like the present, and we need to quieten the gossip about your recklessness with Mrs Durrant, what better than an engagement announcement to a young lady who happens to be greatly in love with you? If you had not noticed.'

Gerald caught his breath, he was acutely aware of the embarrassment he had caused his parents, and Gloria was rather special. Apart from her stunning beauty, he found her fresh and lively, very different from the women he was usually acquainted with. She had undeniably caught his attention at their first meeting, and more so at Filkes wedding. Hence why he made certain he called on her at the hotel the following morning in an effort not to lose contact with her. So far, it had worked out very nicely.

'What about Mr and Mrs Armstrong? Do you think they will approve?' Gerald asked.

'I am quite sure they will, dear, I shall make certain of it,' his mother replied.

Gerald pondered for a while, smoking his cigarette. He contemplated the consequences of giving up his bachelor life but also considered his parents' feelings and his own ambition of becoming a consultant like his father. He began to think about the advantages of coming home to a beautiful young wife every evening and smiled to himself, so he decided to do his parents' bidding and make the proposal. Perhaps marriage to Gloria might not be too much like hard work.

'Alright, I agree,' he said to them, who both sighed with relief, 'I will ask her.'

'A sound decision, son,' Marcus said.

Gerald suddenly thought. 'What about a ring? I can hardly propose without one.'

'Worry not, that is already taken care of, it has always been my wish that my grandmother's ring should pass down through the family. There did use to be money in the family once upon a time. Your great grandmother, Charlotte, married into the Napier's of Portsmouth, tragically her husband was killed at the Battle of Waterloo, and the family fortune died with him. Poor Grandmother was left at the mercy of the cousins, but she always wore her precious emerald and diamond engagement ring until the day she died and bequeathed it to my mother and then in turn to me. I will go upstairs and fetch it, I am certain that Gloria will be delighted,' Edith replied.

She returned after a few minutes with a small leather ring box and passed it to her son. Gerald opened it, and his eyes met with an exquisite dark green emerald, encircled by rose-cut diamonds, set in platinum with a rose gold band, it was truly dazzling.

'Mama, are you sure?'

'Yes, Gerald, a beauty like Gloria deserves a beautiful ring, and I hope that she will treasure it as much as Charlotte did.'

And so, Gerald re-entered the sitting-room where the sound of music drifted from the gramophone, he looked at Gloria. 'She really is beautiful and fun to be with, go on man, do it, marriage might not be all that bad,' he thought to himself and went towards the small group of smiling people. He picked up a glass of champagne from the tray on the sideboard, and presented it to Gloria, kissed her cheek, took her by the arm and led her through to the study.

'Why, Gerald, what is this? Spiriting me away from the party in this manner,' she giggled as he sat her on the sofa and then sat down beside her. He took her hand.

'I am conscious of the fact that we have only known each other for a few months,' he said, already the expression on Gloria's face began to change from wide-eyed to curious, 'however, I am enchanted by you, Gloria, and if you are willing to wait for me to finish my studies, I would be honoured if you would take this into consideration and agree to become my wife.'

He took the small box from his pocket and presented the stunning ring to Gloria. She was speechless, in one sentence, her wildest dream had come to pass, and now she was lost for words. She just looked at Gerald, her love.

'Say something, darling,' he implored, at which Gloria looked straight into his eyes and whispered,

'Yes, yes, Gerald, I will.'

He bent down on one knee and placed the ring on Gloria's finger, it fitted perfectly, and the emerald shone almost the same colour as her eyes.

'Do we have to wait?' she asked.

'Yes, I'm afraid we do, it is one year out of a lifetime together, think of it in that way.'

With this, he swept her onto her feet and kissed her full on the lips, he felt her melt in his arms, and Gloria thought her heart would burst.

Gerald was aware he must now ask James's permission for Gloria's hand and went in search of him, leaving Gloria with his absolutely delighted parents.

He found both James and Frances sitting on the Monks bench in the hallway, enjoying a quiet moment, away from the noise of the gramophone and seized the opportunity to speak to them.

'Ah, splendid, here you both are, enjoying a little peace and quiet, I presume. May I speak with you a moment?' He offered James a cigarette, but he declined, saying that he preferred his cigars. Gerald resumed. 'Sir, I know that I have not been acquainted with Gloria for a great many months......

He continued to say all the lines required of him to ask for James's permission to marry Gloria.

Throughout the little speech, Frances's face was lighting up at each sentence, whereas James kept his composure until it was his turn to speak. He had a mixture of feelings with regards to the proposal, of both surprise and relief that any man was willing to take on his feisty daughter, combined with some bewilderment of how she had managed to attract a man from Gerald's social standing. Still, the young man seemed genuine.

'Well, Gerald, you have indeed caught me by surprise,' James said, 'Gloria is still very young, she does not turn eighteen until

November. I would most certainly not agree to a marriage until you have qualified and proven that you can support her. I think a long engagement will be required to slow matters down a little, other than that, I have no objection to the marriage, as I am sure my wife will not either.'

Frances was beaming, nodding her head in agreement and already working on the guest list.

'Of course, sir, that was my intention all along, and I thank you for agreeing to the engagement.'

The two men shook hands, after which Gerald returned to Gloria and his parents to report the glad tidings. He then offered his arm to his new fiancée, and they headed towards the sitting-room to impart the news to the family and friends gathered therein. With a smile that lit up her face, Gloria re-entered the room with Gerald, what a life she was going to have, as far as Gloria was concerned, she now had it all.

The room was full of smiles, everyone expressing their delight at the news and congratulating the happy couple, it was all quite overwhelming, but Gloria was in heaven. She proudly showed her ring to Frances and Fleur, who fussed over her, holding her hand and moving it around so that the light caught the diamonds, making them twinkle like stars. Clara and Lilian were already acquainted with the ring, having been told its story numerous times as children, nevertheless, seeing it on Gloria's long slender finger added another dimension to its beauty.

'Well met, old chap,' Antony said to his friend as they stood together smoking cigarettes.

'Let us hope so,' Marcus replied, 'a year is a long time for a young couple to wait, I think we might have to find a way of keeping Miss Armstrong entertained over the coming months. Something to ponder over, I believe.'

A notice was placed in The London Daily News. *"Dr and Mrs Marcus Phelps of Finsbury have pleasure in announcing the engagement of their only son, Gerald Napier Phelps, to Miss Gloria Elizabeth Martha Armstrong, youngest daughter of Mr James Armstrong."*

Over the next few weeks, Gerald observed Marcus and Filkes at the hospital but would see Gloria as often as time allowed. The late summer weather had remained warm, and she would cycle over to the hospital so they could meet up for a picnic lunch in the park. Any evenings Gerald had free, they would endeavour to go out for dinner or the theatre.

All too soon, the summer gave way to autumn, which also brought September and Gerald leaving for Durham terribly close for Gloria to contemplate, she would miss him dreadfully. Even though she could telephone and write letters, she wanted to be married already and with him every day. Why could they not marry before he went away? Every time she was close to Gerald, her body ached for him, and she was certain he felt the same way, how would they endure being parted for so long?

'There is a party at the doctors' mess on Saturday night, they are always so much fun, according to Filkes, shall we go and celebrate our last evening together before I return to Durham?' Gerald asked.

Gloria thought it an absolutely marvellous idea, and as her sister and Filkes would be there too, her parents could not possibly object. There was a degree of protest when the subject was mentioned, but as usual, Gloria used her powers of persuasion to dispel any doubts that her father possessed. Thus, she dressed in her new dark red silk dress overlaid with delicate black lace decorated with black beads and sequins, in which she looked exquisite.

As predicted, there was music, dancing, plenty of champagne and cocktails at the party, and a fine time was being had by all.

Gerald's friends, Joseph and Gordon, were also there, the two young men who were at the theatre when Gloria first met Gerald.

'You know, old girl, he looked everywhere for you that night, was in a dark mood for the rest of the evening, rather spoilt our fun you know,' a somewhat inebriated Joseph professed, 'could not stop talking about you for weeks afterwards, the next thing we know he is engaged to you. Took us all by surprise, you know, never thought he was the marrying type, but I can now see what all the bother was about, you are a peach.' He tottered away to find more champagne.

Gloria was trying her utmost not to laugh but failed miserably, and as she turned to Gerald, she declared that she had never had so much fun in all her life. He looked at his beautiful fiancée and took her hand. 'Come with me, Gloria, there is a quiet little restroom down the corridor where we can find a little privacy, I will be away the day after tomorrow, and we shall not see each other for six weeks, come on, darling.'

The champagne had gone to Gloria's head, and although she knew it was terribly wrong, her feelings for Gerald were so intense, she allowed him to lead her away from the party.

A large sofa was situated in the dimly lit, oak-panelled room that Gerald led Gloria into, they sat down together and looked into each other's eyes.

'I love you, Gloria, do not be afraid.' He kissed her tenderly. Before long, there was no holding back from her feelings, and Gloria succumbed to him.

CHAPTER 4

The cold afternoon in Durham the following January had been hastily arranged, Gloria had left London without saying a word to a soul, not even Fleur. She caught the early train to Durham where Gerald was waiting for her on the platform, from whence they took a hansom to a small, terraced house a few miles out of Durham, where a friend of Gerald's had agreed they could stay for a couple of days. Here, Gloria changed into her wedding dress, she had secretly purchased a simple ivory satin and lace gown, along with a lace-trimmed hat decorated with pink silk flowers. Not the dress she had dreamt of, but under the circumstances, it would have to do.

And so, there they stood outside the register office, Gloria shivered and pulled her woollen winter coat closely around her.

'Are you alright, darling?' Gerald asked tenderly, 'what a predicament we have got ourselves into, you will be missed at home by now.'

'I left a letter on the mantelpiece late last night. Papa will have a fit, and poor Mama will be heartbroken, but at least we will be married and our baby legitimate, that is one less scandal to deal with. Please say it will turn out alright in the end,' Gloria said.

'I suspect it will be rocky for a while, but hopefully, they will eventually come to terms with it, and I am sure when Gerald junior arrives, he will make up for everything, for he will be as adorable as his mother.'

'So, it will be a boy then?'

'Yes, I am certain of it, in fact, you will have all sons, what would we do with a headstrong daughter? I have all on keeping up with you,' Gerald teased.

Joseph and Gordon arrived at last, and the small party entered the door of the register office and waited to be called through. It was a short ceremony, nevertheless, as the registrar asked if she, Gloria Elizabeth Martha Armstrong, will take Gerald Napier Phelps to be her lawful wedded husband, and he placed a gold band on her finger, she could not have been happier. They spent their wedding night at Gerald's friend's house after an intimate dinner at the Royal County Hotel, and for a while, they put aside the consequences of their actions and were blissfully happy in each other's arms.

Gloria awoke the next morning to find Gerald already up and sitting by the window smoking a cigarette, deep in thought. She thought how handsome he looked in his burgundy paisley dressing gown, his dark brown hair all tousled. She stretched and sighed. 'Good morning, husband.'

Gerald grinned, remembering their night together. 'And how is the lovely, Mrs Phelps, this morning, may I ask?' smiling at his beautiful wife.

'At this moment, I am very happy, darling, I wish we could stay here forever and not have to go home and face the music,' Gloria replied.

'But face it, we must, my sweet Gloria, your parents will be furious, and my father, well, we will have to face him too.'

The expression on Gerald's face darkened, he hated upsetting his father and was relying on Gloria's charisma to help soften the blow. A little more subdued than a while earlier, Gloria began to pack her bag. She had brought her grandmama's carpetbag with her to travel light, and as she carefully folded up her wedding dress, she contemplated how Lizzie Huxley would have dealt with her predicament. She had only died a couple of years ago, and Gloria knew that out of any of her relations she could have confided in, it would have been Grandmama Huxley, the thought made Gloria sad and miss her very much.

'A penny for them, darling,' Gerald said softly.

'I was just wishing that my grandmama was alive, she would soon have made everything right, she always did.'

Gerald kissed her. 'Come on, we had better get our skates on, or else we will miss the train.'

The powerful locomotive hurtled down the tracks heading for London, not much was said during the journey, the motion of the train was making Gloria feel a little nauseous. Resting her head on Gerald's shoulder, she tried to sleep. She awoke as they pulled into St Pancras station, there were steam and noise everywhere, jarring Gloria's senses. There was no need to find a porter as Gerald could carry both of their bags. He hailed a cab, and before long, they were heading towards Draycott Place, where no doubt the Armstrong household would be in an uproar.

Needless to say, the atmosphere was very unpleasant indeed. James ranted and raved, Frances was crying, Gloria was crying, Gerald was trying to reason with his new father-in-law, but to no avail, James was in a fury.

'Get out of this house, girl, you are a trollop! No better than those actresses you aspire too, I never wish to see you again. As for you, young man, you are a disgrace. GET OUT OF MY HOUSE, LEAVE NOW, BOTH OF YOU!' he yelled, his face purple with anger.

Frances was pleading with her husband, but it was no use, he was enraged, and there would be no talking to him for hours.

Gerald and a distraught Gloria left the house, the cab had been waiting with their luggage, and Gerald instructed the driver to take them to his home. Gloria had stopped crying and said, 'I have never seen Papa so angry, and now your parents already know what we have done after he visited them. I am so sorry, Gerald, he has a terrible temper, I cannot forgive him for the things he said, it was dreadful.'

'My father is a wise man, and I am certain he has dealt with much worse than this situation in his career.' Gerald replied.

'It was shameful, what is your father going to think of me now.' Gloria was angry and embarrassed.

'I suspect he will be more disappointed in me, and hopefully, Mama will be secretly pleased that she is to have her first grandchild.'

The meeting went more or less as Gerald had predicted, Marcus delivered his speech on how disappointed he was at their not being able to wait until they were married but concluded that what is done is done. A small announcement of their marriage in the paper would quell any gossip, the baby would be early. Edith fussed over Gloria and took her into the sitting-room, ringing for the maid to bring some tea. She arrived a few minutes later with an enormous tray of tea and biscuits.

'Thank you, Polly, that will be all,' Edith said. 'We must look after you, my dear, and the little one, all this excitement is not good for either of you.'

Gloria was overcome with Edith's compassion, wishing that her home were as loving and peaceful, but then this was her home now. Marcus had made it clear that she and Gerald would live with them until he reached a respectable point in his career when he could afford to move into their own home.

They were to have the rooms above the surgery in the adjoining house. Their bedroom was decorated with candy stripe wallpaper below the dado rail, with cream painted lincrusta above and contained a large brass bedstead covered with a flower-patterned quilted spread. One of the smaller adjacent bedrooms had been converted into a bathroom and another a sitting-room cum study, in which a magnificent mahogany desk sat by the window. All in all, it eluded an air of tranquillity, just the ambience required for the young couple to adjust to their new life together.

A carrier had been sent to Gloria's home to fetch her clothes and personal items, at least her father had allowed that. She imagined how he would have probably relished in watching the maid pack everything away, cursing her with each item.

'Why can you not be more like Marcus?' she thought to herself.

Gerald had already missed a week of lectures and desperately needed to return to Durham. 'Mama and Papa will take good care of you, darling. I have to catch up on my studies if we want to make a decent life for ourselves and Gerald junior,' he said.

'Still adamant it will be a boy, are you?' She placed her hand on her stomach, which since the previous week, had just begun to round slightly. 'I do not mind, either way, as long as it is healthy, I just wish my mother would send a message, I have never known Papa to be this angry for so long, even Fleur has not contacted me, and I swear that will be Papa's doing. I will visit her myself after you have gone to Durham, I miss her terribly.'

'Just be careful, Gloria, please do not do anything that will raise your blood pressure,' Gerald warned.

'I just want to talk to her, she is my sister,' Gloria replied.

'If you must, but take a cab, you are not to ride that bicycle.'

'Giving me orders now, are you? Just because we are married, it does not allow you to tell me what I can or cannot do.'

She affected one of her extravagant head flicks and started to laugh, Gerald strode over to her, swept her up in his arms and deposited her on the bed. 'Now, Mrs Phelps, what am I going to do with you?' He kissed her.

Gerald returned to Durham, and Gloria tried hard to establish a routine for herself, Edith was so kind, as were Clara and Lilian, introducing Gloria to their friends. Although they were very gracious, admiring her beauty and congratulating her on her marriage, they were middle-aged ladies with whom she had nothing in common. Gloria had not been living in London long enough to have established any friendships, and since meeting Gerald, her life had been a whirlwind, leading to her present situation. She had attempted to see Fleur, only to be informed by their maid that Mrs Allen was out of town and would not return for another two weeks.

'My entire family has disowned me, even Fleur, it is not as if I have murdered anyone or stolen the crown jewels or something equally as criminal, I fell in love and got pregnant,' Gloria thought gloomily.

She passed the time reading and sewing a sampler for when the baby arrived. Marcus had insisted she take a brisk walk each day to keep herself fit.

'Put some real colour in your cheeks, my dear, women in my home village in Somerset walked miles each day when they were with child, I am a great advocate of fresh air and exercise, you must not stay cooped up in the house, Gerald will be home soon,' Marcus said.

He spoke with such gentleness and wisdom, it was no surprise that patients came from all over London to see him. Gloria was humbled by the generosity and compassion the Phelpses had shown her, she had never felt this loved by her own parents, only her grandmama.

'Gloria, how would you like to help me in the surgery?' Marcus asked one day. 'I think my patients would benefit from being greeted by a pretty face. You can book my appointments, file the notes and keep on old man company in between patients. What do you say, dear?'

'That is very kind of you, Marcus, I would like that very much, and I do need to learn something about what you doctors get up to so that I may help Gerald once he is qualified,' Gloria replied.

'Then it is settled, you may start tomorrow morning after breakfast.' He kissed the top of her head and returned to his rooms.

The next two weeks flew by for Gloria as she learned how to file, book appointments, and most of all, she enjoyed talking to the patients helping them feel at ease. With her dazzling smile and bright conversation, it was not difficult. Many of them were children as paediatrics was Marcus's specialism, they also warmed to her. This made her realise just how much she was looking forward to becoming a mother, promising herself that her child would always be shown love and affection openly, to grow up feeling loved and wanted. She was already nineteen weeks gone and had a small bump showing. Gloria also knew that Fleur would be home any day soon and her darling Gerald at the weekend. She longed to see him and thanked Marcus for understanding that she needed something to occupy her time while he was away.

Even though Gloria was forever hopeful that a letter would arrive from her mother, it would be too much to expect a phone call, but alas, nothing had arrived since the Phelpses had taken her in. Part of her was saddened by this, nonetheless, she was happy and content and accepted her lot for now.

Dinner that evening was quiet, just Marcus, Edith and Gloria, they retired to the sitting-room to play some records on the gramophone. Gloria sat for a while listening to a recording of a selection of songs from *A Country Girl* when she suddenly felt unwell. 'I think I might go up early tonight,' Gloria said to her in-laws, 'I feel awfully tired, I think an early night is called for.'

Marcus looked concerned and moved over to Gloria, who was sitting on the sofa opposite. He felt her forehead. 'You do seem a little warm, my dear. Come, Edith, help Gloria upstairs, settle her in, and I will pop up later to check on her.'

Gloria was only too happy to oblige, she certainly felt most peculiar and ready for a lie-down. Edith placed her arm around Gloria's shoulder and helped her upstairs, however, just as they reached the landing, Gloria buckled over, clutching her stomach and let out a scream.

'Marcus, Marcus, come quickly, something is terribly wrong,' Edith shouted.

Gloria was groaning and holding her stomach as she collapsed on the floor, blood oozing through the muslin dress she was wearing.

'MARCUS!'

He raced up the stairs as fast as he could and knelt down beside Gloria, she was in a great deal of pain and bleeding heavily. Marcus scooped her up in his arms and carried her to the bedroom.

'Tell Polly to bring up towels and hot water, I must try and stop the bleeding, I fear she will lose the baby. Edith, please go and wait downstairs, you must not witness this.' he said.

Two hours later, a weary Marcus came back downstairs and slumped into his favourite armchair.

'How is she, Marcus?' Edith asked.

'She is sleeping at the moment, I have given her a sedative, the poor child is exhausted, and I am afraid the baby is lost,' Marcus replied.

Edith gasped, putting her hand over her mouth. 'The poor darling…… Gerald will be devastated.'

'She has lost a great deal of blood, and we must keep a watchful eye on her for infection. Pour me a brandy please, my dear, I am in dire need.'

Edith returned with the drink, and Marcus swirled it around the glass silently.

'What is it, dear?' she asked her husband.

'I am contemplating whether I should send a message to Mrs Armstrong, she is her daughter after all, not ours, it might just bring them to their senses knowing what Gloria has suffered, I should leave word for her sister too. It is often the mind that takes time to heal after the loss of an unborn child, and being at odds with her family is certainly not going to help,' he said.

The couple discussed the matter and concluded that nothing could be lost by sending a message in the morning, but much might be gained. Marcus also telephoned Gerald at his rooms in Durham and imparted the devastating news.

'I must return home immediately,' Gerald said, 'my poor, sweet Gloria, what have I done to her?'

'These things happen, it is no one's fault, son,' Marcus replied, 'but I think she will need you at her side.'

They talked for a little while longer, and Gerald said he would catch the morning train to London.

Marcus spent the night dozing in the chair by Gloria's bed, checking her temperature every two hours and making sure she did not start haemorrhaging again. She kept murmuring Gerald's name in her drugged sleep, and Marcus's heart felt heavy indeed. A part of him felt responsible for the situation the young couple had found themselves in, as he had encouraged the engagement before Gerald was ready to settle down, added to which Gloria was only eighteen years old.

'The pressures of society are too tiresome, maybe someday in the future, all men and women will be equal, but I doubt I will live to witness that day.' These thoughts were passing through Marcus's mind when he heard Gloria stirring, he walked over to the bed and held her hand.

'Gloria, dear, it is Marcus, how are you feeling?' he asked.

'Where am I? What has happened? I feel dreadful and so tired.' Her voice was quiet and weak.

Marcus spoke gently. 'I am afraid I have bad news for you, my dear, you have suffered a terrible miscarriage, I was unable to save the baby, it was far too small. You are lucky to be alive, Gloria, I am so very sorry.'

Gloria's eyes welled up with tears, and she began to sob uncontrollably. She wept for half an hour with Marcus stroking her hair, he had already grown extremely fond of his young daughter-in-law, and this was a bitter blow for them all. Eventually, Gloria's sobs subsided, and she looked at Marcus with red-rimmed eyes. 'Was it a boy or a girl, were you able to tell? Please, I want to know.'

'It was a girl, but she had not formed properly, that is why you miscarried. Please, you must rest now, I will tell Polly to bring up some chicken broth, you must try to eat and regain your strength,' Marcus said gently.

'Gerald had wanted a boy, we said how troublesome daughters can be, and it looks like he was correct.' She began to cry again.

Gerald arrived home in the late afternoon, filled with a combination of guilt for having seduced Gloria in the first place and extreme concern for her well-being. He did love her in his own way, and the moment he stepped through the front door, he rushed upstairs, having the sense to enter their bedroom quietly, to see Gloria asleep looking pale and wan. He leaned over the bed and kissed her very gently. Her eyes fluttered open, and recognising Gerald immediately, she smiled and reached out for his hand.

'Hello, my darling,' he said softly.

'I am so sorry, Gerald, I lost our baby, it was a girl.'

'I know, darling, I know. Everything will be alright, Papa said you will be able to conceive again, we will just have to make a boy next time.'

Gloria's eyes welled up again, but she also tried to smile.

'You always manage to make good out of bad, which is one of the reasons why I love you so much…. and other things.' She gave a small mischievous grin.

Gloria's recovery went well, she was young and strong, and alongside her new family's love and care, she was soon feeling much improved. Inevitably, Gerald had to return to Durham very soon after Gloria was out of danger. He had already missed vital study time and needed to work extremely hard over the following months if he were to achieve his goals.

News of her miscarriage did prompt Frances to visit her daughter, and the two attempted to re-build some bridges. Sadly, James was adamant he never wanted to lay eyes on her again, uttering that it was God's punishment for her sins and that she had always been a troublesome child.

'Let the Phelpses discover her true colours, they might not be so sympathetic towards her,' he had yelled at Frances as she left their flat on her way to visit Gloria.

Fleur had also returned home and visited her sister as soon as she read the note containing the dreadful news. Both Fleur and Frances were made most welcome by Marcus and Edith. Their sympathy and generosity left Frances feeling acutely embarrassed and ashamed by her husband's behaviour. He was an impossible man at times, she had thought angrily.

Gloria was so pleased to see her sister, talking together made her feel a little less lonely in the world.

'Papa was beside himself with anger when he read your letter, I thought he was going to have a stroke, you could have confided in me,' Fleur admonished.

'I wanted to, but I thought you might persuade me not to go. Gerald had already bought the licence and made all the arrangements, I had to go, I wanted to go, I love him,' Gloria replied, with a resolute firmness in her voice, despite laying on her bed looking pale and tired.

'You are so impetuous, Gloria, I had a feeling something like this would happen. When I could not find you at the party that night, I suspected Gerald might have lured you away somewhere, but what is done is done, and despite losing the baby, you are still Mrs Phelps, and Gerald is a fine-looking husband.'

'Indeed, he is, and I am indebted to Marcus and Edith, I have never met such wonderfully kind people. The most important thing now is for Gerald to qualify and start his career, he will be a consultant like Filkes in no time,' Gloria gushed.

'Speaking of Filkes, I have something to tell you,' Fleur said somewhat reluctantly. 'The reason we were out of town was to view a house. Filkes has been offered a consultant position at the Ramsgate General Hospital, it is an opportunity he cannot afford to turn down. It does mean we will have to leave London, I am so sorry, darling.' Gloria's face dropped. 'You can visit us often once you are up and about, it is only a train ride away after all, and we have purchased a lovely house overlooking the sea,' Fleur added.

'No, you cannot desert me, you are all I have, Gerald is away so much, and now I have lost my baby. Please, do not go, I have nothing, Fleur, please.' She pleaded with her sister, who was awfully distressed herself, not wanting to leave Gloria, especially at the moment, but the life of a doctor's wife meant they must go where their husband's work takes them.

'We are keeping a flat in London, I will come up as often as possible, and we are not leaving for another six weeks. I am sorry, darling, it should have been good news, but instead, events have rather taken the shine away, and I now feel terribly guilty.'

The sisters discussed their plights at great length for an hour or so and parted company rather sad but with plans in place. A bereft Gloria lay in bed and cried herself to sleep.

Over the coming weeks, she gradually regained her strength and resumed her work in the surgery. It kept her busy, and even when her mother telephoned imparting the news that they were returning to Cambridgeshire, her father being tired of London, Gloria took the announcement with little emotion. It was of no consequence what her parents did now, her father had disowned her, and her mother kept her distance.

It would not be long until summer arrived, meaning Gerald would complete his finals and graduate.

'He will be home soon.' Gloria hugged the pillow next to her in bed and day-dreamed of Gerald's home-coming.

CHAPTER 5

The graduation ceremony at Durham was absolutely splendid, and Gerald cut quite the dashing figure in his cap and gown. Gloria was, of course, overcome with pride and had attended the event with Marcus and Edith. That evening they all dined at the Royal County Hotel, where only eight months earlier Gloria and Gerald had sat together for their first dinner as man and wife. So much had happened during that time, and Gloria now felt a somewhat wiser woman and eager to begin her life as the wife of Dr Gerald Phelps.

On their return to London, Gerald commenced the first part of his practical training at St Thomas's Hospital, he spent six months as House Physician, followed by a further six months as House Surgeon. He completed his training with excellent results, and to add to the celebrations, Gloria announced she was pregnant again.

'Yes, darling, it is true, and this time it will be a boy, Gerald junior, he will be healthy, strong and the image of his father.'

She had broken the news earlier in the year, and true to her word, Gerald Gabriel Maddox Phelps was born on the 13th of September 1904, and he was perfect.

For a while, life was idyllic, baby Gerald, whom they decided to call Gabe to save confusion, was very content, and motherhood suited Gloria well. She doted on him, vowing to keep her promise that he would grow up feeling loved and wanted, not permanently at war with his parents, well, not with his mother anyway. Gerald was to study in Dublin for a year, a fact that they had argued about bitterly.

'But he is only three months old, how can you go away and leave us so soon? I shall miss you dreadfully, please can we not just spend some time together, when was the last time we went to the theatre?' Gloria said.

'Stop being so selfish, if you want all the finery of being a doctor's wife, then I have to study more to provide you with that life, I am going, and that is the end of it,' Gerald snapped.

The row had carried on until baby Gabe started to cry.

'Now look what you have done, shouting at me like that,' Gloria retorted.

She flicked her head and went through to the nursery in the adjoining room to soothe her crying son. It had been the first real argument between them, and she was distressed and confused.

As a peace offering, Gerald came home the next evening with tickets for *Lady Madcap* at the Prince of Wales theatre in an attempt to console Gloria. He tried hard to explain to her that it was out of necessity for his career that he go to Dublin, not by his own choice, and on his return, he would soon be in a position to set up his own Harley Street practice and eventually move into their own home.

'It is one year out of our whole life together, please be patient,' he said.

'I do understand, darling, I miss you, that is all, and so does your son.' She was nursing him as they spoke, and Gerald looked down at his baby son, who gurgled and smiled. He had dark hair and olive coloured skin like his mother.

'He is a fine specimen of a child, is he not?' Gerald teased.

'You have been spending too much time with Dr Stevenson in his laboratory,' Gloria scolded. 'Gabe is not a specimen, he is our beautiful, perfect child, and if his father really does have to go away for a while, then so be it, we will both be here waiting for him when he comes home.'

Gerald kissed his wife, relieved that they had managed to restore peace.

Edith had been more than happy to take care of her grandson for the evening, ushering her son and daughter-in-law out of the front door, telling them that she was more than capable of looking after a baby.

The theatre was at full capacity that evening, and for Gloria and Gerald, it was a welcome escape from the pressures of the last few weeks. Gloria's slender figure had already returned, and her new gown made from white mousseline de soir fabric decorated with black Chantilly lace turned heads as she had entered the theatre on Gerald's arm.

'You are so beautiful, my darling, we knew it would not be easy, but life always finds a way of turning out, you will see,' he said.

The family celebrated Christmas together at the Phelps's house, Edith had kindly invited Fleur and Filkes for a few days, and Clara and Lilian had also come to stay. They fussed and cooed over Gabe, who loved every minute of the attention he received, rewarding each person with a smile and kick of his legs as he lay in his cradle. A feeling of tranquillity rested over the household, and the new year of 1905 was welcomed in with a toast of champagne, followed by a rowdy rendition of *Auld Lang Syne*.

A week later, Gerald was on his way to Dublin, leaving a tearful Gloria standing in the hallway holding Gabe in her arms, she held up his chubby little arm, waving it towards his father as he walked out of the front door.

'It will quickly pass, my sweet Gloria, I will write and telephone when I can. Goodbye, darling,' he said. A moment later, he climbed into a cab and was soon out of sight.

For a few weeks, Gloria went through the motions of life, she adored Gabe and spent as much time with him as possible, but there was an air of sadness about her, and once again, Marcus suggested she resume helping him at the surgery. She refused at first, saying how she did not wish to leave Gabe with a nanny, but his gentle powers of persuasion eventually succeeded. They employed a lovely young woman called Beatrice Smalley as a nanny for Gabe, and Gloria agreed to work in the mornings when the surgery was busiest. Before long, the depression around her began to lift, and her emerald eyes sparkled once more.

She also made friends with a woman of a similar age, who had arrived for a consultation with Marcus, named Lucy Carnegie, whose husband was a solicitor on Lombard Street. She was blonde and pretty, not a classic beauty like Gloria, but she had a captivating smile and a mischievous personality. The two young women had warmed to each other instantly as they chatted together in the reception of the surgery, consequently, they had arranged to meet for tea a few days later at Lyon's Tea Shop on Sloane Street.

It was her first outing without Gabe, and Gloria felt anxious about leaving her son with Beatrice whilst she was away from the house. Nevertheless, Edith encouraged her to go, saying that some young female company would do her good and Gabe would be just fine with his grandmother and Beatrice. So, a cab was hailed and Gloria, looking as lovely as ever in a pale grey taffeta afternoon dress, set off in the direction of Belgravia.

Lucy was already waiting for Gloria at a table by the door, so they could see the comings and goings of the various ladies that frequented the tea shop.

'It is the best view, Gloria, one can have so much fun. Now, what shall we have? The tea and scones here are delicious, what do you say?' Gloria agreed, and they ordered.

The afternoon flew by as the two young women spoke about themselves to each other, their marriage circumstances could not have been more diverse. Lucy's parents had arranged her marriage to Albert Carnegie based on the grounds that he was an upstanding gentleman in society, wealthy enough to keep her in a comfortable lifestyle, and as far as they were concerned, that was enough. She confessed she did not love him but was very fond of him, and because his work kept him extremely busy, it gave her the freedom and money to keep herself well entertained.

'You must come to one of my soirées, we wait for an evening when our men are away or at their clubs, and we have drinks, play cards and have immense fun,' Lucy said.

Gloria was not too sure at this early stage and replied, 'Thank you, but I do not think I could leave Gabe at the moment, he is too young, maybe another time.'

'Of course, my apologies, I have no children of my own, I doubt I will with Albert, but never mind. So, tell me, how did you meet your delicious husband? I saw his photograph on the wall in the reception,' Lucy said.

Gloria panicked a little inside, she did not want to give too much away to her new friend and decided to divulge most of the story but leave out about their elopement and her miscarriage. Indeed, it still upset her whenever she thought about that horrible night and talk about it was something she definitely did not want to do.

For another hour or so, they discussed the latest fashions and society gossip, both women read The Tatler, and Gloria confessed her love for the theatre. Just then, she caught sight of the time on the tea room's magnificent walnut grandfather clock, it was already five o'clock.

'My goodness, look at the time, I really must go, or I will miss Gabe's bath time, he loves splashing about in the water, he never stops smiling, he is such a happy baby. I have enjoyed our tea together, thank you so much for inviting me. Perhaps you might like to take a walk in the park one afternoon with me, I usually go every day with Gabe, today has been an exception,' she said.

'Yes, I would like that, then I can take a peek at this little marvel you keep talking about, is he as handsome as his father?' Lucy asked playfully.

'Not at all,' Gloria replied, 'he is twice as handsome.' And they laughed together.

Gloria's life brightened up somewhat with Lucy for company, spring had arrived, and they strolled in the park, took tea, and soon became firm friends. During one afternoon outing, they spotted a billboard advertising a funfair the following Saturday, so they decided to make a day of it with a picnic lunch. Gabe was now sitting up and would be able to join them on the picnic blanket.

Although her days were passing pleasantly, her nights were increasingly lonely, she missed Gerald tremendously, not having his warm body by her side in bed each night was becoming increasingly hard to bear. She kept every letter he wrote and often sat in bed with the pillows plumped up around her reading them again and again. 'Come home soon, my darling,' she whispered and kissed the latest letter she had received that morning.

The funfair was delightful, there was a merry-go-round, a roller coaster ride, a helter-skelter, Punch and Judy, a freak show and all manner of tents with a variety of amusements. Gloria and Lucy wandered around and were enjoying themselves immensely, and so was Gabe, as he sat up proudly in his perambulator, smiling at his mother.

'He is rather adorable, I must say, makes me feel quite peculiar inside, perhaps I could persuade Albert....' Lucy said wistfully.

It was just then that Gloria spotted a sign - *Madame Burton,*

Fortune Teller, advertised outside a brightly coloured tent. It suddenly reminded Gloria of her grandmother, she told Lucy all about her and decided to pay Madame Burton a visit.

'Lucy, would you mind looking after Gabe while I go in? I have not had my fortune read since Grandmama passed away, she always made it such fun.' Lucy agreed, and Gloria entered into the darkness of the tent.

An old, dark-skinned gypsy woman wearing a red patterned headscarf and enormous gold hooped earrings was seated behind a table covered with a black velvet cloth, on which sat a crystal ball and a pack of tarot cards that had been dealt.

'Come in, my child, what is your name?' Madame Burton spoke with a thick Romanian accent and looked quite daunting.

'Gloria, Madame Burton.'

'Sit, sit, show me your hands.'

Gloria took off her gloves and held out her hands, the gypsy seized them and began studying them in great depth.

'You are lonely woman, yes? I see the life you have now will change path, there will be death.' Startled, Gloria attempted to pull her hands away, but the gypsy woman gripped them tightly and carried on talking. 'There will be many men in your life, but you will never find true happiness.'

'Stop, please, I do not want to hear anymore.' Gloria was frightened, this was not how her grandmama had read palms.

'He is not what he seems, be warned,' the gypsy added.

That was enough, Gloria jumped up out of her seat, glaring at the woman before her.

'I do not believe any of this, none of it is true, here take your silver sixpence as I do not wish to be cursed also.' She snatched up her gloves from the table and hurriedly left the tent, stepping out into the sunshine with a haunted look on her face.

'Whatever is the matter, Gloria, what happened in there?' Lucy asked, looking very concerned.

'It was nothing, just a silly old gypsy woman trying to scare me. Please, can we find the refreshment tent? I am in dire need of a cup of tea.'

Gloria took the handle of Gabe's perambulator from Lucy and looked at her beautiful son, he must have sensed his mother's distress because he started to cry.

She picked him up and hugged him. 'There, there, it is alright, just your silly Mama being over-emotional, I think it is time Papa came home, do you not think?'

The fortune-telling escapade put rather a damper on the rest of the day, and although Gloria tried to shake off the dark mood that had descended over her, before long she asked Lucy if she minded if she took Gabe home, it was his nap time, and Gloria felt a headache coming on.

'I will telephone you tomorrow,' Lucy told her, 'I have no idea why you will not tell me what the gypsy woman said, they are known to be charlatans, you must not believe anything she told you, understand?'

'I will be alright, Lucy, thank you, we will talk tomorrow.'

The women parted company and walked in opposite directions to their homes.

Gerald telephoned from Dublin that evening, and Gloria had never been so happy to hear his voice.

'What is it, darling? I can sense there is something wrong, is it Gabe?' Gerald asked.

'No, our son is fine, he is growing every day and becoming rather heavy to hold. Nothing is really wrong, I just miss you terribly, please can you come home for a few days, darling,' Gloria implored.

'I know, my sweet Gloria, I just might be able to find some time during the Easter break, it would be good to see London again, Dublin is overcome with such poverty and disease, and of course the best thing about London is my wife and son are there.'

They talked for a few more minutes, and Gerald hung up.

Gloria slept fitfully that night, dreaming of men walking past her, staring at her and then jumping off cliffs. Next, baby Gabe was sitting in his perambulator, and it began to roll towards the edge of a different cliff. Try as she might, her dream legs would not work, and she was unable to run and save him, she tried to scream, but nothing came out of her mouth……

She woke and sat bolt upright. 'Gabe,' she called out and dashed into the nursery to make sure her son was alright. He lay there in his crib, sleeping soundly, and Gloria dropped to her knees, breathing heavily.

'Pull yourself together, Gloria,' she chided herself, 'it was a bad dream, nothing more, nothing is going to happen to anyone.' She went back to bed and eventually fell asleep. She was awoken in the morning by the gusty cries of Gabe demanding his breakfast.

True to his word Gerald did make it home for Easter, the whole Phelps household was so pleased to see him. Gloria stood in the hallway with Gabe in her arms, gazing at her husband, her heart full of love. 'How can my life go wrong? Look at him, look at his wonderful family, Madame Burton has told me untruths, I do not believe her.'

All this was passing through her brain as Gerald walked towards her. He kissed her full on the lips and then circled his arms around his wife and son.

'By Jove, it is good to see you,' he said.

The family took tea in the sitting-room, where the conversation was lively and animated. Gloria sat closely beside Gerald with Gabe on her lap, he kept pulling at his father's jacket sleeve as if trying to attract his attention.

Marcus laughed. 'I think you had better remind your son of who you are, old chap.'

At which, Gerald turned to look at his baby son, who instantly smiled at him.

'Here take him,' Gloria said, 'he is not going to break.'

Gerald took his son and bounced him up and down on his knee, which made Gabe squeal with laughter.

That night Gloria lay in Gerald's arms, blissfully content, no nightmares disturbed her sleep, and when they woke, she fetched Gabe from the nursery and put him between them as they sat up in bed waiting for Polly to bring their breakfast. Gloria looked at her two men and vowed that she would never let anything take them away from her.

CHAPTER 6

'Come on, Gabe, you can do it, walk to Papa.' Gloria watched with delight as fifteen-month-old Gabe's chubby little legs carried him safely into the arms of his father on the opposite side of the sitting-room. Gerald swung his son into the air and held him up to see the glittering decorations on the enormous Christmas tree that had been delivered a few days earlier. He had finished his studies in Dublin at last and returned home in time to celebrate Christmas with his family. Gloria's dark cloud had lifted, and she felt at peace once more. Gerald was to commence his first Senior House Officer position at St Thomas's as general surgeon for two years, after which he would decide upon his speciality.

He worked long hours, but Gloria was learning to accept her lifestyle, despite Gerald not being at home much, however, at least he was in London and not hundreds of miles away. She was grateful that he had boundless energy and when not at work, was able to devote equal time to his family, consequently, by March 1906, Gloria was pregnant again, much to the delight of everyone.

Regrettably, the pregnancy did not progress well, Gloria was sick for weeks, and before she had even reached her third month, she suffered another miscarriage. In her own private thoughts, poor Gloria was adamant that the gypsy woman had put a curse on her, not that she could confess this to anyone. Fortunately, Gloria recovered physically quite quickly, but emotionally it was another mental scar that had to be hidden deep in her subconscious. It emerged in her dreams on nights when she was alone while Gerald was working, and she would wake, bathed in sweat and trembling.

Gerald and Marcus both observed how pale and withdrawn Gloria had become, they were sat together in the sitting-room after dinner one evening discussing what could be done to cheer her up.

'You know, she has not been to visit her sister in Ramsgate for months, the change in scenery and the sea air would do her the world of good, do you not think?' Gerald spoke quietly to Marcus, not wanting Gloria to overhear their conversation.

'Yes, son, I agree, but encouraging her to leave you and London will not be an easy task, you know how wilful she is, the trick is to make Gloria think it was her own idea. My, my, the psyche of women, there should be a study done on it.'

The two men laughed loudly, which attracted Gloria and Edith's attention, who were listening to the gramophone at the other end of the room.

'What is it that you two find so amusing this evening?' Edith called out.

'The title of my latest book, it is a mystery entitled *The Female Brain*,' Marcus replied with a feigned serious look on his face.

'And just what is that supposed to mean, my dear? Have you not realised yet that our brains are far superior to yours? Why we can even perform more than one task at a time.'

They all laughed, and Gloria thought about how she could answer the telephone in the surgery, at the same time swing around and reach notes out of the filing draws and inform the next patient when it was time for them to go into the practice room, amongst other things.

The merriment lifted Gloria's mood for a while, so much that she suggested they play a game of Whist, to which they all agreed.

The Phelpses had a lovely rosewood card table that opened to reveal the green baize lined surface inside.

Marcus dealt the cards and said, 'You know, Edith, when was the last time Clara and Lilian came up, or you went down to visit them? You always say there is nothing quite like sister talk and company, do you not agree, Gloria?' It was an attempt to spark her into thinking of Fleur. 'That last postcard Fleur sent you from Ramsgate showed such a beautiful view of the beach and the sea, it certainly made me wish to inhale that fresh sea air.'

His words did hit home, especially as Gloria missed her sister's company a great deal, and despite their keeping a flat in London, Fleur rarely visited, the fact was, she longed for Gerald's company more. She listened to Marcus and Edith talking about the marvellous times they had when Gerald was young, playing on the beaches in Somerset.

'I can remember him at about seven months old sitting on that old, crocheted blanket we used to have, do you remember, dear? He was sitting up one moment, and when I next looked around at him, he had fallen forwards and was face down in the sand. He never cried, just looked extremely surprised and began to examine the sand with his hands after we had propped him back up again. How we laughed,' Edith said.

'Really, Mama, I am sure Gloria does not want to hear amusing anecdotes about my childhood, it is Gabe we should be making memories for,' Gerald replied, a little embarrassed.

Gloria suspected what was happening, and it made her think of her own childhood, they never did anything fun as children. Perhaps it was time she visited Fleur and let Gabe sample some sea air and sand.

'Gerald, darling, would you mind awfully if I did spend a few weeks with Fleur, I think it is also time for our son to experience something new, Fleur has been pleading with me for ages to visit, but I did not want to leave you.'

'Mind, Gloria, it is just what the doctors have ordered for you. I shall be terribly busy myself over the next few weeks, I am about to start my rotation at The Women's Hospital, and there will be a great number of night shifts to endure. Please go, Gloria, I wish to see that lovely complexion of yours with some colour once more,' Gerald said.

Thus, the arrangements were made, and Gloria found herself aboard the train for Ramsgate with Gabe on her lap and Beatrice to assist her, once they reached their destination and were settled in, Beatrice was to return to London the following day.

Gloria spent the whole summer at Ramsgate, she had not realised just how tired and depressed she had become. They went for walks on the beach every day and even bathed in the sea. Gabe ran around in the sand barefoot, laughing and falling over, only to pull himself back up and continue on his journey shouting, 'Mama, Mama,' at the top of his little voice, he was a very content and happy child. By the end of August, Gloria recognised how much her health had improved both mentally and physically. The long evenings talking with Fleur had helped tremendously, but now it was time to return to London and her husband.

They arrived home two weeks before Gabe's second birthday, whose appearance had altered somewhat during his holiday at the coast. His chubby legs had slimmed off with all the exercise, and as he had inherited the Huxley complexion from Gloria, his angelic face was now tanned, as was his mother's.

'Well, I hardly recognise either my wife or child,' Gerald remarked as his son clattered through the hallway running towards his father, 'look at you both.'

'I am sorry, darling, we are both rather brown, I know, but I do feel surprisingly well, and Gabe has had the most marvellous adventures. Fleur has one of those Brownie cameras, and we have dozens of photographs to show you, we must get one.' Gloria hurried over to her husband and kissed him lovingly.

Then, picking up his son, Gerald said, 'Come on, let us find your grandparents, they have missed you sorely. Are you coming, darling?' He held out his hand to Gloria, who was standing, looking at her husband and son.

'No, she is wrong, my life is perfect,' Gloria thought to herself. 'Coming, darling, I was just admiring my handsome men and wondering why I deserve you both,' she said.

'No, it is I who should be grateful, my sweet Gloria, and tonight I will demonstrate my gratitude once Gabe is asleep.'

'Why, Dr Phelps, whatever do you mean by that?' Gloria pretended to be shocked. She took Gerald's outstretched hand and walked with him to the sitting-room where Marcus and Edith were waiting.

Gerald kept his promise that evening, and two months later, much to everyone's delight, Gloria discovered that she was pregnant once more. This time there were no complications, and she gave birth to another healthy son on the 29th of June 1907, they named him David Ralph Phelps. Gloria sat up in bed, cradling her new baby son, exhausted but very happy and asked Gerald to tell Edith to bring Gabe upstairs to meet his baby brother. He ran over to the bed, saying, 'Mama, baby' over and over again.

'Yes, Gabe, he is your brother, David, come and see him.'

The little boy stretched up to see and managed to clamber up on to the bed. He knelt beside Gloria and peered at the tiny bundle in her arms, and bent over to kiss his baby brother on the cheek.

'Well, it looks as if those two will get along swimmingly,' Marcus said, and the family all smiled.

Gloria wrote to her mother with news of the arrival of her second grandson, but even that never prompted Frances to visit, she always had some excuse or another for not being able to make the trip. It continued to sadden Gloria that her parents could not forgive and forget her early folly, so she satisfied herself by thinking that it was their loss, and they would have to live with it. Fleur was overjoyed but also a little envious, she and Filkes had been trying for a baby ever since they married with no success. Nevertheless, she was happy for her sister and arranged to come up to London to visit in a few weeks once Gloria had recovered from the birth.

Christmas 1907 found the Phelps family once more celebrating with a full house of guests. Clara and Lilian came up from Somerset, Fleur and Filkes were also invited. Antony Stevenson had joined the party, not to mention the latest member of the family, baby David, who was growing rapidly and beginning to sit up.

The post-Christmas luncheon traditional cigars were passed between the men as they sat chatting in the sitting-room whilst the ladies listened to the gramophone and played with the children. Gabe doted on his baby brother, he had the most easy-going temperament for a child.

'I wonder how David will be as he grows, he seems content, I am very fortunate to have two such children, it would never do for them to be like I was as a child, no wonder my father despaired of me. I cannot thank you and Marcus enough for everything you have done for me these last four years, you treat me as if I were your own daughter, and for that, I am truly grateful.' Tears of emotion welled up in Gloria's eyes as she spoke.

Edith took her hand. 'If I had been fortunate enough to have had a daughter, I would have wished for her to be just like you, dearest Gloria, you have rekindled an old lady's love for life, it is I who should be grateful.'

73

The two women smiled at each other with great fondness until their moment was interrupted by a little voice saying, 'Grandma, Grandma, come play.' Gabe was trying to pull Edith up from the sofa to see his new brown Steiff teddy bear, whom he had named Teddy, of course.

The bear was sitting in between Clara and Lilian on the sofa opposite, Edith joined her sisters, and Gabe stood facing them. Dressed in his sailor suit, he looked adorable as he pointed at his bear and tried to sing *Doctor Foster went to Gloucester*. Encouraged by his grandmother and great aunts, the whole charade brought about laughter and squeals of delight from Gabe, so much so that his father came over to find out what all the noise was about.

Marcus and Antony were left puffing on their cigars. 'Who would have imagined our little plan could have worked out so well,' Antony said to his friend,

'Yes, she is every the beauty we anticipated and such a wonderful mother, she has very little help from Beatrice, insists on raising the boys herself,' Marcus replied.

'Ah, modern women, what is the world coming to, old chap?' Antony smiled as he spoke, the two men were very liberal and supported the increasing movement towards equality for women.

The new year of 1908 was icy cold with a deep frost, nonetheless, Gloria and Gerald braved an evening out at Daly's Theatre to watch a performance of *The Merry Widow,* which they thoroughly enjoyed, after which Gerald had made a reservation for dinner at The Ritz. Gloria loved London and could not imagine ever living any place else, she soaked up the atmosphere of the dining room, with its glittering chandeliers and the golden statue of Poseidon. She looked as beautiful as ever, dressed in a black velvet gown with the new-fashioned wing sleeves made from embroidered net. Gerald ordered a bottle of champagne.

'What are we celebrating?' Gloria asked.

'Well, I have some news to impart, my darling.'

The waiter brought a bottle of Roederer Cristal and poured each of them a glass in the crystal flutes placed on the table.

Gloria's face dropped. 'You have to go away again, is that what you are going to tell me?'

'No, on the contrary, I have been offered the most wonderful opportunity at the Middlesex Hospital as registrar surgeon. I am to take up the position next week. I wanted to have all the details finalised before I told you, is that not news worth celebrating?'

'Indeed, darling, it certainly is.' Gloria was thrilled and thought how proud she was of him, admitting to herself that although she wished he were home more, he was achieving the ambition he had always desired ever since she first met him. They clinked glasses and toasted his success.

'A few more years, and we will be able to move into our own home, would you like that?' Gerald asked.

'Very much so, your parents are far too generous towards the boys and me, we cannot expect them to support us forever, and I would like nothing more than to have our own home. I love you, Gerald.' Gloria smiled her most enchanting smile, and over dinner, they drank the whole bottle of champagne.

The Phelps household carried on in much the same way, there was a warm, happy atmosphere all around, they celebrated David's first birthday and Gabe's fourth. Gloria worked in the surgery as often as she could, having her hands full with two boys to raise, so she did concede in allowing Beatrice to help her a little more. In the afternoons, she took walks in the park and often met up with Lucy. She spent July with Fleur in Ramsgate, which Gabe was very excited about, and David, who was not yet walking, thoroughly enjoyed sitting in the sand attempting to help his brother build sandcastles.

All too soon, another Christmas was celebrated, and the new year of 1909 welcomed in. Gerald was highly thought of at the hospital and gaining an excellent reputation as a skilled surgeon.

The summer of 1909 brought further marvellous news, Gloria was pregnant again, and on the 23rd of February 1910, she gave birth to Dwight Frederick Phelps. Three splendid sons and a successful husband, Gloria had all she had ever dreamt of. Once again, she wrote to her mother, and once more, she excused herself from visiting because James had been taken ill. Gloria did not know what to believe until the next day when Fleur telephoned and tearfully told her that their father had died from gastritis. An ulcer in his stomach had burst, and he bled to death internally, he was only fifty-one years old. Gloria was stunned into silence, she did not know how to feel, he was her father after all, but he had shown no mercy to her over the years, refusing to speak or even acknowledge her, what was she to do now?

Dwight was only a few days old, and Gloria had not yet recovered from his birth sufficiently to be able to travel for the funeral. She sent her mother a telegram, insisting that she ask their neighbour, Mrs Smedley, if she may receive a call on her telephone. Frances seemed typically calm and collected when they spoke, her personality set by her drilled in discipline, preventing her from expressing any emotion, but something in the words that she said saddened Gloria greatly.

'He became a tyrant after you eloped with Gerald, forcing me to move back to the country and never see you again. He attempted to intercept my letters to you, and many times he succeeded, after a while, it just became easier not to try.'

'I am so sorry, Mama, how could he do that to you? But please, you will visit me after the funeral, you have no reason not to meet your grandsons now, and I know that Marcus and Edith will make you welcome, please come,' Gloria implored. Eventually, Frances was persuaded, and she arrived two weeks later.

The reunion was somewhat reserved, but as predicted, Marcus and Edith made Frances more than welcome, expressing their condolences on the loss of her husband and all the usual utterances. Polly brought tea and cakes into the sitting-room where Gloria and Frances were endeavouring to rekindle some semblance of an attachment to each other, but it was not easy. Their relationship had never been strong prior to their estrangement, it would take a long while for bridges to be re-built.

'Would you like to meet your grandsons?' Gloria asked.

'Very much so, thank you,' Frances replied.

Gloria called for Beatrice to bring the boys downstairs, although five-year-old Gabe was already sitting on the landing, curious to take a peek at the mysterious grandmother who had come to visit. Beatrice passed Dwight into Gloria's arms, and Gabe stood quietly by his mother's armchair with David beside him. They were handsome boys, dark hair and olive-skinned, and Frances could not help but feel a tug on her heartstrings when she saw them.

'Boys, say good afternoon to your grandmama Armstrong,' Gloria instructed.

'Good afternoon, Grandmama Armstrong,' they said in unison with a small bow. David, who was now almost three-years-old, could not quite pronounce Armstrong, it came out as "Arm mom", but everyone kept a serious face.

'I am very pleased to make your acquaintance, Masters Gabe and David,' Frances said.

'And this is the new arrival, Dwight.' He lay blissfully asleep in his mother's arms.

The afternoon passed pleasantly enough, Gloria observed her

mother and tried to read her. She appeared taken with the boys, but an air of sadness and indifference surrounded her as if she had lost her reason to live. James's temper and mental cruelty had sucked the life out of her, and despite the family enjoying a splendid dinner together that evening, Frances politely said thank you but insisted she go home in the morning when asked if she would care to stay for a few more days.

Gloria and Gerald lay talking in bed that evening. 'Poor Mama, she is much changed, I hope that over time she will recover her own self. I will send her photographs and regular reports of the children, perhaps something will put a light back in her eyes.' Gloria spoke with sadness in her voice. 'I fought with my father permanently, I vow I will never let that happen with our boys, we must always try to reason with them, Gerald.'

He pulled Gloria under his arm and kissed her. 'We will do our utmost, my sweet Gloria.'

Just then, lusty cries came from the nursery. 'Someone is hungry again,' Gloria sighed and climbed out of bed to go and feed Dwight.

The first flowers of May were endeavouring to bud in the garden, the weather was decidedly inclement for the time of year with persistent rain, and hail an inch deep was reported at Epsom. Gloria was longing to take a walk but instead had to placate herself by reading the latest issue of The Tatler, it was Friday the 10th of May 1910. Marcus and Edith were visiting her sisters in Somerset, and the house was tranquil until suddenly, there was a great commotion in the hallway as Polly came clattering through the door.

'Mrs Phelps, Mrs Phelps, the king's dead,' she shouted.

Shocked, Gloria jumped up from her chair and hurried to the hall where Polly had already attracted the attention of Beatrice, who was holding David, the two young women were in floods of tears.

'Aye, 'tis true, the king died late last night while we was all in bed, I heard it at the market where I was buying tonight's vegetables, what are we to do?' Polly sobbed.

'My goodness, the announcement last night said he was gravely ill but dead, this is terrible news, poor Queen Alexandra, how dreadfully distressing.'

Gloria attempted to calm the two young women, despite feeling distraught herself, Edward had been a very popular king despite reigning for only nine years.

'Come now, Polly, calm yourself and go and make tea for us all, I will join you in the kitchen in a moment. Beatrice, take David with you, and I will go up and see if Dwight is awake.'

When Gerald returned home that evening, the household was in a state of disorder, dinner was served late, and the boys sensed something was amiss because of the air of distress about the house. Gabe had learned of the King's death at school, but he was only five years old, and unable to grasp the emotional effect it had taken on his mother and nanny.

The king's funeral took place two weeks later, Gerald, Gloria and the boys waited amongst the vast crowds of people outside Buckingham Palace as the funeral procession slowly made its way to Westminster Hall. The Archbishop of Canterbury conducted a small, private service for close family members, after which the procession went on to Windsor Castle. A full funeral ceremony took place in St George's Chapel, where the king was laid to rest. He had been one of the most popular monarchs in history, only time would tell how the new King George V would fare.

Gerald's excellent reputation increased as he worked at various hospitals within London, and he soon announced that he was to take his own rooms on Harley Street. Two years later, by the beginning of 1912, he was financially in a position to purchase his own house in which to contain his growing family.

'Gerald, darling, this is wonderful news, how exciting, my own home, where are we to live?' Gloria was so thrilled, the thoughts of choosing décor and furnishings and overseeing her own household meant the world to her.

'We are to view a promising property tomorrow morning, just a short walk away from here on Lloyd Square,' Gerald told her.

'Gerald, thank you, they are delightful, I am beside myself.'

The house they viewed had four storeys with four bedrooms and two large reception rooms, the kitchen was situated on the lower-ground floor, which also led out into the garden, and there was an additional room on the top floor. It was already very tastefully decorated in Art Nouveau style, which Gloria would be content with, provided she may order new soft furnishings and have a maid of her own. All of this was arranged, and a young girl named Kate Clay was employed.

The last day at Granville Square was dreadfully emotional, after all, her life since marrying Gerald had taken place there, her sons were born there, and she had been very content. Still, they were only moving a short distance away, which meant visiting each other would never be a problem.

The family settled in very quickly, and with much persuasion on Gloria's part, her mother agreed to visit for a few days to see the new house. The visit was strained as their relationship had never been consolidated since her father's death, and they remained polite and unemotional with each other. Frances was thankful that Gloria had found happiness, but London was too much for her, she preferred the quiet of the countryside.

All was well in both Phelps households, and before Gloria knew it, a year had passed since they moved to Lloyd Square. She felt at ease with the world until one evening, whilst watching Gerald as he sat reading the newspaper, the expression on his face darkened, and she suddenly felt her inner peace and quiet disturbed.

'You know, Gloria, there is unrest on the other side of the channel, I have been contemplating volunteering for RAMC again, I could help out a great deal as a surgeon if war broke out,' he said with great sincerity.

'You do not really think that will happen, do you, darling? Surely not,' Gloria replied with a worried expression.

'I fear we may be drawn into it and have to prepare for the worst.'

'Gerald, please, do not say such things, it is too horrible to contemplate.' Gloria felt troubled and wished to change the subject.

'Nevertheless, I will call on my old major and offer my services, one never knows what the future might bring. Now, come on up to bed, Gloria, you look in need of some attention.'

She looked over at her husband, and even after ten years of marriage, she still felt the same rush of love when he spoke in such a manner.

'Well, darling, we have gone and done it again,' Gloria told her husband one evening in early June. Gerald lifted his head from the newspaper he seemed permanently attached to these days.

'Done what, Gloria?'

'We are to expect an arrival around Christmas time.' She smiled, holding her hand over her stomach.

'Good heavens, we are going to need a larger house at this rate,' he exclaimed.

'Are you happy, darling?' she enquired.

'Of course, I am happy, shall we have another son, do you think?'

'I do hope so. Do you remember us saying that girls would be nothing but trouble?' They laughed together.

He actually arrived a little after Christmas, on New Year's Day

1914. After much deliberation over names, they agreed upon Julian Piers Huxley Phelps, and he was as handsome as all his brothers. Gloria lay in bed holding her new arrival, with the other boys sat around her. Gabe was now nine years of age, David six and Dwight three.

'He is not very big, Mama,' Gabe commented.

'Babies are small, darling, you were smaller than Julian when you were born.'

Her eldest son frowned a little and then said, 'But I am the tallest now though, am I not?'

'When I am nine, I will be even taller,' David proclaimed, and the boys began to squabble over who will be the tallest and then the fastest runner and the cleverest at school, Dwight sat on the bed watching his brothers intently until Gloria intervened.

'Boys, stop it now, you will wake Julian. Now run along to Beatrice and get ready for bed. Kisses all around and sleep tight all of you, my beautiful boys.'

How she adored her children, it was moments such as these that Gloria remembered Madam Burton's words that day and told herself once again. 'I knew she was wrong.'

Gerald had already visited RAMC H.Q. on the King's Road to see his old major, Hugh Sansome. He was now a Captain and welcomed Gerald with a firm handshake.

'Good to see you again, old chap, I always knew you would do well, you were an excellent student,' he had said.

Hugh was in his early forties, of stocky build with a strong square face, twinkling blue eyes and a perfectly groomed moustache, he signed Gerald up there and then as a volunteer. He had invited Gerald and Gloria for dinner, and since that evening, never failed to inquire after her and the boys at every RAMC meeting.

'Damn fine woman you have there, Gerald, and four sons to

carry the Phelps name through, Margaret and I have only managed daughters so far, six of them would you believe.'

It had been an enjoyable dinner, and despite Gloria not having a great deal in common with Margaret, they were able to talk enthusiastically about their children's accomplishments whilst the men discussed medicine and politics.

A dark cloud was looming over Europe, the newspapers were filled with reports of the assassination of Archduke Franz Ferdinand and his wife in Sarajevo and the Balkan crisis, but it was Germany's invasion of France and Belgium that finally brought Great Britain to a decision. On the 4th of August 1914 at 11 pm, Britain declared war on Germany.

CHAPTER 7

'What does it all mean, Gerald? Are we safe? What about the boys?' Gloria was decidedly un-nerved and unsure of how being at war with Germany would affect her world. Gerald explained as best he could and tried to reassure her that everyone was confident it would all be over by Christmas.

'Beatrice's brother has already volunteered, and he is only just turned eighteen years of age, she told me he wanted to see some of it before it was all over. It is all so dreadful, darling. Gabe keeps asking me what is happening, and I am unsure of what to say, please will you talk to him,' Gloria pleaded.

'I will have a man to man chat with him soon, but you know I am awfully busy at the hospital preparing for the injured soldiers to arrive, we are expecting hundreds of them, and they are dreadfully wounded,' Gerald replied.

As soon as the war had broken out, Gerald had been called up to one of the Territorial General Hospitals situated around London, he was now an experienced surgeon and his services in great demand. But the sheer scale of the devastation of human life was a shock even for some doctors, many of whom had treated injured men from the Boer War and other recent conflicts. The modern heavy artillery and machine guns ripped men apart, and there had already been 263,000 soldiers wounded at the Battle of Marne, 81,000 of whom had died.

Gloria attempted to keep her life as normal as possible for the boys' sake. Gabe and David attended Clerkenwell Boys' School, which was only around the corner from their home. She walked them there every morning with Dwight scurrying alongside his brothers, trying to keep up, whilst Beatrice pushed Julian in the perambulator. From school, she would walk to Marcus and Edith's house to help in the surgery as often as possible.

Marcus was incredibly busy since many civilian doctors, like Gerald, were being employed by the military, and Gloria barely saw her husband. He worked days and nights attempting to attend to his own patients alongside tending to the wounded soldiers at the Territorial Hospital, the lives of everybody were being turned upside down.

It was soon clear to see that despite hope the war would be over by Christmas, this was not going to happen, nevertheless, Marcus and Edith insisted that the whole family congregate at their home to celebrate Christmas to keep up with tradition. Although the tree was not quite as large as last year, it had been beautifully decorated with silver ribbon bows, holly, ivy, mistletoe and plenty of sugared candies by Edith, Gloria and the boys. Julian had sat next to the box of decorations, pulling them out and examining them thoroughly.

'Look, Mama, Julian looks like the Raj of India,' David said, pointing at his baby brother. Everyone laughed when they saw that somehow, he had managed to wrap a paper garland around his head like a turban and began to cry when he was unable to pull it off.

'My poor darling, what have you done to yourself?' Gloria unravelled the garland and picked him up from the carpet, she bounced him up and down to soothe him. Peace was restored just as the doorbell rang, Polly opened the door to greet Clara and Lilian, who came in with armfuls of presents for everyone.

Gerald insisted he work at the Territorial Hospital on Christmas morning. 'I must ensure that my last intake of patients are in a stable condition before I come home, I promise to be on time for lunch, I certainly do not want to miss my share of that enormous plum pudding Polly has rustled up.' He tried to smile.

'Please try, darling, the boys will be so disappointed. David and Dwight have no understanding of what is happening, and Gabe is learning far more than I wish at school. He asks so many questions that I cannot answer, it is fortunate that Marcus is here to come to my rescue.'

'I know, but we must all do our bit to save Britain from the Huns, and you, my sweet Gloria, are charged with keeping my family safe and try to prevent my father from working himself into the ground,' Gerald told her.

'And what about you, darling? I must keep you safe too,' Gloria replied.

'I am fine, please do not fret.' He pulled Gloria towards him by her still slender waist and kissed her. 'Damn all of this, it will change us all, I cannot imagine Britain will be the same country again, the atrocities and loss of life will be catastrophic if this war continues.' He held Gloria tightly and then left for work.

He returned home a little later than promised. Still, all was forgiven as they tucked into roast turkey filled with chestnuts, pork and apple stuffing, served with gooseberry, apple and bread sauces followed by the eagerly awaited plum pudding. Polly came through into the dining-room carrying the plate on which the steaming, brandy-soaked pudding sat and carefully placed it in the centre of the table. Marcus struck a match with which he set it ablaze, and large portions were served all round.

'Does anyone have the lucky sixpence?' David asked as he scooped a huge spoonful of pudding into his mouth. A chorus of "Not I" echoed around the table when all of a sudden, seven-year-old David stopped in his tracks. 'Ouch,' he cried and spat his pudding back in his bowl.

'David! where are your manners?' Gloria scolded.

He poked around in his pudding bowl and came out with not only the sixpence but also one of his front teeth that had become wobbly a few days prior, the coin had knocked the tooth out.

'Look what I found,' he said, grinning with a gap in the top row of his teeth, 'I will be double lucky, I got the sixpence, and the tooth fairy will also visit tonight.' He looked enormously proud of himself, which made the family laugh.

After lunch, everyone gathered in the sitting-room, and Gloria wound up the gramophone to play a new record of Christmas carols she had purchased, they all sang along, and for a day and a night, the war was forgotten as they celebrated Christmas 1914.

Although the new year of 1915 brought about Julian's first birthday, a happy event for the Phelps family, the war continued to rage. The first Zeppelin bombing raids on the east coast brought about the deaths of innocent civilians. It was reported as *wanton and insignificant*, and it struck fear into the hearts of the English people, not knowing if they could be safe in their own homes.

The newspapers reported the day to day events of the war, which Gloria found impossible to read, she left it for Gerald to read her snippets in the evenings when he was home and attempted to relax in his favourite armchair. More often than not, he fell asleep with a glass of brandy in his hand, and Gloria would have to gently take it and place it on the table beside him. So as not to disturb him, she would cover him with a blanket and let him sleep for as long as possible before his next round at the hospital.

The war was relentless, April reported the "gas barbarity" that had taken place in Ypres. Gloria was horrified to learn that the Germans had released poisonous chlorine gas over the trenches, killing some soldiers instantly, leaving others to die agonising, lingering deaths.

She did read about the sinking of the Lusitania by a German torpedo, and in the privacy of her bedroom, once her children were asleep, she wept uncontrollable tears, grieving for the deaths of the 1,198 civilian lives, and then broke her heart over the ninety-four children that had perished with them.

She awoke the next morning with red-rimmed eyes but immediately climbed out of bed, wrapping herself in her favourite sage green velvet dressing gown and went to check on her own beautiful boys. Gabe and David were asleep on the floor beneath a tent they had made from their bedsheets, the eiderdowns and pillows were a mattress, she smiled. 'Maybe I should let them join the Boy Scouts when this wretched war is over,' Gloria thought to herself and went across the landing to look in on Dwight and Julian.

They had the room opposite, and Beatrice slept in the smaller adjoining room, she had already arisen after hearing Julian cry when he woke up. Over the years, Gloria had become very fond of Beatrice, she helped quietly in the background, always aware that Gloria wished to raise the children herself as much as possible, they had a mutual understanding that had developed over time. Gloria watched her lift Julian out of his cot, speaking quietly to him, he soon smiled at her, and she carried him over to the dressing table that was utilised for washing and changing him. Dwight was still sleeping, and Gloria walked over to Beatrice.

'Good morning, Mrs Phelps, he had a bit of an unsettled night, maybe he just had a bad dream, we all seem to be having them at the moment,' she said.

Gloria took over washing and changing her son. 'Have you never thought of finding a husband and having children of your own, Beatrice?' she asked.

'No chance of that now, is there? They'll not be any young men left soon if this war goes on, they'll all be dead,' Beatrice replied.

Gloria felt eternally grateful that she had found Gerald long before this ghastly time, her main fear now was keeping him. Only the other evening over dinner, he spoke about how many doctors in the Corp were being drafted abroad to the field hospitals. She lived in dread of this happening to Gerald.

Gloria longed for summer to arrive, maybe the sunshine would lift people's spirits. She had hoped to spend a few weeks with Fleur at Ramsgate again, except Gerald had advised against it on account of the increasing number of Zeppelin bombing raids on Britain's coasts. Instead, Fleur came up to London, and the mixture of her sister's company and the warmer weather cheered her up somewhat. Lucy joined them on numerous occasions, they took long walks in the parks with the children, went boating on the Thames and talked about the war as little as possible, except for how it was affecting their husbands. Fleur spoke about how hectic life was for Filkes, some of the larger hotels in Ramsgate had been converted to hospitals caring for the wounded, keeping him equally as busy as Gerald. On the other hand, Albert had joined the Royal Flying Corps. He already had a keen interest in aviation prior to the war and taken flying lessons, his transfer to the corps was a simple application for transfer.

'I must say, he looks rather dashing in his uniform,' Lucy remarked, 'how those flying machines get up off the ground is a mystery to me, but Albert loves it, the views you see from the sky are astonishing, he tells me, cannot say that I wish to try it myself.'

David turned eight years of age that July and Gabe eleven in September, summer had passed through to autumn, and the nights began to close in. The boys returned to school, and Dwight joined his brothers for his first year at Clerkenwell. He had been very excited about wearing his school uniform, and Gloria felt as if she would burst with pride when all three boys lined up in the sitting-room to have their photograph taken with her box brownie.

'Why I think you must be the most handsome trio I ever laid eyes upon, now chins up, eyes towards the camera.'

The click, click sound of the shutter was very familiar in the Phelps household, as Gloria wanted to capture every moment of her sons' development over the years. She had dozens of photograph albums, all kept in a bookcase in the sitting-room.

Their lives retained a certain normality and routine, and for once in a long time, Gerald was home for dinner and did not have to work that night. The boys were allowed to stay up late so they could spend time with their father, they played charades and blind man's bluff, the latter of which caused poor little Julian to be tripped over on numerous occasions as he toddled around trying to join in. He had learned to walk in the summer but was still finding his feet, eventually, the game had to be called off when he fell over and bumped his head. Gloria was trying to pacify him when they all heard a loud bang from outside, which started Julian crying again.

'What the devil was that?' Gerald sounded quite alarmed and went over to the window to take a look outside, in the distance, he could see flames and smoke, they heard more loud bangs, which scared the boys.

'What is it, Papa?' Gabe asked.

'I have no idea,' his father replied, 'but something is on fire in the direction of The Strand and Aldwych.'

More thunderous bangs followed, which made the whole family, along with Beatrice and Kate, venture outside to investigate what was happening. All eyes were fixed into the distance and were met with a chilling sight. Shaped like a colossal silver cigar, a Zeppelin moved silently through the sky, the loud bangs were the explosions coming from bombs being dropped indiscriminately on populated areas of London, only one or two miles away from Lloyd Square.

Totally outraged, Gerald grabbed his sons and pushed them towards the front door, 'Get back inside,' he yelled, 'and go down to the kitchen, we will be safer down there.'

'Is it a Zeppelin, Papa?' both Gabe and David shouted.

'Hurry up, do as I say, come on, Gloria.' She stood staring at the gigantic machine in the sky, clutching her youngest son to her chest and stunned into silence. 'Gloria, Gloria, damn it, woman, come on!' Gerald's expletive shook her out of her daze, and she hurriedly made her way into the house.

The frightened group of women and children huddled together whilst Gerald paced around muttering angrily to himself about how despicable the Huns were, bombing innocent civilian people, and how he wished this terrible war to end now before the loss of human life reached millions. Gloria had never seen her husband so agitated, the war was changing him, over the months, he had become quiet and withdrawn. She tried hard to rationalize his long silences with his being over-tired, but there was more to it, and with every attempt to talk to him, he replied with the same answer. 'You would not understand, it is not for you to understand.'

After about half an hour, Gerald instructed everyone to stay put while he went up to establish if it was safe to come out, he soon returned. 'The Zeppelin is gone, but it appears as if there has been much damage in the distance. Now, come on, boys, it is way past your bedtime.'

'But Papa, can we not go and see?' Gabe pleaded.

'Certainly not! What you will see is not for boys of your age, now go on with your mother and try to get some sleep,' Gerald snapped.

Gabe, David and Dwight obeyed their father and made their way upstairs, Beatrice settled Julian into his cot, whilst five-year-old

Dwight sat on his bed wide-eyed with bewilderment.

'What happened, Nanny?' he asked.

'There, there, poppet, nothing for you to worry about, snuggle under the blankets, and close your eyes.' The little boy did as he was told and soon fell asleep while Beatrice stroked his dark brown hair, humming quietly.

On the other hand, Gabe and David in the room opposite had become exceedingly over-excited, and Gloria was having difficulty persuading them into their pyjamas.

'Did you see how enormous it was? I have never seen anything so huge, how does it fly? Who steers it?'

They talked incessantly until Gloria had to scold them, something she never liked to do, she preferred to try and talk reason with them, but tonight that was never going to happen. The two boys were quiet immediately, knowing they had pushed their mother too far.

'Sorry, Mama,' they both said. Gabe still followed with, 'but please can we go and see tomorrow after school?'

'I doubt your father will allow it, now go to sleep both of you.'

She gave each of her eldest sons a kiss and tucked them in, 'Good night, my darlings,' she said and turned off the light as she left.

Downstairs, Gerald was on the telephone, the hospital had rung, requesting he come immediately as there had been many people badly injured and killed.

'My father has been called in also, I think it would be best if my mother comes and spend the night here with you and the boys, neither of you should be alone tonight.'

'Yes, of course, poor Edith,' Gloria replied.

'I would not worry too much about my mother, she was brought up on a farm, and she once told me she could shoot birds eating the peas in their garden from twenty yards, so I think you will be safe with her.' Gerald said.

Marcus and Edith arrived at that moment, and the two doctors left together in a cab to the hospital. The two women wearily made their way to the sitting-room and poured a stiff brandy each. They discussed the evening's dreadful events, and Gloria spoke of her fear for the boys and how helpless she felt.

'I wish there were something I could do other than keep house and take care of the children. Gerald and Marcus work so hard, Gabe, David and Dwight are at school, Beatrice and I only have Julian during the day. I know Marcus lets me help at the surgery out of the kindness of his heart, he has it running like clockwork without me, I need to do something more,' she sighed and sipped her brandy.

'I heard from Mrs Bancroft next door that her daughter works as a clerk in the Civil Service, you are excellent at typing and book-keeping now, perhaps you could enquire there?' Edith replied.

'You know, I rather think I might, thank you.'

The devastation of the Zeppelin air raids was evident everywhere in the city, the National Penny Bank had gone up in flames and theatres were damaged on The Strand. Gerald had returned home that following morning exhausted. He described some of the horrific injuries that innocent people had sustained, it made Gloria sick and all the more determined to find some form of employment to help the war effort.

The following day she called at the Bancroft's house to speak to Dorothy with regard to applying for a position at the office where she worked. Dorothy was in her mid-twenties, a kind-hearted, homely looking girl with light auburn hair and freckles. She was more than happy to introduce Gloria to her supervisor, and within a few days, Gloria had a desk, a typewriter and a huge pile of papers requiring two copies of each. Before long, Lucy joined them, and the three women took their work very seriously indeed.

Gerald was vaguely pleased that Gloria had found "something to do", as he put it, not that he took much notice of her anymore. He had taken a flat near the Territorial Hospital, the constant travelling back and forth was wearing him down being his justification. Therefore, he paid very little attention to Gloria's new role, which disappointed her somewhat. The war was changing everything, and Gloria felt as if her life was slowly slipping away from her.

CHAPTER 8

Another Christmas and New Year's Day passed with relatively subdued celebrations in both Phelps households, and 1916 brought continuous death and destruction in Europe. The newspapers reported daily with details of the lost and missing men and the events of all theatres of war. Gloria found the use of the word theatre to describe war utterly offensive.

Gerald rarely came home, and she often wondered how he mustered up the energy to keep going. Even though she missed him enormously, she tried hard not to complain, her main difficulty was trying to explain to the boys where their father was.

The war raged on, and conscription was introduced in January. All single men between eighteen and forty-one years of age were liable to be called up for military service. The Battle of the Somme stole the lives of 19,240 men on the first day, and by its end, the total amounted to 420,000. Tragically, Lucy's husband was amongst the casualties, he was shot down on the Western Front. Lucy was grief-stricken for days, both Gloria and Dorothy did their utmost to console her. Gradually, over the weeks, her despair lessened, and she returned to work sad but understanding of the thousands of other grieving widows there were across the world.

The lives of everyone seemed to drift along in a never-ending hope that one day the war would end, the spark of life had long been extinguished, and even Gloria began to feel numb and emotionless. Despite everything, the boys were doing well at school, in fact, Gabe was top of his class in all subjects. He soaked up information like a sponge and if truth be known, was ready to start Westminster School, but as his thirteenth birthday was not until next September, he reluctantly accepted that he would have to wait.

A brief glimmer of hope that peace might be made between Germany and the Allies shone for a short while in December 1916. Unfortunately, it came to nothing, and the war resumed. There were food and coal shortages, Marcus and Gerald commented on the increase of tuberculosis, polio and rickets amongst the poverty-stricken Londoners. In actual fact, a large proportion of men drafted were already infected with primary tuberculosis, which would be missed at their examination. Consequently, these soldiers went on to develop a secondary infection from the damp, cold, unsanitary conditions of the trenches, disease was rife.

1917 brought no respite, and on the day in April when Gerald broke the news that he had been promoted to Lieutenant-Colonel and was to be sent to France in command of a field hospital, Gloria could stay strong no longer and broke down.

'Please, Gerald, do you have to go? What about the boys? What if something happens to you? It would be too much to bear. I do not want you to go,' she sobbed.

'I have no choice, Gloria, please do not make this any harder than it is already, we must all make sacrifices.'

He was too tired for her tears, and in the current climate, he was beginning to find her emotional character draining. His expertise was desperately required in France, he had felt very honoured at being promoted and eager to help save lives at the front line instead of mending those already saved at home.

The following week, Gloria stood with her boys, Marcus and Edith, on the platform of Victoria Station, tearfully waving Gerald goodbye. He turned to his eldest son. 'Gabe, take care of your mother and brothers and do as Grandfather tells you, I expect to hear excellent reports from your headmaster, and keep practising your Latin verbs, my boy.'

'Yes, Papa,' Gabe replied, holding up his chin, endeavouring to be brave.

His father ruffled his thick brown hair and did the same to David and Dwight. Julian was only two-years-old and had no real comprehension of the events taking place, Gloria was holding him on her hip as he looked around the noisy train station wide-eyed. Gerald put his arm around Gloria and kissed her. 'Be strong, much suffering awaits me in France, and it will be some time before I am home again. Take care of my sons.'

He kissed his mother on the cheek and shook his father's hand firmly, Marcus pulled his son towards him and patted him on the back. 'Take care, old boy, and return safely to us all,' he said. And with that, Gerald turned and walked towards the open door of the first-class train carriage, he stepped up, turned to wave to his family one last time and then sat down next to another RAMC officer.

The tram journey home was a subdued affair, no one spoke much, and the older boys were terribly upset at seeing their father go away. Julian sat on Gloria's lap, looking out of the window, she held him tightly as if clinging on to the lives of everyone she loved. She had felt confronted with a turning point in her life as she watched Gerald walk away from her on the platform, and suddenly Madame Burton's words pushed their way into her thoughts. *You are lonely woman, yes? I see that the life you have now will change path, there will be death.* Gloria started and felt the colour drain from her face, Edith had been watching her.

'Are you alright, my dear? You have gone dreadfully pale,' the older woman whispered, not wishing for the boys to overhear.

Gloria replied with sadness in her voice. 'What is to become of us all, Edith, when will this wretched war be over? I have a bad feeling in my heart.'

Edith took Gloria's hands in hers. 'We will survive, we have to, you have four splendid sons relying on us, and they all deserve the best chance in life we can offer them.'

Her words were wise and full of belief, once again, Gloria pushed Madame Burton's words deep into the dark recess of her mind and attempted a smile at her mother-in-law.

'Shall we take a detour to the funfair at Battersea Park and let the boys and we enjoy a little light relief? I quite fancy a turn on the shooting gallery and imagine a Hun in my sights,' Edith said with a twinkle in her eye.

She was in her seventies, straight and proud and in full possession of all her faculties. Gabe had overheard the last part of the whispered conversation and piped up, 'Really, Grandmama, can you shoot a gun?'

'Indeed, I can, young man, I was an excellent shot in my youth, now let us proceed henceforth and see if an old lady still has a good eye.'

Edith Phelps certainly did have an excellent eye, three bullseye shots in a row and a much-deserved round of applause from the crowd that had gathered around them. The stallholder was equally impressed and awarded her with a large stuffed dog made from beige fur with black floppy ears. A much cheerier party returned to Granville Square, it had been decided that Gloria and the boys were to live there while Gerald was away. They clattered their way into the hallway, shouting excitedly to each other, which roused Marcus from his study, he had not wished to visit the funfair as he had much work to catch up on at home.

'My goodness, what a din,' he exclaimed.

'Look, Grandfather, look what Grandmama won on the shooting gallery,' Dwight shouted excitedly, holding up the toy dog, 'his name is Jip'.

Marcus frowned at his wife over the top of his spectacles and then shook his head, smiling. 'Still got it then, old girl?' he said.

'It would appear so, husband dear,' Edith replied modestly, and for the first time in a long time, laughter rang out in the house.

Life soon fell back into its usual routine, the boys went to school, and Gloria continued her job at the Civil Service. Fortunately, Beatrice stayed with the family and took care of Julian while Gloria was working. Many girls had left service to work in the munition's factories or as conductresses or even drivers on the buses, trams and underground trains, and this included Gloria's maid. Thankfully, Polly remained with Edith, she was in her forties and quite happy to stay in regular employ with the Phelpses.

Gerald wrote to Gloria as often as possible, his letters were brief and filled with the horrors of war. Thankfully, he had remembered to arrange a telegram for Gabe to wish him good luck on his first day at Westminster, much to Gloria's relief. Her eldest son looked incredibly handsome as he stood before her in his brand-new school uniform, although only of average height, he was well proportioned with an athletic build.

'Eyes to the camera, darling,' Gloria said and clicked the shutter of the much-used box brownie. Not wanting Gerald to miss anything while he was away, she made certain that as many moments as possible were captured, so she could show him when he returned home. 'Make it soon, my love,' she whispered to herself.

Every now and again, a sense of doom overwhelmed her. She lay awake with too many troubled thoughts for her to sleep. Somehow, sleep would eventually come, and she would rise the following morning summoning up the strength and resolve to make it through another day, if only for her sons' sakes.

A week before Christmas 1917, a letter from Gerald arrived with the most wonderful news the family could have wished for, he had been granted leave to return home for Christmas, everyone was over-joyed. He could not say on what day it would be, it all depended upon available transport.

It was seven o'clock Christmas Eve when an exhausted Gerald walked through the front door of Granville Square, he dropped his bag on the hall floor as his four sons rushed towards him.

'Papa, Papa, you made it in time for Christmas,' they chorused.

He knelt on one knee as each boy threw their arms around him, almost pushing him over.

'Steady on, chaps, you almost knocked the wind out of my sails.' He hugged each one tightly.

Gloria, Marcus and Edith stood in the hallway watching the touching scene, and as soon as Gerald was able to tear himself away from his sons, he turned his head upwards to look at the rest of his family, the face that greeted them shocked Gloria immensely. It was thin and drawn, with dark shadows under his glazed eyes, she put her hand over her mouth as she gasped.

'Gerald, darling, what have they done to you?' she implored, rushing over to him as he attempted to untangle himself from the numerous arms and legs that encompassed him. He stood up, and Gloria embraced him, kissing him gently. 'You look exhausted and famished, come through and warm yourself by the fire, Polly managed to rustle up some coal and wood, there is such a shortage.'

Gerald flopped down in the armchair by the fireplace, he was in his RAMC uniform, and whilst part of her felt proud of the sacrifices he was making, Gloria despised what the war had done to her husband. Polly brought him through a tray of cold chicken, pickles and bread, accompanied by a steaming pot of tea, everyone else had already dined earlier, and Gerald said he was too tired to eat much anyway.

Nearly four-year-old Julian stared at his father, saying nothing, however, Gabe, David and Dwight were so full of questions to the point where Gloria could sense they were pushing Gerald too far.

She cut in. 'Come now, boys, give your father some peace, he is exhausted, I am sure he will relate his adventures tomorrow, besides if you do not go to sleep, Father Christmas will not bring you any presents.' That gained their attention, and they instantly fell silent. 'Now say goodnight to your father, grandmama and grandfather, hasten your way upstairs, and I will be up in a few minutes.'

They marched out of the room in order of age, followed by Julian bringing up the rear, totally out of step with his brothers as they made their way up the stairs.

'That behaviour should not be encouraged in boys so young,' Gerald snapped, 'a fifteen-year-old boy died on my table last week, not much older than Gabe, had one of his legs blown away. I was unable to save him, crying out for his mother at the end, stupid boy had lied about his age when he joined up. It is all so futile.'

The room fell deathly silent. Marcus walked over to the drinks cabinet and poured a large brandy for himself and one for his son.

'Here, drink this up, old boy, and then I think sleep and rest are required.' Gerald took the glass from his father and made short work of the rich, warm liquid that burned his throat as he swallowed. Marcus always had such a calming influence on every situation, and this was no exception.

'My apologies, I am most dreadfully tired, I think I will go up. Goodnight, I will see you in the morning.'

Gloria had not spoken a word, the change in Gerald was alarming, she was unsure of what to say, so she just stood up, put her arm through his and silently led him up the stairs.

They walked in silence until they reached their bedroom when Gloria spoke. 'I will just check on the boys, darling, and be with you shortly.'

Gerald pulled away from the hand slipped through his arm, she watched as he walked through the doorway, he looked as if he held the weight of the world on his shoulders, and Gloria felt helpless.

Beatrice was attempting to settle Julian and Dwight into bed, it was Christmas Eve after all, and they were very excited. Gloria sat on the bed beside Julian and stroked his hair, he had inherited curls from somewhere in the family line and looked like a little cherub snuggled up in his eiderdown. Dwight was sitting up, bright-eyed and wide awake. 'I am too excited to go to sleep, Mama,' he said.

'Well, if you do not sleep, Father Christmas will know, and he will not leave you a present,' Gloria said seriously,

'But, Mama -' Dwight started to speak, however, Gloria put her finger to her lips.

'Hush now, lie down and count sheep, you will be asleep in no time.' A somewhat disgruntled Dwight pulled his eiderdown over his head and began counting.

'One sheep, two sheep, three sheep.'

'Count them in your head, darling,' Gloria said, 'now good night both of you, I will see you in the morning.' She kissed them and then crossed the landing to Gabe and David's room, they were fully aware that Father Christmas was not real, but fortunately, both were mindful that their younger brothers still believed. Their conversation stopped when Gloria entered, which alerted her to the fact they were talking secretively about something.

'No secrets from your mother, boys, what is the matter?' she asked.

They both looked very serious, Gabe spoke. 'What is the matter with Papa? He looks most unwell.'

Gloria forced a smile. 'Papa is just tired from the long journey, darlings, nothing to worry about.'

'But we heard him shouting about someone dying, Papa never usually shouts at anyone, are you alright, Mama?' Gabe replied.

'Less of this talk now, come on to bed, you both have the latest issue of Boys' Magazine to read, and we do have Christmas to celebrate tomorrow, so lights out at nine o'clock, and I will see you in the morning.'

They all bade each other good night, and Gloria closed their door behind her. She stood motionless for a moment, her heart racing, Gerald had changed immensely, and she was unsure of how to help him. In the past, she would have teased him and used her charms to lift him from black moods, but this was something entirely different.

She crept quietly into her dressing room and changed into her silk nightdress, it was cold, making her shiver, so she slipped a robe over the top. Taking a deep breath and mustering up a smile, she entered the bedroom that Gerald had not frequented for many months, to her surprise and to some degree of relief, he was fast asleep on top of the covers in full uniform, exhausted. Gloria took a spare blanket from the oak chest at the bottom of the bed, covered him gently, and then lay her robe on top. Knowing it smelt of her perfume, she hoped the aroma might remind him of her while he slept. Climbing in beside him, she curled her body around his, closed her eyes and tried to sleep.

It must have been the early hours of the morning when she was stirred by Gerald talking incoherently in his sleep, he was hot and sweating. Gloria watched his closed eyes moving from side to side as he dreamt of what she knew not, but from the expression on his face, it was nightmarish.

'My poor darling, what hells have you witnessed?

Now that she was awake, Gloria took the opportunity of slipping into the boys' bedrooms to put a small gift in the stockings they had hung over their bedposts. In past years, she and Gerald had crept into their rooms together, placed presents at the foot of their beds and were then woken early by shouts of delight that Father Christmas had been. This year was a more sober event, and Polly was to place their main presents under the Christmas tree once the boys were all fast asleep.

It had been hard to purchase much at all this Christmas, and trying to avoid military-themed presents had been nigh on impossible. Even though Gloria had no desire to encourage it, the older boys had all expressed their want for some lead toy soldiers. After much searching, Gloria had come across a set of RAMC figures complete with doctors, nurses, a stretcher-bearer and an ambulance. 'Perfect,' she had congratulated herself.

In addition, she purchased a Meccano set each for Gabe and David, for Dwight a drawing pad and a large pack of Crayola crayons, as soon as he could hold a pencil he had loved drawing and colouring, and for Julian a pull along toy dog named Prince as a playmate for Jip. Even though she was unsure if Gerald would be home for Christmas, she had bought him a silver cigarette case engraved inside with the words - Love Always, Gloria.

Morning broke to the excited voices of four boys who had all congregated in Gabe and David's room to delve into their stockings and discover the contents. It was nine o'clock, and Gloria gently roused Gerald from his sleep, he woke slowly and then started as he realised where he was, noticing that he had slept fully dressed in his uniform.

'Welcome back, darling,' Gloria murmured, 'you have been out for hours, and you were having what looked like the ghastliest nightmares.'

'It is a nightmare, I cannot tell you.' His voice was hoarse, so she fetched him a glass of water from the nightstand.

'But you are home now, darling, and it is Christmas morning. Why not dress in something comfortable today, out of this horrid khaki, and there are four boys eager to see their father. I will instruct them to keep the noise down if possible.'

Gerald complied, and within an hour, he was washed, shaven and dressed in a brown tweed suit, looking fresher than the night before. He joined the family in the dining room, where they were all partaking of poached eggs on toast. The large willow pattern teapot sat in the centre of the table, and that was the first thing Gerald desired, he had not tasted a decent cup of tea since he left for France.

All faces turned towards him as he wished them good morning, he was relieved there was no mention of his outburst from the previous evening, and the family enjoyed a pleasant breakfast together. They kept the conversation light for the sake of the boys, and as soon as they were allowed down from the table, Gabe, David and Dwight rushed into the sitting-room to set up their hospital, with Julian bringing up the rear dragging Prince along behind him by a collar and lead. It was quite a comical sight as Prince kept falling over, and Julian had to stand him back up, then the whole process was repeated enough times before the little boy gave up, picked the dog up by its ears and followed his brothers into the other room.

Gabe called to his father. 'Papa, Papa, please come and help us set up the field hospital we had for Christmas.' Gerald looked sharply at Gloria.

'Go and have a look, I thought it was rather fitting under the circumstances,' she said.

Everyone followed through into the sitting-room, and Gerald

made his way over to the small table that his sons were using to set up the toy figures.

'Help us, Papa, please, where shall we put them? What does your hospital look like?' David asked.

Gerald's face began to turn an angry shade of red when he saw what his sons were playing with, how could a tin of little lead figures possibly relate to the gruesome sights he was witnessing day after day, week after week.

'Not now, David, I need to talk to your grandfather,' he growled.

'But, Papa, we have not seen you for ages, we want to hear about your adventures in France.'

'Not now, I said!' His voice had risen harshly, 'And there are certainly no adventures to be told.' He turned his back on his family and strode towards the study, leaving them all in stunned silence.

'What has happened to him, Marcus?' Gloria asked, 'that is not Gerald, he has barely spoken a word to me since he came home, what can be done?'

Marcus frowned. 'The horrors of war have happened, Gloria, and sometimes it cannot be undone, I will try and speak to him. In the meantime, encourage the boys to play with some of their other presents if you can.'

Lilian came to the rescue and suggested a game of *Pin the tail on the donkey*. Everyone found that an agreeable choice and a welcome distraction from the gloomy atmosphere that had descended upon the Phelps household.

Marcus followed his son into the study and found him standing by the fireplace, smoking a cigarette. 'May I join you?' he asked. Gerald jumped, startled from his thoughts.

'Yes, of course.' He offered a cigarette from the silver case Gloria had given him, Marcus lit it and inhaled deeply.

'Care to talk, old chap, it might help.'

Gerald scowled. 'No, Father, I do not wish to talk about it, you would not understand, no-one can understand, you would have to be there.' He stubbed out his cigarette in the ashtray on the mantelpiece. 'Now, I suspect there will be some kind of luncheon to be had, let us get Christmas over and done with so that I can return to my work in France.'

Marcus thought it wise to let the subject rest, he could see Gerald's nerves were more than frayed at the seams and did not want to push him over the edge.

'Damn this war, when in hell's name will it ever end?' Marcus spat the words out.

'Perhaps when there is no-one left to kill,' Gerald replied.

Gerald remained in the study until lunch was served, and Marcus made his way back to the sitting-room where Edith had managed to pin the donkey's tail onto its head, much to the amusement of the boys who were laughing hysterically.

Polly had worked her magic in the kitchen, turning out a more than adequate Christmas fayre and of course, her famous plum pudding. Sadly, there was an air of melancholy during the whole affair, and Gerald soon excused himself and retired to his bedroom, declaring he was tired and needed to rest. Gloria made to stand up and join her husband, but Marcus gently pulled her back down and whispered in her ear, 'Let him be for a while, my dear, he is in a very vulnerable position at present, and I feel he needs to work his way through it alone.'

Reluctantly, Gloria agreed, and the rest of the family attempted to continue the Christmas festivities for the boys' sakes.

Antony Stevenson joined the party in the evening, he always managed to cheer up a situation with his morgue sense of humour. He was busy relating the case of a chap who died from drinking a poisoned bottle of vintage port he had received as a gift. The challenge had been to ascertain whether he was the intended victim or whether it was some unknown person from twenty years earlier, the port having been poisoned when it was initially bottled.

'Turned out the poor chap was the victim of unfortunate circumstances, the poison had been administered some years prior. Whoever had been targeted at that time had a lucky escape, or perhaps they suffered their end through some other dastardly deed,' Antony said.

Gloria was sitting opposite Antony, and just as he had finished his gruesome account, she spotted Gerald standing in the doorway, smoking a cigarette and watching his family intently. The moment he realised that Gloria had seen him, he turned away and walked out into the hallway. She could take no more, excused herself and made towards Gerald. He began to move away from her, so she called out.

'Darling, please wait, talk to me, have I done something wrong?'

'You see, there you go again, it is always about you, never a thought for anyone else,' he snarled. Gloria was utterly taken aback.

'Gerald, how can you say that? How cruel of you.'

'Life is cruel, Gloria, now run along back to your little party and leave me in peace.' He walked into the study, slammed the door behind him and locked it.

Gloria was left standing alone in the hallway, totally stunned as to what had just taken place, the despicable war had stolen her husband, and she felt totally and absolutely desolate. Slowly, she made her way back to the sitting-room, where a decanter of sherry sat on the walnut sideboard, she poured herself a large glass and sat down heavily on the sofa, almost spilling her drink. She must have been sitting there for quite some time sipping her sherry, struggling to untangle the thoughts that were racing through her brain when Edith's voice broke into them.

'He is my son, and I share your despair, my dear.' The two women sat in silence, neither of them knowing what to say.

Gerald stayed in the study and never came up to bed. Gloria and Beatrice had seen to the boys, with Gloria trying her utmost to reassure Gabe and David, mainly, that their father was over-tired and that he would soon be back to his usual self. Deep down inside, she sensed doom and conceded it not to be so.

She barely slept herself, and as morning broke, went downstairs to see if Gerald had come out from the study. All she found was a note on the mantelpiece informing her that he had gone to the Territorial Hospital and would spend the night at the flat. Alongside the message lay the silver cigarette case Gloria had given Gerald for Christmas. Clutching both to her chest, a feeling of utter despair overwhelmed her, and she began to cry, fearing that Madame Burton's fortune was coming to pass.

Gerald returned later in the morning to say his farewells, he gave his mother a kiss, stiffly shook hands with his father and four sons, and left for the train station to return to France. He never even acknowledged Gloria as he walked out of the front door.

CHAPTER 9

The beginning of 1918 was a sorry affair, Gerald never remembered either Julian's or Dwight's birthdays. Indeed, no communication was received from him whatsoever until a telegram arrived for Gloria one morning at the beginning of March. She opened it with trembling hands, not knowing what to expect, it read.

'WE REGRET TO INFORM YOU LT. COLONEL G. N. PHELPS INJURED DURING BOMB RAID ON T.H. NO. 4. NATURE OF WOUNDS NOT YET RECEIVED WILL SEND FURTHER PARTICULARS WHEN RECEIVED.'

Slowly, she walked into the sitting-room, where Marcus and Edith were having coffee. When they saw the expression on her face and that she was clutching a piece of paper in her hand, they feared the worst.

'The hospital has been bombed, Gerald is injured, that is all it says.' The words came out in a curiously calm manner, and Gloria felt numb as she passed the telegram to Marcus.

'Sit down, dear,' Edith said, who had herself turned ashen. Gloria sat next to Edith on the sofa whilst Marcus headed for the hallway to make a telephone call, he returned a few minutes later.

'Nobody has heard anything yet, but Captain Sansome assured me that if any details come his way, he would inform us immediately.'

'So, we just sit and wait?' Edith asked.

'I am afraid so, my dear.'

Gloria looked at the time on the grandfather clock, it was already gone nine, and she was due at the Civil Service at half-past. 'I should get my skates on, or I will be late for work.' She spoke in the same matter of fact manner.

'Yes, you should, dear, we ought to carry on as best we can until we have further news,' Marcus replied.

Gloria went to the hall and put on her coat, picked up her embossed leather handbag from the table and left the house in silence. Lucy and Dorothy were wonderfully supportive after Gloria broke the news to them, they said all the right things, attempting to bolster her up and when Lucy said, 'He will be home in no time, darling, mark my words.' They found her reply most unexpected.

'I am not sure he will come home, not to me and the boys anyhow, not a single letter has arrived since his return to France, I fear I have lost him.'

She described his behaviour at Christmas to her exceedingly dismayed friends, who both agreed that it must be the effects of the war and that, of course, he will come home. Gloria put on a brave face but was not at all convinced.

Four more days past with the same routine, take the boys to school, go to work, bring the boys home from school, tea, dinner, bed, then on the fifth morning, another telegram arrived. Gloria opened it in trepidation of the information it would contain.

'LT. COL G N PHELPS TRANSFERRED TO NO. 53 WIMEREUX IMPENDING SURGERY. SHRAPNEL INJURY RIGHT LEG. WILL KEEP INFORMED.'

'My poor Gerald, will you ever return to me?' Her life was turned upside down, and she felt powerless to change anything. Her beloved husband was injured in a hospital in France, moreover, he seemed oblivious to her existence, and her heart was breaking. She sat in the hallway, motionless until Edith came through.

'Did I just hear the Post Office boy?' She stopped when she saw Gloria sitting on the Monks bench.

'What is it, dear? What is the news?'

Gloria handed her the telegram, which Edith read quickly.

'At least he is away from it all now, away from the bombs and butchery,' she said pragmatically, 'he will be home soon, I am sure of it.'

Gerald returned to England four weeks later and was admitted to the very place where he had himself treated hundreds of wounded men, never anticipating that he might return as one himself. Marcus had been allowed to visit him in his capacity as a doctor. When he came home that evening, he explained to Gloria and Edith the extent of his son's injuries and an account of the horrendous night when the hospital was bombed.

'I read the report, and Gerald was actually off duty that night in the officers' mess. Evidently, they heard the sound of aircraft engines in the distance and went outside to take a look in which direction they were heading. It did not take them too long to realise they were coming for them. Half a dozen Zeppelin-Staakens dropped bombs over the hospital, causing indescribable destruction, death and injury. There was chaos everywhere, and of course, Gerald rushed into the thick of it to help the wounded.

'He and two nurses were running along the duckboards when a bomb exploded close by, throwing them off into the mud. Gerald was hit in the leg, shattering his femur, he is extremely fortunate not to have lost his leg. Later it was discovered that one of the nurses had fallen into a bomb crater, and it had taken her all night to climb out, sliding in the mud and what she thought was slime, only to discover later that it was blood.'

They sat in stunned silence for quite some time until Edith spoke in a low voice. 'What kind of despicable, inhuman beasts bomb the sick and wounded? They are animals.' Her hands were shaking. 'Something has to be done to end this war now, I want my son.'

Inside her head, Gloria thought, 'And I want my husband.'

Gloria and Edith were allowed to visit Gerald briefly the next day and were deeply shocked by his appearance, he was deathly pale and obviously in a great deal of pain. His leg was inside a cage covered with a blanket to protect it while it healed. The two women sat on either side of his bed, attempting to make conversation, but very little was said. Edith did most of the talking, telling him how relieved Clara and Lilian were that he was home in England and dreadfully concerned about his injury. Gerald could scarcely look Gloria in the face, although he did eventually ask after his sons. She was able to report that the older boys were all excelling at school and how Julian was so desperate to join his brothers she had persuaded the headmaster to take him this September before his fifth birthday.

'They are clever boys and take after their father,' she added, hoping for some sort of response.

'They will be just grand,' Gerald muttered and drifted back to sleep. The shot of morphine the nurse had administered earlier had done its job, leaving Gloria and Edith looking at Gerald as if he were laid out in a coffin.

The two women were very distressed during the tram journey home, discussing the dramatic change in Gerald and what they could do to aid his recovery once he was home. They would ask Polly to make a bed up for him in the study until he could manage the stairs, and he would easily be able to navigate the downstairs rooms in his wheelchair. But Gloria felt cold inside, and her fear of losing Gerald at the foremost of her mind, however, she kept her thoughts to herself, not wishing to add further to Edith's angst.

She loved Gerald profoundly and desperately wanted her husband home, vowing not to give up hope, having learned of many men returning from the war awfully disturbed in their minds from the traumas they had witnessed. Undoubtedly, with love and care from his family, Gerald would recover if only he would let her close again.

Gloria had been granted time off work, so she may visit Gerald more often. It was very difficult as some days he refused any visitors, and on others, a glimmer of his former self would surface for a short time, giving Gloria some hope. But then the bitterest of blows was delivered when she walked into the ward one afternoon to see a young woman perched on Gerald's bed. They were holding hands and talking intensely, then, as she stood up to leave, she leaned forward and kissed him passionately, full on his lips.

A sledgehammer hit Gloria in her chest. She turned away and leant against the doorway, breathing heavily, her heart palpitating wildly. 'NO, NO! How could he do this to me? He loves me, I know he loves me, it must be a mistake.' Her mind was in turmoil.

Gloria watched the woman walk towards the doorway and eyed her up and down, thinking her quite ordinary with mousey brown hair tied back in a loose chignon. As she came closer, Gloria noticed the long, jagged pink scar across her cheek, marring whatever attractiveness had ever been in her face. She passed by Gloria and hesitated for a moment as if recognising her and quickly turned her eyes away, hurriedly exiting through the door.

Gloria's heart was pounding, having no idea what to do or say, she certainly did not want to make a scene in the ward but was determined to find out who this woman was to Gerald and if she was the reason he was now so indifferent towards her. Taking a deep breath and steeling herself, she gracefully walked over to her husband. At thirty-three years of age, Gloria was an exceptionally beautiful woman, you would never know she had borne four children, her waist was as slender as when she was eighteen years of age, and she held herself with poise, grace and composure.

'Hello, Gerald.'

'Gloria, I was not expecting you this afternoon.'

'No, I could see that you were not,' she said with a hard edge to her voice.

Before Gerald had the chance to respond, Gloria carried on talking, saying how Marcus had told them the marvellous news that Gerald would be discharged next week and that his leg had healed well, what was required now, was to regain his strength with physical therapy. He may walk with a slight limp, nevertheless, he should recover the full use of his leg. The wonders of modern surgery, Marcus had remarked.

'Stop it, Gloria, I know you saw her, I am not a fool,' Gerald said.

Gloria flushed and held her head high. 'What is it that you wish to tell me, Gerald? Come on, spit it out.'

Gerald shook his head. 'I cannot do it any longer, Gloria,' he said.

'Do what?' she demanded.

'I cannot return to my old life, to you and the boys, I am not the same man you fell in love with, he was destroyed in France.'

Gloria's eyes welled up with tears of anger more than any other emotion. 'But you have not even given any of us a chance to help you. Is it her, that woman, does she understand you?'

'You would never understand, you were not there, Lavinia was. She dragged me through the mud to safety after the bomb exploded and was herself caught by shrapnel, you saw the scar on her face. We are bound together through that horrific experience, you, Gloria, are from a different world, and it is one that I no longer have any use for.'

The whole sordid conversation had taken place in whispers, but

Gloria could take no more humiliation and stood up to leave.

'You are going to throw away fifteen years of marriage and our family for her? Well, I will let you explain to our sons, I cannot, as I do not understand myself. Goodbye, Gerald.'

She turned and walked away, not daring to look back lest the tears that burned her face betrayed her true emotion, her heart was broken.

Somehow, Gloria made it to the outside world, she gulped in deep breaths of fresh air to calm her nerves and found a bench to sit down on before her legs buckled beneath her. She felt nauseous, and although the May air was warm, she shivered, no coherent thoughts would enter her head, and at that moment, she felt utterly wretched and very alone.

A gust of wind roused her, and when she looked at her gold fob watch, she realised that half an hour had passed by without her even noticing. The reality of the situation hit home once more, and it sickened her to the very core of her being. Her thoughts ran wild.

'Fate will not forgive you for this, Gerald, what you are doing is unforgivable, you will pay for your actions somehow, Madame Burton was right all along, you are not what you seem.'

Pulling herself together with tremendous effort, Gloria made her way to the tram stop and went back to Granville Square. Fortunately, it had been arranged for Beatrice to meet David and Dwight from school as Gloria was quite late back. When the boys heard their mother come in, they dashed into the hallway asking, 'How is Papa, when is he coming home, when can we see him?'

She braced herself and replied, 'Too many questions all at once, you will see your father quite soon, I think, now run along and get washed up for tea.'

'Yes, Mama,' they chanted.

As she watched her beautiful, innocent sons run off to do her bidding, she thought to herself, 'Does he not realise how hurt his sons will be. Gabe especially idolises you and has a great desire to be a doctor himself, you are making a grave mistake husband, I hope you know what you are doing.'

Her mind was in chaos, nevertheless, she began planning what to do next and decided that moving back to Lloyd Square and being independent of Marcus and Edith was a priority. She had no way of predicting what their reaction would be when the news was broken to them that her marriage was over, and their beloved son had taken up with another woman. And she did just that as they sat together in the sitting-room after dinner. Relating the whole painful episode to Marcus and Edith broke her heart once more, their first reaction was one of disbelief. Through her tears, Gloria reassured them that it was absolutely true, and it would be impossible for her to live at Granville Square once Gerald was discharged from hospital. She also insisted that he would have to take full responsibility for informing his sons of his actions.

'Calm down, dear, surely we can find a way of working this through,' Edith said.

'I think not, your son looked at this Lavinia how he used to look at me. No, he made it perfectly clear that I did not fit into his life anymore,' Gloria sobbed.

'Marcus, you must talk to our son, make him see sense, please,' Edith begged.

'Certainly, I will try, I sensed he was deeply troubled when he returned from France at Christmas, but I had not foreseen this disturbing outcome, and you know that you are like a daughter to us, we will not see you and the boys suffer in any way.'

Marcus's words were indeed comforting, nonetheless, she was equally aware that she must be in a position to secure her independence if blood family bonds tied closer. Not that she had experienced that with her own family, quite the opposite, in fact. This thought made her groan inwardly when she thought of her mother and how she would probably relish in her prediction that her marriage would not last. Furthermore, what will Fleur's reaction be? How she wished her sister were here to talk to.

Somehow, Gloria went through the motions of the next few days, a carrier was booked to return hers and the boys' things to Lloyd Square, and she began the seemingly impossible task of hiring a maid when most of the young women were now doing war work. There were very few replies to her advertisement in the newspaper. Eventually, a young Belgian refugee about twenty years of age made an appointment, her name was Rosa, and she spoke excellent English. She explained how she had taken care of her father and younger siblings in Belgium after her mother died and was no stranger to hard work. They had fled to England at the start of the war, and Rosa needed money to care for her ailing father. Gloria appreciated her candidness and hired her there and then.

'I have Beatrice to help with my younger sons, so the housekeeping and cooking will be your main duties, I am a modern woman and will treat you with respect.'

'Thank you, Mrs Phelps, I am indebted to you,' Rosa replied.

'That is settled then, you can start tomorrow, the house has been locked up for many months and will require a good clean and airing, I can meet you there at a quarter past nine after I have walked my children to school.'

The boys were not too keen on moving back to their own home, they liked living with their grandparents and did not understand why they must leave, except for Gabe. At almost fourteen years of age, he had the intuition to know that something was very wrong with his mother. As her firstborn, they had a special bond, and when he found her alone in the sitting-room one evening, he asked if he may join her.

'Of course, my darling, come here and sit with me,' she said. 'What is wrong, Mama? I know there is something, is it Papa, when is he coming home?' he asked with concern in his voice.

'My dear boy, my Gabe, how I love you so.'

'Mama, please tell me what the matter is, I sense that Papa is not the same anymore, is it because of his injury?'

'Something like that, darling, yes, and it means that he will not be coming home to us again.'

Gabe tried to comprehend what his mother was telling him as she explained that as his father had been away for such a long time, probably not much would change and that he must not fret but continue to study hard at school and make her proud.

'Will we ever see Papa again?' he asked his mother.

Pushing back her tears, Gloria replied, 'Of course, my darling, he will be living at Grandpapa's, so you and your brothers can all visit him there.'

Gabe threw his arms around Gloria's neck and held her tightly.

'I love you, Mama, I will always take care of you,' he said.

A tear spilt over her eyelid as she held her son, she blinked another tear away, then looked at him and forced a smile.

'When this nightmare war is over, I think life for everyone will be very different, not just ours. Perhaps it will be the beginning of something better, the deaths of so many must surely not be in vain.'

They sat together in silence, Gabe with his head resting on his mother's shoulder. Gloria gazed into nothingness, she had no idea what their future would be, her mind was a blank, at this moment in time, she just felt broken.

CHAPTER 10

'THE WAR IS OVER.' The words were blazoned across the headlines of every newspaper. Dense crowds of people gathered outside Buckingham Palace to celebrate the signing of The Armistice at eleven o'clock on Monday the 11th of November 1918. Gloria was amongst the throng with her sons, Beatrice and her dear friends, Lucy and Dorothy. Maroons were fired, and at the sound of each detonation, the crowds shouted - HURRAH. There were loud renditions of *God save the King* and *Rule Britannia*. The mass of people began to jostle, requiring Gloria to hoist Julian up on to her hip, as he was in danger of being crushed amongst the hundreds of legs around him.

'Look, Julian, can you see the Union Jack flying on the palace?' she said to her youngest son.

'Yes, Mama, I can, why are there so many people?' the little boy asked. She kissed his cheek.

'Because we are at peace once more, my darling, sweet Julian,' she replied.

'Will Papa come home now?' he asked.

The words hit her hard. 'That I cannot say.' She held her son tightly as if she imagined someone reaching out from the crowd and stealing him away from her.

The last few months had been enormously gruelling for Gloria, and when she learned that Gerald had moved out of Granville

Square to take a flat with Lavinia in Kensington near to his rooms, her heart broke for the hundredth time. There had been no contact with him, all communication regarding arrangements for the boys had taken place through Edith, and fortunately, their relationship remained undamaged by Gerald's affair.

'I have to admit, Gloria,' Edith told her one day, 'it is not the first time Gerald has caused a scandal over a woman, but when he met you, it seemed as if you and he were perfect for each other. Marcus and I both encouraged your courtship, and even when you eloped, we took it as a sign that you were destined to be together. I love my son, and I love you as a daughter, and I confess I cannot understand why he has done this to you.'

Gloria was extremely touched by her words and took the older woman's hand. 'Edith, you have been more of a mother to me than my own, and I will be eternally grateful for your love and friendship. I wrote to my mother hoping for some empathy, but she replied with words that implied, I told you so. Even Fleur has kept her distance. Now, come on, let us have a sherry and celebrate once more the end of the most horrific of times and toast to a brighter future for us all,' Gloria said. Inwardly she doubted that would come without difficulty.

Arrangements for Christmas were decidedly awkward, and not wanting to disappoint the boys, Gloria agreed to take them to Granville Square mid-morning. They could all have lunch together and celebrate as the family had always done, then in the evening, Gerald could spend time with his sons while Gloria returned home. In actual fact, an evening of cocktails and playing cards with Lucy and Dorothy had been planned, and the three friends were very much looking forward to letting their hair down in the privacy of Gloria's home.

All over the country, there was an air of euphoria that four years of war were over at last, and despite there not being many turkeys for sale, chickens were plentiful. Polly, as usual, had performed her magic in the kitchen and produced a splendid meal. A huge brightly decorated Christmas tree stood in the sitting-room where the boys presents had been placed, and they had opened them with great enthusiasm, leaving a mountain of wrapping paper on the floor.

Gloria and Edith had shopped together for hours as toys were in short supply courtesy of the war. Yet, they managed to arrive home with further additions to Gabe and David's Meccano sets, a box of the new Lotts building bricks for Dwight, and for Julian, an elephant money box. It made him squeal with laughter when each time he put a coin in the slot and pulled the elephants tail, it swallowed the money. However, their special Christmas treat was to be an outing to the Drury Lane theatre to watch *Babes in the Wood* at the matinee the following day. Gloria had not been to the theatre in a very long time and decided that a pantomime would be just the tonic required to bring some laughter back into their lives.

The family were having such a marvellous time, playing games and singing along to the gramophone that Gloria lost track of the hours, it was when she heard Polly greeting someone in the hallway that her heart sank, it was Gerald. She had meant to be gone before he arrived. Slight panic welled up inside her, she had not laid eyes on him since that fateful day at the hospital and was amiss as to how she must face him.

'It is I who have been wronged,' Gloria told herself, pulling on all of her inner strength, 'I will hold my head high and make my farewells as soon as possible,' she resolved.

He entered the room dressed in military uniform, as he had remained attached to the Territorial Hospital as consulting surgeon, and her reaction to seeing Gerald, who was indeed still her husband, took her by surprise. Despite walking with a cane, he looked no different, he was as handsome as the day she met him seventeen years ago, and her heart lurched.

'What have I done to make him leave me? I have not changed, I take excellent care of our sons, why, why I do not understand, I will never understand.' These thoughts raced through her head as the boys all shouted. 'Papa, Papa, Christmas greetings to you.'

They dashed towards him, except for Gabe, he held back for a moment watching the expression on his mother's face as he tried to gauge her feelings. While his younger brothers were fussing around their father, Gabe moved over to Gloria.

'Are you alright, Mama?' he said quietly.

She looked into the face of her beloved son, he was a fine young man, and her heart filled with love for him.

'Yes, darling, I am quite well, you must go and welcome your father, and I will see you tomorrow, good night.' She kissed the top of his head and said her goodbyes to everyone quickly, then braced herself to pass by Gerald so she may go to the hallway and leave for her own home. His look burned through her as she walked towards the sitting-room door.

'Good evening, Gloria,' he said. 'How are you?'

'How do you think I am - Gerald, you have ruined my life,' she hissed.

He flinched at the ferocity of her delivery.

'I am sorry, Gloria, but you will never understand.'

'You are right, Gerald, I will not, try to explain to your sons, they do not either.'

Before any more could be said, Gloria kissed her boys goodnight and walked to the hall to don her hat and coat, she left the house quickly and quietly and stepped out into the street. It was snowing again, which added to Gloria's misery, she hated the winter.

She pulled her coat collar around her neck and walked the short distance back to Lloyd Square, hurrying her pace until she reached her doorway. She had given Beatrice and Rosa the day off to be with their own families for Christmas, but the lights had been left on, and a fire made up in the sitting-room. Gloria took off her hat and coat and threw them on the chair in the hall, she went straight through to the drinks cabinet and poured herself a large sherry. She stood by the fire, warming herself, and on the mantelpiece in front of her face stood a framed photograph of her and Gerald taken on their fifth wedding anniversary. Putting down her sherry glass, Gloria picked up the picture, they looked so happy, a beautiful couple people always commented. Immense anger welled up inside her, and she violently threw the photograph across the room, smashing it against the sideboard.

'I am cursed, I must be, maybe my father was right about me all along. To hell with you, Gerald, I hate you.'

She downed her sherry in one and picked up the shattered photo frame, there was a long crack in the glass that purely by chance had cut Gloria and Gerald in two, she smiled ironically to herself.

'Well, Gerald, you have got what you wanted, I hope you sleep well at night with your precious, Lavinia!'

There was a loud knock at the door, and Gloria remembered that Lucy and Dorothy were coming round for drinks. She hurried to open the front door clutching the broken photograph frame, her two friends burst through the door singing, *We wish you a Merry Christmas* and showering her with hugs and kisses. They were already quite squiffy from their Christmas celebration at Dorothy's house, the Bancrofts certainly knew how to put on a luncheon party, and this year had been no exception.

'Why, Gloria, what have you there? Come on, show Lucy, I hope you are not moping over Gerald.'

Gloria smiled at her friends. 'No, on the contrary, Gerald has been served his just deserts, look.' She held up the frame.

'Damn shame, darling, he never did deserve you,' Lucy said solemnly. 'Now, come on, where is the champagne? The least we can do is drink up his supply of Roederer Cristal. We are to forget men this evening, who needs them anyway.'

'Mrs Phelps, Mrs Phelps, wake up.' Gloria opened her eyes and groaned. 'Mrs Phelps will be here with the children soon,' Rosa said as quietly as possible, imagining that Gloria must be feeling somewhat delicate. Rosa had arrived early that morning to prepare breakfast, and after witnessing the glasses and empty bottles in the sitting-room, realised that her mistress must have enjoyed quite a party with her friends. She tidied up while the ladies slept upstairs, and by half-past eleven, thought it was time to rouse Gloria.

'I rather think we overdid it last night.' Gloria said, holding her forehead. 'What time is it, Rosa?'

'Just after half-past eleven, ma'am,' she replied.

'Are Lucy and Dorothy awake yet?'

'Not yet, would you like me to wake them?'

'No, leave them be, Rosa, let them sleep. Can you bring me some strong tea and aspirin, please? I have the most dreadful headache.' Gloria was looking at Rosa with one eye closed.

 Rosa smiled to herself as she left the bedroom, it was the first time since her employment at Lloyd Square that she had seen Gloria enjoy herself, and it pleased her. She knew not the full circumstances of Gloria's separation from her husband but sympathised with her. As far as Rosa was concerned, Gloria was one of the most agreeable women she had ever encountered and would do anything for her.

Gloria pushed back her eiderdown and rolled out of bed, she sat for a moment and then made her way unsteadily to the bathroom.

By the time Rosa returned with the tea tray, Gloria had splashed cold water on her face, tidied up her hair a little and was sat in her chair by the window.

'Thank you, Rosa, would you mind drawing a bath for me? I really must pull myself together, we are going to the theatre this afternoon, what will Mrs Phelps think of me in this condition?'

An hour later, a much-revived Gloria made her way downstairs and found Lucy and Dorothy in much the same state of disarray as Gloria had been earlier.

'One too many champagne cocktails, I think,' Dorothy said with a pained look on her face, Lucy just raised her arm in the air and waggled her fingers.

'Has Rosa brought you some strong tea or coffee?' Gloria asked.

'Yes, thank you, we are on our second pot. We had fun though, did we not.' Dorothy replied.

'Indeed, we did,' Gloria confirmed.

Rosa made them all buttered toast, and once they had eaten something, the three friends soon recovered. Eggs and bacon would have been lovely, only Gloria wished to save her rations for her sons.

Edith arrived with the boys at two o'clock, only a short while after Lucy and Dorothy had left. The house was spotless once more thanks to Rosa, and an excited party left for Drury Lane in great anticipation of *Babes in the Wood.* Marie Blanche was principal boy, with the "Babes" played by Stanley Lupino and Will Evans. Gloria had procured them front row seats in the grand circle, and it was Julian and Dwight's first outing to the theatre. They both sat wide-eyed, mesmerized by the music, the singing and brightly coloured costumes, they enjoyed every moment of the performance.

'I have not laughed so much for years, I feared my corset would break.' Edith remarked to Gloria.

The boys talked about the pantomime incessantly, and Gloria

felt a great sense of satisfaction seeing her children so happy, it was a precious moment.

Two days later, Gloria received the most devastating news, Dorothy had died of the Spanish flu. Edith called round the moment Mrs Bancroft had tearfully told her.

'How can it be, Edith, she was here on Christmas day with Lucy, we had the most marvellous time, she was quite well, please tell me it is not true, she is one of my closest friends.' Gloria was very distressed and in a flood of tears.

'I am terribly sorry, but it is so, her brother Tom is gravely ill too, but Marcus thinks that he might pull through. He told me there are hundreds of people dying all over London, they say those affected are perfectly well at breakfast and dead by dinner, it is frightful,' Edith told her.

'Poor Dorothy, poor dear, Dorothy, why is life so cruel? She was a good, kind person. I must send my condolences to Mr and Mrs Bancroft.'

Dorothy's funeral was held three days later at St James's church, it was a small gathering of just family and close friends. Gloria and Lucy grieved for their friend and found it impossible to imagine how Dorothy's family were feeling. They had lost their eldest son in the war and now their only daughter to a deadly disease that was rampaging across the world, leaving millions of people in its wake.

The war may have been over, but 1919 dawned with the Spanish flu still raging and soldiers returning from the trenches expecting to take up the jobs they did beforehand, and for Gloria and Lucy, this was just so. When they learned that they were no longer required at the Civil Service, they were outraged.

'But what are we to do now?' Lucy asked the pompous man named Mr Peabody, who had returned to his manager position.

'What do you think, ladies? Return to your husbands and

domestic duties, and let the men do the work,' he said, peering over the top of his spectacles.

Well, that was like waving a red rag at a bull for Lucy, she was infuriated, and in no uncertain terms informed the "horrible little man" that she no longer had a husband to return to, he was killed in the war and did he not know that the women had been far more productive in this office than the men had ever been. She was appalled at the notion that women were now of no use and ranted on for at least five minutes before pausing for breath, at which point Mr Peabody dryly said, 'Are you quite finished, madam? If you wish to take the matter further, I suggest you speak with the prime minister.'

Incensed, the two friends glared at Mr Peabody, whose eyes had already returned to the papers on his desk, they turned heel and marched out of the office as loudly as their heels would allow.

'Mr Pea Brain, I say,' was Gloria's response.

'I have a good mind to join those suffragette women and chain myself to a railing, something really does have to be done, even if we wanted another man, there are none, four years of futile killing saw to that.' Lucy was furious.

The disgruntled duo decided that a visit to Lyons would have been just the ticket to cheer them up. That was not possible either, as people were being warned to keep away from public places for fear of being infected with the flu. So, they returned to Lloyd Square and asked Rosa to rustle up some tea and scones instead.

'Not quite The Ritz, darling, but we can pretend,' Gloria lamented.

They sat contemplating their futures, it was not as if either of them needed any money. Lucy had her trust fund, and Gerald supported Gloria and the boys, a matter Marcus had seen to immediately. However, she had enjoyed working and with all four boys at school, being on her own in the house she knew would drive her to distraction, there must be something else to do. All these thoughts swirling around her head suddenly made her feel glum.

Lucy was in a similar position, she too needed a distraction from being alone. She pondered for a moment. 'Leave this one with me, darling, let me see what I can come up with, surely there are some fun things to do now this wretched war is over.'

Within a few weeks, Lucy had herself and Gloria employed at Selfridges on the perfume and make-up counter, life was looking up for them at last. Gloria's attractiveness served her well in the store, gentlemen purchasing perfume for their wives or lady friends would make towards her, and she would welcome them with her dazzling smile and easy charm. The only downside was the aching legs and feet suffered by the middle of the afternoon from standing at the counter. Gloria tolerated the discomfort as the work passed the most part of her day while her boys were at school.

There were still many lonely moments when she hoped the life she was living was a nightmare and that one morning she would wake up with Gerald beside her, loving her, but then reality would come crashing down and bring her back to earth.

Gloria missed her sister dreadfully, and whilst they spoke on the telephone regularly, Fleur had not been up to London since Gerald had deserted her, it was as if she did not want to be associated with any scandal. The last time they talked, tentative arrangements were made for them all to visit Ramsgate during the summer holidays, something Gloria was in desperate need of, apart from the fact that Julian had not yet seen the sea or walked barefoot in the sand. The thoughts of the fresh sea air and warm summer days cheered Gloria up, and as the first spring flowers appeared in the Lloyd Square gardens, her spirits began to lift.

This feeling was shattered when Edith paid her a visit on the first

Sunday in May, with the painful news that Gerald was expecting a child with Lavinia. Poor Edith sat on the sofa beside Gloria, her hands trembling.

'I felt it my duty to inform you, dear, Marcus and I were only told yesterday by Gerald, he behaves as if Lavinia is his wife, it was a huge shock to us both, but you know Marcus, he takes everything in his stride.'

This was too much for Gloria, she was devastated. Fighting back tears of a mixture of anger and anguish, she said, 'What next, is he going to divorce me and marry this trollop! You must know that I did nothing to provoke any of this, I loved your son from the instant I met him all those years ago. If my only mistake was succumbing to him before we were married, then let me be struck down, I paid dearly for that when I lost the baby.'

Gloria was beside herself, Edith tried to calm her and poured them both a stiff brandy,

'At least Gerald left his best Martell behind,' Edith said as she passed Gloria the glass, it made her smile a little, and she told Edith how she and her friends had drunk a fair few bottles of his Roederer Cristal collection since his departure.

The brandy helped calm Gloria's shattered nerves, and she talked with Edith about the boys and her own prospects for the future. David would be joining Gabe at Westminster next year, and her concern was that their father would continue to pay for his sons' education. Edith once again reassured her that Marcus would always take care of matters even if anything untoward happened to Gerald, and to reinforce the arrangement, he had instructed his solicitor draw up a document.

'We love them as if they were our own.' she added.

'There is no reason for them to know of an impending half-sibling either unless we have to,' Gloria said, 'I do not wish for them to be upset any more, especially Gabe, he senses my every mood. I do have to be on my guard, he has taken it upon himself to take care of his poor mother, he is such a darling, it is hard to believe he will be fifteen this September, how time flies.'

Indeed, time did fly, and the summer holidays arrived, but hopes of spending a few weeks in Ramsgate were dashed when Fleur announced that she and Filkes were to tour the continent for the summer, he was taking a sabbatical for a while. It all seemed very convenient in Gloria's eyes.

Autumn came and went, and November started with cold northerly winds and sleet on some days. Gloria's mood sank with the falling temperatures, and November also brought the arrival of Gerald's daughter, Justine Phelps.

'Ha, a girl, and he has given her his name, what a cosy little set up they must have, her pretending to be Mrs Phelps, it is totally outrageous!' Gloria spat out the words when she learned of the birth from Edith. 'We always said girls would be trouble after I lost our first baby, perhaps they will reap what they have sown,' Gloria added bitterly.

Marcus and Edith felt helpless, Gloria's plight had been brought about by their own son, and they felt powerless to help her. Apart from her friend, Lucy, she appeared to have no-one else to turn to, the whole situation was tragic.

CHAPTER 11

1920, the dawn of a new decade, but for Gloria, it began much the same as the previous year, except for a most welcome visit from her sister. Filkes was delivering a talk at the Royal College of Surgeons, and they had come up to London for the first time in ages. He was also aware that Gerald would be attending and was mindful of the fact. Fleur had finally come to terms with Gloria's marriage breakdown and understood that the fault lay entirely with Gerald, and the news of his illegitimate daughter had shocked her immensely. Sadly, she had been unable to conceive and confessed to feeling envious of Gloria and her sons on numerous occasions, this being one reason for her not visiting more often. However, considering events over the last two years, she promised that would change from now on.

Filkes escorted Fleur and Gloria to dinner at the Criterion that evening, a pleasure Gloria had not enjoyed in quite some time. Something else she had not done in a long time was purchase any new clothes, so her choice of outfit had to be made from the array of dresses already in her wardrobe. After much changing from one to another, Gloria finally settled on the black satin and georgette dress whose last outing had been to the theatre with her boys when they watched *Babes in the Wood*. A single string of pearls was enough to embellish her outfit, and as she reached into her jewellery box to put on her emerald engagement ring, she faltered and looked in the dressing table mirror.

'What are you going to do with your life?' she asked her reflection, 'it has been two years, Gerald is not coming back. You are thirty-five, there must be someone else out there, I do not wish to die a lonely old woman.'

She turned her head from side to side, then peered at herself closely in the mirror. There were a few lines around her eyes, but no crow's feet, thank goodness, her hair remained thick and glossy, and from the admiring looks she received from gentlemen in the store, she knew that men still found her attractive

'For goodness sake, what man in their right mind will want a married woman with four children? You are quite mad, Gloria.'

At that, she pushed the ring on to her finger, deciding to wear it for its beauty, not for any sentimental reasons, picked up her fur wrap and made her way downstairs to wait for Fleur and Filkes to arrive in a taxi. During the journey, Gloria asked Filkes if Gerald had spoken to him at the conference.

'Indeed, he did, he was polite, asking after Fleur and overall behaved in a gentlemanly manner, I reciprocated the courtesy. Mind you, I did not wish to linger and made my excuses as soon as possible. He looked well enough, despite walking with a cane.'

Gloria sighed. 'What polite society we appear to move amongst, all of Gerald's acquaintances must be aware of our estrangement and his illegitimate child, yet no-one dares speak a word. I have not the means to divorce him, despite his infidelity, what am I to do? hope that he dies.'

'Gloria!' Fleur exclaimed,

'I apologise, that was dreadful of me. Can we forget about Gerald tonight and enjoy our dinner? I have not dined out in ages.'

The school summer holidays arrived, and Gloria had arranged a surprise visit to Ramsgate for all of her boys to coincide with the summer bank holiday, that way, she would have three days off work to enjoy some time at the seaside with her family. Six-year-old Julian was beside himself with excitement as he had never seen the sea or walked on the beach. He had been told the many stories of his brothers' seaside adventures and wished very much to experience one for himself. The long train ride was his first escapade, and he marvelled at the speed at which the carriages were carried along the tracks by the powerful engine at the front.

'How fast are we going, Mama?' Julian asked.

'The train can reach a hundred miles per hour,' Gloria replied.

'I like going fast, can it go any faster?'

'I think this is quite fast enough, darling.' It pleased her to see her son so excited, they were all desperate for a change of scenery.

Fleur was waiting for them at the train station in her new Crossley Manchester car, she waved frantically and sounded the horn to attract their attention.

'Mama, look at Aunt Fleur!' Gabe said in disbelief, 'she has a motor car.'

'My goodness, this is a surprise, whatever next?' Gloria gasped.

She instructed the porter to take their luggage over to the waiting vehicle as she ushered Julian along. He was busy staring at the enormous locomotive waiting patiently on the tracks, hissing steam every now and again.

'Come on, Julian, make haste or Aunt Fleur will go without us.' She took her youngest son by the hand and gently pulled him away.

'I like trains, can I drive one when I grow up?' he asked.

Gloria smiled. 'Maybe one day, but now you must hurry up.'

Gabe had already seated himself in the passenger seat beside Fleur, asking her numerous questions about how to drive and made her promise to teach him when they arrived home.

'Some of the older boys at school already have their own motor cars, I wish I could,' he said.

'Do well at school and university, and you will achieve great things, Gabe,' his aunt told him, 'do you still wish to be a doctor?'

'Not now, Aunt Fleur, not since Papa left home, I find it very difficult to speak to him, Mama has been so dreadfully hurt and upset, I think I might study law instead.'

'That is also an honourable and profitable occupation, I think you will do extremely well.'

Fleur flew down the roads, requiring Gloria to hold on to her new red velvet cloche hat and, more importantly, on to Julian as tightly as she could to prevent him from standing up in the car and falling out.

He was shouting at the top of his voice. 'Whooosh, faster, Aunt Fleur, faster.' David and Dwight clung to the seat, looking a little less calm than either of their brothers.

They soon arrived at Fleur and Filkes home, it was a large, elegant house overlooking the beach with an enormous lawn and a row of chestnut trees at the bottom.

After some refreshments, the boys were allowed to go out to the garden and play, it was familiar, of course, to Gabe and David, although it had been a few years since their last visit. They ran outside, noisily showing their younger brothers the summer house and the best trees to climb. Gloria and Fleur sat in the garden with a glass of lemonade, watching the boys running around playing tag and laughing.

'I had so wished for my home to be filled with children like yours, Gloria, but it has not happened. Filkes and I have visited various doctors and succumbed to all manner of tests, but to no avail. Perhaps it was just meant to be this way.'

'I am very sorry, Fleur, it all seems wrong for both of us, you have a wonderful husband and no children to share him with, and here

I am with four beautiful boys and no husband, what mixed up affairs life throws at us.'

The long weekend flew by, and Gloria took reels of photographs with her new Kodak Autograph camera, still determined to capture on film her sons growing up.

Monday afternoon was approaching fast, and it was time for them to leave for the train station and return to London. Julian was pleading with Gloria to let him stay, he had reminded her so much of that first summer she had brought Gabe to Ramsgate, running barefoot up and down the beach, not minding the sand between his toes in the slightest bit, his face all sticky with ice-cream.

'No, darling, we cannot stay, I am very sorry,' she said.

Julian began to cry. 'Why, Mama, I like it here with Aunt Fleur, please, please.'

Fleur understood her sister's dilemma and felt sorry for her, so on the spur of the moment, she declared, 'Then stay you will, all four of you, I am having a most marvellous time and insist you keep your Aunt Fleur company for a few more days.'

Gloria was taken aback. 'No, Fleur, I cannot expect you to do that, it will be too much for you.'

'Nonsense, Gloria, why they almost look after themselves, and I have your handsome eldest son to assist me, what do you say?'

There was a chorus of PLEASE, at which Gloria agreed with one exception.

'I will send Beatrice to you on the next train, believe me, you will need an extra pair of hands.'

Gloria returned to London, and Beatrice duly departed to Ramsgate. The house was still and quiet, and Gloria found it most strange, so she placed a record on the gramophone and sat down in the armchair to relax. On the table beside her lay the latest copy of The Tatler, and flicking through the pages, she came across the fashionable hairstyles of the American film stars. Her eyes were drawn to the new bob style that Louise Brooks was wearing.

'I think a visit to the salon is required, new decade, new look, new Gloria, then let me discover what life will throw in my path,' she said to herself.

Some of the women at work had already cut their long tresses, much to the disgruntlement of Mrs Stanley. She was the shop floor manager, an older woman who disapproved of the racy young women of today. However, she did not want to dismiss half of her ladies on the grounds of fashion, as some other businesses had done but did draw the line at any dress hems being above calf height.

A couple of days later, Gloria walked into Selfridges and was met with astonished looks from her work colleagues. They immediately passed complimentary comments. When Mrs Stanley caught sight of her, she shook her head, saying, 'You too, Mrs Phelps? Whatever next, it was never like this in my day.'

Gloria nearly started to laugh when she thought Mrs Stanley sounded just like her old Aunt Esther, expecting her to "humph." Fortunately, Mrs Stanley just sighed and returned to the counter.

When finally there was a lull in the volume of customers, Lucy made her way over to Gloria. 'Well, you are a dark horse, I must say, keeping this a secret from me,' she said, pretending to be miffed. 'You look glorious, it has taken years of you, I am quite determined to book in with Anton as soon as I finish here this afternoon, then we will have an evening out together while your children are away.'

'Why not,' agreed Gloria, 'who is there to tell us otherwise.'

Gloria's thoughts for an evening's entertainment were mostly the theatre and a musical, on the other hand, Lucy was adamant they should try a night-club.

'Come on, darling, Murray's on Beak Street is only a cab ride away, and they have a brand-new cabaret show named *Murray's*

Frolics, it will be so much fun. We can have dinner, a few drinks and be entertained all in one place,' she said.

Slightly hesitant, Gloria agreed, on the premise that a visit to Harrods for a new dress was a necessity, and on that, they both decidedly agreed.

An extensive shopping trip resulted in a gorgeous olive embossed silk dress for Lucy, with a matching feather stole. Her hair was now styled in an Ira Claire bob, and it suited her perfectly. For Gloria, a satin dress comprised of an abstract pattern in shades of purple, pink, black and cream, that was overlaid with delicate black lace. Both of their dresses came just below the knee, rather daring they thought for a pair of thirty-five-year-old women with no husbands to escort them. But these were modern times, so they adopted an attitude of derring-do and made their way to Murray's.

They had the most fabulous night, although dancing had been off the menu, as neither Gloria nor Lucy had learned the Charleston or Foxtrot. Instead, they sipped cocktails, watching the cabaret intently and enjoyed every minute of the singing and dancing. They promised they would have a night out together more often, and Gloria had not been in such high spirits in a long time, perhaps her life was turning for the better at last.

The next weekend Beatrice arrived home with the boys, they clattered in through the front door like four bulls in Selfridges china department, dropping their bags on the floor and kicking off their shoes, shouting, 'Mama, Mama, we are home.' The noise would have raised the dead.

Gloria came through into the hallway to a rapturous welcome from her sons. Throwing their arms around her and all talking at once, they said how much they had all missed her.

'One at a time, my darlings, I cannot make out a word any of you are saying.' She had to raise her voice above the commotion. 'Go through to the sitting-room, and I will ask Rosa to bring some lemonade and biscuits, now go on, all of you.'

When she returned, the boys were all seated, and Gabe said with surprise, 'Mama, you look different, you have had your hair cut.'

'Yes, darling, do you like it? I thought your old Mama needed to move with the times a little.'

'You always look beautiful, Mama.' To which David and Dwight both voiced their agreement on the subject.

Julian sat on the sofa with a big smug smile on his face. 'Look, Mama,' he said, 'we bought you a present from the seaside.' He handed her a box wrapped in pretty pink paper, with a blue bow tied around it.

'What a lovely surprise,' Gloria exclaimed, 'what is it?'

'Open it, Mama,' all four said in unison.

Gloria carefully untied the bow and unwrapped the paper, she took off the lid of the cardboard box and carefully removed its contents. To her delight, it contained an exquisite scallop shell with a small figurine of a woman inside. She was dressed in a silver-grey evening gown decorated with a tiny pink flower and stood on an array of little sea-shells, to Gloria, it was one of the sweetest trinkets she had ever seen.

'I chose it because she is pretty like you, Mama,' Julian added. A small tear of joy welled up in the corner of Gloria's eye, and she hugged her youngest son tightly.

'Thank you, my darlings, I will treasure it always.' She looked at her four sons and was overcome with such a feeling of love and pride, she thought her heart would burst.

They each told her of their Ramsgate adventures, and much to Gloria's alarm, her sister, had shown Gabe how to drive.

'It is so thrilling, Mama and not too complicated once you have learned which foot pedals to press and how to change gear, you really must ask Aunt Fleur to teach you, then we could have our own motor car.' He was very proud of himself.

'And where would we drive a motor car in London? The trams and underground trains are much easier,' Gloria replied, a little nervous of the thought.

'But we could drive into the countryside and see lots of different places at weekends, it would be wonderful.' Gabe said.

'I will ponder over that idea while you ponder over how we would purchase a motor-car,' Gloria replied.

Then David spoke up. 'Ask Papa to buy us one, he never takes us anywhere, so why should he not, then we could.'

His words hit Gloria hard, it was the first time he had spoken of his father with such a bitter tone in his voice, perhaps his leaving had affected her sons more than she had imagined. Gabe came to the rescue.

'Thinking about it, David, perhaps Mama is right, where would we keep a motor-car anyway, and we can always catch a train to go places,' he said.

He was showing a great deal of maturity and empathy for their plight, David just shrugged his shoulders and picked up his lemonade, Dwight never said a word, and Julian, through a mouthful of biscuit, said, 'I like trains.'

Various milestones were reached throughout the year, Gabe celebrated his sixteenth birthday, David his thirteenth, and he joined Gabe at Westminster. Dwight and Julian continued their schooling at Clerkenwell, although Dwight preferred to draw and paint rather than study Algebra or Latin.

Julian lived in awe of the world around him, already fascinated with his toy cars, trains and aeroplanes and of course, being the youngest, he was doted on by his brothers. With his cute cherub face and dark curls, he was adorable, and Gloria's heart melted when he would smile and say, 'I love you, Mama.'

He was the least affected by his father's absence, he had never really known him. Gabe had already formed his own opinion of his father, and both David and Dwight seemed indifferent as to whether they saw him or not. It was a most disagreeable situation, but overall, for the most part of the year, everyone in Gloria's life seemed to have been more at peace. Indeed, Gloria had accepted her situation, embracing the freedoms women were now experiencing, and being a woman over thirty-years-old, she now had the right to vote. The pre-war class system was breaking down, and financially, many upper-class families were crippled by the cost of the war alongside lack of income from the Empire and declining farming rentals. Exceptionally high taxes and death duties also took their toll, forcing many of them to sell their stately homes and belongings, the glittering days of the Edwardian era were over.

Sadly, unemployment amongst the working classes remained high, but thankfully for Gloria, whilst ever Gerald supported her and the boys, along with her job at Selfridges, she could continue to enjoy a comfortable lifestyle.

CHAPTER 12

The lifted spirits of everyone carried through into 1921 with a special celebration for Gloria and the girls held at Murray's. Mrs Stanley had resigned, and Gloria had been promoted into her position. She felt very proud that by her own doing, independent of any man's influence, she had achieved something in her life.

'I hope we can wear shorter dresses from now on,' said Evelyn, one of the younger women.

'And some brighter lipstick,' Sophia added.

Gloria put on an air of superiority and replied, 'I think not ladies, shorter dresses would never do.' She paused for a moment, 'I believe we must all wear trousers, then we can have lower heels and not have such dreadfully aching feet by the end of the day.'

'Hip, Hip, Hurrah for Mrs Phelps,' the girls cheered.

There was much clinking of glasses and toasts of champagne, after which Gloria groaned, saying, 'Please, do not call me Mrs Phelps,' she paused for a moment, 'Madame Gloria will do.' They all burst into a fit of giggles.

Gloria fitted her new role like a glove, the girls loved her, and even though Lucy had felt a teeny bit jealous at first, she quickly realised that Gloria's strong personality combined with her beauty and elegance, very soon transformed the perfume and make-up department into a far more welcoming and attractive shopping experience for the customers.

Alas, for Gloria, her life always seemed to run in a series of immense ups and downs, and at the beginning of May, she experienced one of its most tragic episodes. Edith, the woman who had been the mother she never had, suffered a stroke and died at her home in Granville Square at eighty years-of-age. Gloria was grief-stricken. With immense difficulty, she broke the news to her boys that their beloved grandmama had passed.

'But how can that be? We were having tea with her only yesterday, and she was quite well,' Gabe said, desperately holding back tears of grief. David, Dwight and Julian were openly sobbing, and Gloria felt as if she were losing control.

Beatrice and Rosa came to the rescue and helped calm the younger boys while Gloria sat in shock on the sofa with her eldest son, clasping his hand tightly. Rosa poured Gloria a brandy, which she swallowed without barely tasting it and instructed Rosa to pour her another one and one each for herself and Beatrice, who was also dreadfully upset.

'Poor Marcus, she was everything to him,' Gloria said to Beatrice.

'He will be heart-broken for sure, Gloria,' she replied through her own tears. She had long abandoned calling her Mrs Phelps since Gerald left, the two women were more like friends after all the years they had brought the boys up together.

'Gerald, also,' Gloria admitted, 'despite everything he has done to me, Edith was his mother and the finest woman I have ever known, I loved her dearly.'

Marcus had telephoned that evening with the tragic news, and Gloria wanted so desperately to see him and try to comfort him.

'Thank you for your kindness, dear, but I have Gerald here with me,' he told her.

'That is of no consequence in this situation, Marcus, I can certainly put aside my grievances for him at a terrible time like this.'

Marcus's voice faltered slightly when he next spoke. 'I, I really do not think you should be here at this moment, Lavinia and Justine are with him.'

The words hit hard, and she was speechless for a few moments, Marcus was distressed enough without her presence adding to his grief, she thought, therefore, she agreed to visit him the following afternoon with the boys, once they were all home from school.

Dinner that evening at Lloyd Square was a very sombre affair, no-one had much of an appetite, and hardly a word was spoken except for Gloria informing the boys that they would all be visiting Grandfather the next day.

'What are we to say to him, Mama?' David asked.

'There is not much one can say at times like this, we just have to let your grandfather know how much we all love him and that Grandmama will be terribly missed,' Gloria said.

'Will we ever see Grandmama again?' Julian asked so innocently.

Choking back tears, Gloria replied, 'No, darling, she is in heaven now, but she will always watch over us, and we must always remember her because she was a very special lady.'

The conversation brought about floods of tears once more from everyone.

Gloria and Beatrice put Julian to bed, he lay there with his dark brown curls on the white pillowcase and big brown eyes looking at his mother, at seven-years-old, he could not fully understand why she was so distressed. Gloria leaned forward to kiss him goodnight, and the little boy put his arms around her neck.

'You are not going to die, are you, Mama?' he said.

A pain stabbed her heart, and she held him tightly. 'No, darling, I am not, I will always be here to take care of you, my beautiful boy. Now try and sleep.'

Struggling with her own grief, Gloria crossed to the other side of the bedroom and settled Dwight, he showed her a picture he had drawn earlier that evening of an angel.

'It is Grandmama,' he said quietly, 'I will miss her so much, she was always such fun.'

'I know, darling, we all will.'

Across the landing, Gabe and David were sat together on one of the beds talking between themselves, they looked up as Gloria entered their room.

'How are you, Mama?' Gabe asked, always conscious of his mother's feelings.

'I am very sad, as we all are, and it will be a difficult time for everyone, especially your grandfather and father,' Gloria said.

'It is not fair, Grandmama should have lived forever, what are we going to do without her?' David was bravely fighting back the tears as he spoke, he was nearly fourteen-years-old and desperately trying to be grown-up.

'Somehow we will go on, and remember, she will always be with us in our hearts.' Gloria choked on the words, the emotion was becoming too much for her to bear, but she had to stay strong for her boys. 'Try and sleep, my darlings, and tomorrow we will see how we can help your grandfather, goodnight.'

They climbed into their beds, and she left them to talk. Shutting the door behind her, she leaned against it closing her eyes, and in her mind's eye, she recollected Edith's kind face and her warm smile, causing the grief to well up inside her once more.

The following morning Gloria hated having to send her sons to school, but there was nothing to be done at home, and keeping busy was always the best way of coping in difficult circumstances, she told them. Gabe and David went off together bearing up gallantly, leaving a subdued Dwight and Julian with Beatrice to make their way to Clerkenwell.

Emotionally drained, Gloria caught the tram to work and somehow made it through the day. Lucy was a brick, she knew how much Edith meant to her friend and was quite distressed herself, she too had been very fond of her. Indeed, anyone who ever met her was captivated by Edith Phelps. The heartbreak would take a long time to heal, and Gloria knew that life would never be quite the same again.

They visited Marcus as planned that afternoon, they found him alone in the sitting-room smoking a cigarette, he had cancelled his patients for the day. Gloria had instructed the boys to be on their best behaviour so as not to upset their grandfather, they stood in the centre of the room in silence. At the same time, Gloria went over to kiss Marcus on the cheek and offered her deepest condolences. He looked exhausted and thanked her, but when he saw his grandsons lined up like wax-work models, he raised a smile, saying, 'What is the matter with all of you? Come over here and give your grandfather a hug, I am not going to break.'

Julian and Dwight reached him first, and Julian climbed up on to Marcus's lap, he stubbed out his cigarette so he could circle his arms around his youngest grandson while Dwight perched on the chair wing. Gabe and David stood in front of Marcus and told him how very sorry they were about Grandmama and asked if there was anything they may do to help.

'As long as I have all of you, then that will be all the help I require,' he told them with a warm, loving look.

The funeral took place two days later at St James's church, the last time Gloria went there was for Dorothy's funeral, which added the sadness of losing her friend on top of the anguish she felt for Edith. The church was full of mourners, and everyone stood in silence as the pallbearers carried Edith's coffin into the church, setting it down amongst an array of white flowers.

Gloria positioned herself and the boys on the front row pew at the left end, away from the immediate family. And, as if Edith's death and the funeral had not been enough to cope with, Gerald had the audacity to arrive with Lavinia on his arm wearing a ring on her left hand.

'Why is Papa's nurse friend here?' Dwight asked his mother. 'She lives at the flat with him, and she had a baby. He told us that after the war, she had nowhere to live, so he let her stay with him.'

Gloria could not believe what she was hearing, the nerve of the man, he has never told his sons the truth.

'No... you are not what you seem, Dr Phelps, Madame Burton was right. What further untruths have you imparted to our boys, I wonder,' she thought to herself, feeling somewhat repulsed at Gerald's weakness of character.

These thoughts raced through her head as she tried to think of a reply for her son, fortunately, she was rescued by the organist striking out the opening chords of *Amazing Grace* and all were required to stand and sing, saving Gloria from having to answer.

'*Yea, when this flesh and heart shall fail, And mortal life shall cease, I shall possess within the veil, a life of joy and peace.*'

Gloria choked on the words of the hymn, hoping beyond hope that Edith was at peace, because she had a premonition that from henceforward, life was about to change for the worse.

The next few weeks were awful, Edith left an immense void in everyone's lives, Marcus seemed to be bearing up, keeping far too busy, and Gloria feared he was not allowing himself time to grieve. Lilian stayed up in London living with a friend not too far away on Amwell Street, she fussed over Marcus, making certain he looked after himself, and they had dinner together most nights, she was quite wonderful.

Gloria felt numb most of the time, putting on a brave face for her boys and grieving at night once she was alone. They visited Marcus regularly after school as they had always done, it helped ease the pain of their loss. Once again, they spent two weeks of the summer holidays at Ramsgate, it was becoming an accepted annual custom and certainly helped cheer them all up to some extent.

As always, time is a great healer, and whenever sadness overcame her, Gloria thought of all the unconditional love Edith had shown her over the eighteen years of their acquaintance. These memories made her feel honoured to have known such a magnanimous lady, hoping that she herself could show just a part of Edith's compassion and love towards others.

The warm summer weather and sunshine always raised Gloria's spirits, and by the time the boys returned to school in September, they were all beginning to smile once more. Gabe turned seventeen years of age and entered his last year at Westminster before going up to Oxford to commence his Law degree, something he was very much looking forward to. Then, only a couple of weeks after Gabe's birthday, Lilian invited Gloria and the boys for Sunday tea. She had indeed taken over the running of Granville Square, assisting Polly in the day to day affairs and keeping Marcus company. He found that having Lilian around reminded him of Edith and the years of happiness they had spent together, which comforted him. The atmosphere around the table was quite jovial, both Gabe and David describing in great detail the last school cricket match of the season.

'It was Gabe's last turn at the wicket with the score at 151-148,' David was explaining, 'the bowler sent him a spinner down the pitch, but Gabe managed to wallop it high, sending it off for a six, winning us the match. He played splendidly - ' He was about to continue when the telephone rang in the hallway, and after a short moment, Polly came through to the dining room telling Marcus it was Gerald.

'Excuse me, everyone, hopefully, this will be brief.' He stood up and left the room while the rest of the party carried on tucking into the delicious iced Queen cakes Polly had baked. When Marcus returned a few minutes later, he had an ashen look on his face.

'Whatever is the matter, Marcus, dear?' Lilian asked, 'come and sit down, you look dreadful.'

He spoke quietly. 'It may not be news that you wish to hear under the circumstances, but Gerald has just informed me that Lavinia has been killed in a motor vehicle accident.'

The words stunned everyone into silence. Lilian was the first to speak. 'My goodness,' she exclaimed, 'how utterly dreadful.'

Gloria was unsure what to think, despite who the woman was, it was a ghastly way to die, and she would never have wished her dead. Her only thoughts had been wishing that Gerald had never met her. 'How much tragedy can one family take,' she thought to herself.

'I really must join Gerald at St Thomas's, he is my son, and he is distraught,' Marcus said.

'Of course, you must, we will stay and keep Lilian company until you return,' Gloria replied.

'Actually, I would rather accompany Marcus to the hospital, I would feel of more use there than sitting at home,' Lilian said.

Gloria was a little surprised by her reply but then thought perhaps it would be best she go home with the boys, facing Gerald in this situation if he came back to the house, was not at all in her best interest.

The small party returned to Lloyd Square, Gloria went to the sitting-room and poured herself a sherry, Gabe followed her in, while his younger brothers went upstairs to their rooms.

'Mama, may I join you?' he asked,

'Of course, darling, in fact, why not join me with a small sherry?

I think we deserve one after all of this terrible news.' A surprised but delighted Gabe accepted the sherry at once, he had partaken of the occasional glass before, but not to his mother's knowledge, it was usually at his school friend Freddie's house when they were studying together.

'Helps one think, Gabe,' Freddie proclaimed as he helped himself to his mother's best Jerez.

Gabe sat next to his mother on the sofa, enjoying his sherry. 'What will Papa do now, do you think? he asked. 'I am quite aware of his situation with Lavinia, and so is David. Papa thinks we do not know that Justine is our sister, Dwight and Julian are not old enough to understand, but I am not a fool, Mama, I know what he has done to you.'

'Gabe, my poor boy, why did you never tell me?'

'I did not want to upset you any more than you have been.'

'Well, it is all water under the bridge now, and we have survived, but this turn of events will alter matters for your father, he will have to find someone to care for the child, although I doubt it will impact on our lives,' she told her son.

'I feel sorry for Grandfather, too many sad things are happening to him, he seems lost without Grandmama, and great Aunt Lilian fusses over him as if she is trying to take her place,' Gabe said.

And that is precisely what came to pass, Marcus and Lilian married less than a year after Edith's death at St Mark's church. It was a small, quiet wedding to which Gloria did not attend, she felt her presence would not be necessary. The only guests were Gerald, Clara and a few of Marcus's friends and associates from the medical world, including Antony Stevenson, who had now retired. Marcus himself was in his seventies, though he continued running his practice and teaching at Guy's and St Thomas.

Some thought it odd that Marcus had married his deceased wife's stepsister, but they were actually very content together, regardless of Lilian being nineteen years younger than Marcus. She was possessed of a bright, cheery nature, much like Edith. Through the years Gloria had known Lilian, she came to understand that Edith had been more like a mother to her after she was adopted by the Napier family. Lilian had been betrothed to a soldier in her younger days, but he was killed during the Sudan War, and no other suitor had measured up, thus, she had remained a spinster.

The summer of 1922 was cool and unsettled, leaving Gloria a little subdued as September approached, on the other hand, the fact that Gabe was to begin his studies at Oxford filled her with so much pride she was fit to burst. His father had taken him to Saville Row a few weeks before to have a new three-piece suit made. It was cut in the latest style, with a shorter jacket and slimmer, tapered trousers in olive-green wool with a subtle blue check woven in, the finishing touch being a brown Homburg hat. A new black evening suit was also ordered. It had been the first contact between father and son for a few months, and the conversation was somewhat arduous. It mostly combined pleasantries and what Gabe should expect up at Oxford, combined with stiff comments of how proud Gerald was of his son, nevertheless, they shook hands and parted on reasonable terms.

'Good luck, son, you have grown into a fine young man, and I can see that you are taking good care of your mother.' He attempted to explain and justify why he had deserted Gloria, but Gabe was not interested.

'It matters not, Papa, I do not wish to know or understand, you broke Mama's heart and that I cannot forgive. I am grateful for the financial support you are providing for us all, without which I am fully aware that Oxford would be out of the question, and I sincerely hope that my brothers will be given the same opportunities as I in the future.'

On his arrival home that day, Gloria had been passing through the hallway as Gabe entered through the front door.

'Hello, Mama,' he said and kissed her cheek.

'How was your outing, darling?' Gloria asked.

'It was bearable, but I thought Father looked rather unwell, he had a cold and a bad cough,' Gabe had replied.

'Perhaps he is working too hard. The main issue is you are now suitably attired for your first day at university, and I am very proud of you.'

Gabe collected his suits a fortnight later and put them on to show Gloria, seeing her son at almost eighteen-years of age dressed so grandly, brought a lump to her throat. He reminded her so much of Gerald when they first met that night at the Gaiety Theatre, the same dark hair and handsome face, although Gerald's different coloured eyes had not passed through to his son, Gabe's were both hazel brown.

On the 13th of September 1922, Gabe celebrated his eighteenth birthday in style, dinner at The Ritz with the family. He wore his new evening suit and cut quite the dashing figure with Gloria on his arm. She looked dazzling in a low backed gown with a back sash made from a shimmering, bronze coloured fabric. She wore a glittering diamante clip in her hair and carried a feather boa to complete her outfit, she embraced the new style of the decade, and it suited her well. Heads always turned when Gloria entered a room, and tonight was no exception as the party were seated.

It was a splendid dinner, and after dessert had been served, Marcus ordered a bottle of Dom Perignon to toast Gabe's birthday and his future success at Oxford.

Gabe raised his glass and said, 'I would like to propose a toast to my dear grandfather, without whom our lives would have undoubtedly taken a different path. Since my birth, your love and support have been endless, my only sadness tonight is that Grandmama could not be with us. However, great Aunt Lilian is keeping Grandfather on the straight and narrow, so, let us raise our glasses to Dr Marcus Phelps, my friend, my guide and mentor.' This was followed by the sounds of, 'Cheers, chin, chin,' and the clinking of glasses around the table.

Gabe continued, 'I wish to propose another toast, this time to my mother, my beautiful, glorious, Mama.' His eyes were filled with love as he looked at Gloria. 'You are, without doubt, the most wonderful person in my life, the strongest and most loving being anyone could wish to know. Throughout my eighteen years on this earth, you have never faltered in your love for my brothers or me, you are my rock and foundation, Mama, thank you, I love you.'

Although she smiled radiantly, Gloria's eyes brimmed with tears as she raised her glass to her son. How she would miss him when he moved to Oxford, telephone calls and letters would never replace his presence in the house, her first bird was to fly the nest, and it was an immensely emotional moment.

A few weeks later, nothing could have ever prepared any of the Phelps family for what happened next....

Gerald Napier Phelps was dead.

CHAPTER 13

Marcus was devastated, he had been with his son at the end after a woman telephoned, informing him that Gerald's condition had deteriorated, and he was close to death. Pneumonia had set in after being unable to shake off a cold, and he suffered terribly before he passed away. The woman had cared for him by his bedside, and it transpired that her name was Edwina Yates. She was the nurse who had crawled out of the bomb crater on that terrible night in France when Gerald was injured and had been living with Gerald since Lavinia's death, helping take care of Justine.

Out of the kindness of their hearts, Marcus and Lilian had taken in three-year-old Justine when Gerald became gravely ill, what was to become of her now that he was dead, was quite another matter.

Gabe, David and Dwight had visited their father as often as could be allowed, Julian was very distressed after seeing Gerald so ill and said he was too frightened to see him again. Regardless of their estrangement from him, the three older boys were quite distraught over their father's death, Julian very confused, and Gloria was in shock. It felt as if her life was disintegrating, and she greatly feared for the future.

Gerald's funeral took place four days later at St James's church, at least a hundred people had come to mourn, a mark of his respect and accomplishments amongst his colleagues in the medical world. Marcus was showing immense courage and strength, and although he was now seventy-four years old, he had barely changed since Gloria had known him. Today, though, his appearance was that of a heart-broken man.

Fleur and Filkes had come up to London, and Gloria sat beside them with her boys and Antony Stevenson, who held her hand as they mumbled their way through *Jerusalem* and the *Lord's Prayer*. Earlier, he had successfully steered her away from a confrontation with Edwina, who insisted on sitting with Marcus and Lilian.

'Who the hell does that woman think she is?' Gloria hissed. 'How dare she assume to be his wife. Just how many Mrs Phelpses has there been since he deserted his actual wife and sons!'

Antony had attempted to calm an outraged Gloria.

'The war changed him, it did so to many men, and I cannot fathom why he acted in such a way with you. I have always seen how much you loved him, and my admiration for the way in which you have coped holds no bounds, you are an outstanding woman, Gloria, you are a survivor.'

'I did love him, Antony, with all my heart and soul, and I thought he loved me.' Gloria said sadly.

There was to be a wake held at the doctors' mess in Gerald's honour, to which Gloria felt she had no reason to attend. The last thing she wanted to hear was people saying what a marvellous man he was, what an excellent doctor he was, how much he will be missed, and *what a terrible husband he had been.* No... she took up Fleur and Filkes offer of tea at The Ritz instead.

The mood became rather gloomy, and Gloria began to feel quite emotional when she reminisced about her happy years with Gerald. She wondered why it had all gone so horribly wrong and was very grateful for her sister's company at this present moment in time.

'I must telephone Mama and impart the news, I have not spoken to her in ages, have you, Fleur?' Gloria said.

155

'Yes, about two weeks ago, she sounded older and a little forgetful actually, perhaps I should visit her while we are up in London, will you come with me?' Fleur asked.

'Not this time, I doubt I can face her, I have had far too many conversations with her since Gerald left that ended with, "I knew this would happen, I told you from the start," and I have no desire to hear her say it again, forgive me, darling. Telling her Gerald has died will only add fuel to the fire, I live in dread of what her opinion will be of that.'

Despite the sad atmosphere, the trio enjoyed their Earl Grey tea and beautifully cut sandwiches, followed by little cakes arranged on a white two-tiered china cake stand decorated in a delicate gold and turquoise pattern.

The day after the funeral, Marcus telephoned Gloria and asked that she be present at the reading of Gerald's will. 'I understand how difficult it will be for you with Edwina present and Justine at the house, but you must be there to hear what is said, our solicitor informed me that Gerald changed his will only a few days before he died, and I know not what he has done.'

Gloria was filled with dread, her hands shook as she fastened her coat, picking up her bag, she steeled herself and made her way to Granville Square. She arrived to find a small group of people gathered in the sitting-room, Marcus and Lilian were talking to a tall man with a stoop and thinning hair, whom she assumed to be the solicitor. Clara was there and terribly upset over her nephew's death and also Antony, who greeted Gloria with a kiss on the cheek.

'Stay strong, my dear,' he whispered.

Her eyes fell upon Edwina, who was handing over Justine to Polly, the child was a reasonably pretty little thing with light brown hair and blue eyes and looked more like her mother than Gerald. She began to cry when Polly tried to take her, and even though

Gloria felt hatred towards Lavinia and Edwina, her motherly instinct was too strong to bear any ill will against an innocent child. She wondered what would become of the poor thing now that she was orphaned.

Gloria took a glass of sherry from the sideboard and sat down next to Antony on the sofa, she spotted Edwina lurking in the doorway. The solicitor cleared his throat and began to speak in a high-pitched nasal voice that irritated Gloria immediately.

'We are gathered here this evening to hear the last will and testament of Dr Gerald Napier Phelps, recently deceased.'

'Just get on with it,' Gloria was thinking in her head, 'put me out of my misery.'

The solicitor opened the envelope with a flourish of a paper-knife and began to read.

'I, Gerald Napier Phelps, surgeon M.B. B.S. of Flat 2 Bryanston Court, George Street, London, hereby revoke all former wills and declare this to be my last will and testament. I hereby give to my dear friend, Edwina Yates, all my goods, chattels and other articles situated in and about my private house or flat and all proceeds from the sale of my personal and real estate to be placed in trust by my executors to pay the income of the said Edwina Yates throughout her lifetime..........'

Gloria sat in stunned silence, feeling as if her head were about to explode, the blood pulsed through her temples as she listened to the whining words of the solicitor as he droned on. It was too much, she could take no more and stood up, the words came from her mouth in a torrent.

'How dare he! How could he do this to us? What about my boys? his own sons, the man has left us destitute.'

Gloria was furious, Antony tried to pull her back to her seat, but she shook him off and lunged towards Edwina, who was attempting to slip out of the door.

Gloria screamed. 'You bitch! you and that Lavinia, you stole my husband from me, you plotted and schemed in France, turning him against me, and now I have nothing, you have taken everything.'

She grabbed Edwina's arm gripping it tightly, and was on the verge of slapping the woman across the face, but stopped and looked at her, she was plain and mousey-looking, not worth wasting anger on, so she just pushed her away and glared.

'Take it, have it all, I hope it brings you more happiness than it did me, but I warn you, stay out of my sight – EDWINA!'

She spat her name venomously, Edwina scuttled out of the room and disappeared upstairs somewhere. Everyone sat in silence until the solicitor once again cleared his throat.

'Do you wish for me to continue?' he said.

'Would you mind waiting please while I speak to my daughter-in-law in private,' Marcus asked him.

'If you must, but this is highly irregular,' he replied.

Marcus stood up and guided the incensed Gloria into the study.

'I knew nothing of this, Gloria, please, believe me, you are his legal widow and should be entitled to his estate, but unfortunately, Gerald had the right to change his will if he so desired, I am terribly sorry, my dear.'

'Can it be contested, Marcus?' Gloria asked, totally enraged by the whole situation.

'I doubt it, you have been separated for four years, and you earn your own living,' Marcus replied.

'I cannot support myself and my sons on a shop assistant's income even if I am a supervisor, what am I to do, Marcus?' she said, her voice shaking,'

The blood pounded in Gloria's ears, she felt panic-stricken.

'Try and calm yourself, dear, I have always told you that I would take care of the boys and intend to hold that promise. Nevertheless, even in my financial position, I cannot maintain two large houses, my only suggestion is that you all come and live here with me.'

'No, Marcus, I could not possibly put on you again, there must be another way.'

Marcus calmly convinced her that this was the only solution, and Gloria reluctantly concluded that she would have to accept his gracious offer for now.

'You are far too generous, Marcus, you always have been towards me, I will stay only as long as needs be, I cannot expect you to support a thirty-seven-year-old woman, but if you look after my boys, I will be eternally grateful. You are the kindest, most loving man I have ever known, thank you.'

She kissed his cheek, and he put his arms around her.

'I am truly sorry for my son's behaviour, you did not deserve any of this,' he said gently.

'I cannot go back in there, I need to go home whilst I still have one. Goodnight Marcus, thank you for everything.'

Shaking with anger, Gloria left the house and returned to Lloyd Square, she immediately telephoned Lucy to relate the whole sordid affair. 'I need a large gin martini, please meet me at The Stafford, I have to get away from here.'

Gabe was at Freddie's house for the night discussing plans for Oxford, and she knew she could leave David, Dwight and Julian in the safe hands of Beatrice and Rosa. How she was to tell them all what had transpired she could not contemplate at this moment, therefore, she picked up her handbag and left the house to meet her dearest friend.

Lucy was already waiting outside the Stafford Hotel when Gloria arrived, the doorman tipped his hat as the ladies walked through and made their way to the cocktail bar. They sat at a table and ordered two gin martinis from the waiter who obliged and returned quickly with the drinks.'

'Two gin martinis for the ladies,' the waiter said politely and turned to leave.

'No, stay,' Gloria instructed, she downed her drink in one, gave the surprised-looking waiter her glass back, saying, 'I would like another one, please.'

'Of course, madam, will you be staying for a while?' he enquired.

'For as long as it takes,' Gloria replied. The waiter promptly returned, tray in hand and kept bringing Gloria and Lucy the drinks they requested for the rest of the evening.

'Lucy, do you remember the day at the funfair when I had my fortune told by that wretched Madame Burton?' Gloria said, slightly slurring her words.

'Yes, I do, you would never tell me what she said that upset you so much.'

Gloria went on to relate what the gypsy woman had told her so many years ago, the words were etched in her memory.

'I was so young and naïve, Lucy, I thought my life would be perfect, and here we are, two widows and not another eligible man in sight. What are we going to do?'

Lucy studied the cocktail menu and said, 'I think we each require one of those Fallen Angels.' At which she beckoned their waiter over to the table.

Two very sore heads arrived at Selfridges the following morning, they had left the cocktail bar at midnight and each taken a cab home.

'It was a much-needed diversion though, darling, was it not?' Lucy said to Gloria as they stood waiting for the shop doors to open.

'Indeed, it was, I rather like it there, and I overheard someone saying they were going onto a casino afterwards, maybe we should give that a try, perhaps I could win a fortune and be put out of my misery,' Gloria replied and tried to laugh, but it shook her brain around in her head too much and made her feel giddy.

They managed to survive the day, and as Gloria sat on the tram on her way home, she contemplated the daunting task that awaited her that evening. How she was to tell her sons that they were losing their home and would have to live with their grandfather once more, then inform Beatrice and Rosa that soon, their services would no longer be required. Inwardly she cursed Gerald to the ends of the earth.

Gloria decided to talk to the boys during dinner, she studied each of her sons as they ate the pineapple upside-down cake Rosa had recently discovered the recipe for and wished she knew how they were feeling. Gabe, of course, was a rock, caring more for Gloria than himself, David and Dwight were very quiet, and Julian asked if Papa was now in heaven with Grandmama. *'Hell, more like,'* Gloria had thought to herself but pacified her eight-year-old son with all the words one would say to a little boy. He looked so sad, staring up at her with his big brown eyes, and Gloria's heart broke yet again, she felt despair well up inside her once more but quelled it and began to speak to her sons, she found it almost impossible.

'My darling boys, you know I love you more than anything in this world…..' Her voice faltered. 'I have to tell you something that is going to affect our lives immensely.'

Gabe looked alarmed. 'What is it, Mama? Has something else happened?'

Gloria swallowed and resumed. 'Now that your father has passed away, I am afraid that we cannot stay in our house anymore, we have to go back and live with Grandfather and Aunt Lilian.'

There was a chorus of, 'Why, what for, it is not the same there without Grandmama.'

Gloria attempted to quieten her sons. 'I am truly sorry, my darlings, but it is not by my own doing, if your grandfather had not offered to take us in, we would have nowhere to live at all, so we must be very grateful.'

'What is the real reason, Mama?' Gabe asked.

'I will explain later, but for now, we can carry on as normal in our own house until arrangements are finalised.'

The younger boys grumbled between themselves for a while longer until David persuaded Dwight and Julian that they had enjoyed living at Granville Square when they were small, so it might not be so different now. Meanwhile, Gabe searched his mother's face for a clue as to the real reason for this circumstance. To him, she looked tired and strained, and for the first time, he noticed a few lines around her beautiful green eyes, it worried him.

No one felt like any more to eat after this revelation, Dwight and Julian went up to their room to play, whereas Gabe and David pleaded with Gloria to tell them the truth. They sat together, and she explained that their father had not left any provision for them, and although their grandfather had promised to take care of everyone, he could not keep both houses.

Gabe spoke up. 'Well, I cannot expect Grandfather to pay for Oxford together with Westminster for my brothers.'

'But Gabe, you have worked so hard for Oxford, there must be some other way, perhaps we could apply for a scholarship?' Gloria replied.

With everything that had happened, the fees for Oxford had not occurred to Gloria until now, and again she cursed Gerald for destroying his son's ambition, most probably all of his sons. They talked about the situation they had been forced into, David was very grown-up about everything and surprised Gloria with his maturity. The boys tried to come to terms with the change in their father and why he had not provided for them, but the fact was difficult for anyone to grasp. It always came around to one had to be there to understand, and as none of them had been, it continued to leave everyone in a state of incomprehension.

Marcus and Lilian called on them the following evening and discussed the future arrangements. Gabe repeatedly insisted that his grandfather should not pay for him to go up to Oxford. The two of them debated the subject at great lengths, which led to Marcus jesting that perhaps Gabe take up a career in politics. However, the discussion did lead to him revealing that prior to his desire to take up law, he had thought of becoming a journalist but believed the family would disapprove.

'You know, Gabe, one of my patients is deputy editor of the Kensington Post, if you insist on turning down Oxford, then please, let me speak to Bainbridge and see if he will take you on,' Marcus said determinedly. By the end of the evening, at least one thing was decided upon.

Within three months, Lloyd Square was sold, and bitterly, Gloria had to accept that the equity from its sale must be included in Gerald's estate, all of which Edwina would receive. The immense anger she felt towards Gerald raged inside her for days, she ranted and raved to Lucy on the telephone, who patiently let her friend work it out of her system. Eventually, Gloria calmed down sufficiently, leaving her hatred continually simmering under the surface when she thought of how her sons' ambitions were severely jeopardised by Gerald's actions.

Once again, the extended Phelps family were together under one roof, a situation that left Gloria feeling decidedly uncomfortable. There had been a tremendously upsetting parting with Beatrice and Rosa. Fortunately, they had both found positions elsewhere quite quickly due to the glowing references Gloria had provided for them.

Julian had sobbed for hours after Beatrice left, heartbroken at losing his second mother. He had wailed and shouted about everything being so unfair and ran off up to his room, where Gloria had found him lying on his bed hugging Jip, the stuffed dog that Edith had won at the fair. She held her son tightly in her arms, comforting him, her own heart bleeding.

It took quite some time for the atmosphere at Granville Square to settle. Julian was terribly upset and withdrawn, but gradually with care and love from all around him, he started to recover, and after a while, emerged from the shell he had closed around himself. The promise of a train ride to Ramsgate to visit Aunt Fleur during the Easter holidays cheered him up, and although the seaside had been quite bracing, he returned with Fleur a much healthier and happy nine-year-old.

As promised, Marcus spoke to Silas Bainbridge regarding a job for Gabe at the newspaper, and as luck would have it, an opening had just come up for a junior writer, which Gabe was thrilled about.

'I cannot thank you enough, Grandfather, it is such an exciting opportunity, and I will be earning a wage and able to pay my way.' He shook Marcus's hand with a beaming smile on his face.

'Thank you, but I do not need your money, Gabe, I want you to enjoy life, always save for a rainy day, but after the events of the last few months, I want you to have some fun. Not quite on the scale of those "Bright Young Things" dashing around London, mind you.' Marcus replied with a smile.

'I would like a motor car one day, it was such a thrill when I drove Aunt Fleur's car that time,' Gabe said and began to daydream about which model he would purchase first.

Thus, as 1923 passed, Gabe began his first day at the newspaper office and was given the responsibility of accompanying Perkins to the magistrate's court to report on the day's cases. On his return home that evening, he told Gloria and Marcus how astounded he was at the crimes some people committed. He added that he had enjoyed the day immensely and was looking forward to tomorrow.

There had been one other matter that fell upon Marcus to attend to, that of the orphaned Justine. At present, Edwina was caring for her at the flat. She had agreed to this in the short term, but Marcus knew the situation was in dire need of a permanent solution.

Recently, a letter had arrived for Marcus from one of his old students who had emigrated to New York when he qualified. He was now a successful obstetrician, his name was Gregory Morley, and he and Gerald had studied at St Thomas's together. He had written informing Marcus that he would be visiting London with his wife, Adelaide, en route to a European tour and hoped they could call upon the family and have dinner together. In Marcus's reply, he told Gregory of Gerald's death and his separation from Gloria, attempting to justify the latter with Gerald's change in character during the war. Writing the letter made Marcus feel decidedly melancholy.

However, meeting the Morley's over dinner at Simpson's in the Strand did much to lift his spirits. Adelaide was a wealthy New York heiress, blonde and beautiful. Sadly, the couple revealed that they were unable to have children of their own and had adopted two sons, now aged eight and ten.

Over dinner, Marcus and Lilian talked about Justine and the situation she was in, and without any suggestion on Marcus's part, Adelaide insisted they come and meet her. So, the following morning Justine was brought over to Granville Square, it was a Friday which meant the boys were at school and Gloria and Gabe at work. The four-year-old Justine hid behind Edwina's legs, she was painfully shy and stared at Adelaide wide-eyed.

'Come over here, honey, let me take a look at you. My you're a quiet, timid little thing ain't ya.' She spoke with a strong New York accent, which on hearing it, made Justine's eyes widen further. Adelaide crouched down to Justine's level and held out her hands towards her. 'Come on, sweetie, I ain't gonna bite.' She smiled kindly and beckoned Justine over.

With a slight nudge from Edwina, the little girl moved slowly towards Adelaide.

'She has spoken very little since Gerald died,' Lilian said, 'I think losing him, and her mother has been too much of a shock for her.'

'Well, we can't have that now, can we? What do you say to us getting to know each other a little better? How about a walk in the park with Greg and me? I'll buy you an ice-cream, what do you say, honey?' Adelaide said.

Justine nodded her head and walked towards Adelaide's outstretched hand.

The threesome returned about an hour later, astonishingly, Justine was holding Adelaide's hand and smiling. 'That's settled then, Marcus, we'll take Justine back to New York with us, I always wanted a daughter, we can give her a good life, and she's gotten two brothers at home already.'

Initially, Marcus could not believe what he was hearing, but as the Morley's continued, he realised it was the perfect outcome for Justine. The child had warmed to Adelaide instantly, something she had never done with anyone else.

Arrangements were set for returning to New York with Justine after their European holiday. In the meantime, Marcus could arrange the necessary adoption papers with his solicitor, the whole matter was organised without any setbacks and all paperwork signed on the Morley's return. Marcus and Lilian had waved them off at Southampton, first-class aboard the *RMS Mauretania* after Marcus had promised Justine he would always remember his only granddaughter, and she must not forget her English grandfather.

As the colossal ship left the docks, Lilian was crying and dabbing her eyes with a handkerchief, whilst Marcus felt a huge pang of guilt at handing his granddaughter over to strangers. Nevertheless, he also felt a great sense of relief that Justine would be given the chance of a far better future than she had in England, and for the first time in a long time, a period of stability settled at Granville Square.

CHAPTER 14

'I want to join the RAF.' David had announced a few weeks before his eighteenth birthday, in response to being questioned about his future plans once he left Westminster. 'It would be the most marvellous opportunity, Mama.'

His revelation left Gloria somewhat alarmed, especially when she thought about poor Lucy's husband, who was shot down and killed in the war in his plane.

'This is a sudden turn of events from banking, why the change of heart?' she asked.

'Banking is so dull, I want some excitement in my life, evidently, one can join the Iraq Command, and I could see parts of the world we have only ever seen on maps. It would also mean not having to rely on Grandfather for my allowance, he works far too hard to pay for our schooling, and he is in his seventies now,' David replied.

Gloria had herself been concerned about Marcus over the last few months, he tired more quickly in the evenings and often nodded off in his chair, added to which she had never felt comfortable when they went back to live at Granville Square. Her pride had taken quite a tumble, knowing that she could not provide for her sons without Marcus's help.

Therefore, the matter of David joining the RAF was discussed at great length, and as the war was long over, Gloria put her fear aside and decided if it was David's choice, then she should not stand in his way.

David gained a distinction for his Higher School Certificate and by September had joined 43 Squadron at RAF Henlow as acting pilot officer. He stood in front of Gloria, looking most debonair in his air force blue uniform, and whilst she snapped numerous photographs of him, her heart swelled with love for her son.

'You know, Mama, our motto is *Gloria Finis,* quite fitting, do you not think?' David said, and Gloria held his hands, smiling.

When the day arrived for David to travel to Henlow, Gloria was filled with such a mixture of emotions, it made her head spin, he was the first of her sons to leave home, which panicked her. She also appreciated that he was possessed of a steady personality, level-headed and mature, all qualities that had significantly been in his favour when he joined up. Her two eldest sons were men now, and Dwight not far behind, Julian was already twelve years old and due to start Westminster the following year. All these thoughts suddenly made her feel older and lonely, what would she do when all of her boys were grown and left the nest? Where would she go?

She pushed these thoughts aside for the time being and concentrated on David. The family had dined together the night before, and Gabe, Dwight and Julian said their farewells earlier at breakfast. David attempted a restrained emotional parting with Marcus, both men endeavouring to keep their sangfroid. But eventually, Marcus succumbed to giving David a bear hug, and David expressing emotive farewell words to his grandfather.

'Thank you for everything you have done for us, you are more of a father to me than he ever was. I cannot express my love and gratitude for you enough. I will do my utmost to make you proud, and please do not let Mama pine.'

'I am already proud of you, my boy, and the love is reciprocated, you know that. Now go and learn how to fly those remarkable flying machines, and stay safe,' Marcus replied.

Gloria was sure she could see a glint of a tear in his eye as he patted his grandson on the back.

Mother and son took a taxicab to Kings Cross station, David was to catch the midday train to Henlow and take another cab from the station to the RAF barracks. They stood together on the platform, to Gloria, her son still looked so young, he had barely started to shave. Nevertheless, he was well-muscled and strong from sports at school and grown into a handsome young man, and with his thick brown hair slicked back Valentino style, he looked every bit a film star himself.

The train pulled into the platform and noisily came to a halt, steam seemingly puffing out of all parts of the enormous engine.

'Well, this is it, Mama, thank you for everything, I will write as often as possible, mind you, I am sure it will be awfully busy,' David said.

'Goodbye, my darling,' Gloria said, attempting a smile, 'I will miss you dreadfully, come here, and give your mother a kiss.'

He kissed Gloria's cheek and put his arms around her, saying, 'I will miss you too, I will miss everyone, but this is the adventure of a lifetime. I love you, Mama, goodbye.'

Picking up his tan leather suitcase, he headed towards the train and climbed aboard. He turned to wave to Gloria, and her heart lurched, the last time she waved a man off in uniform, he returned a different person, she desperately hoped history would not repeat itself.

'Goodbye, David,' she shouted, but he could not hear her above the noise of the engine, nor could he see the tears streaming down her face as the train pulled out of the station. Dabbing her eyes with a handkerchief, she slowly made her way to the underground. She had to work that afternoon, and a very despondent Gloria entered the store, which did not go unnoticed by Lucy.

'Bad was it, darling?' Lucy said as her friend positioned herself behind the counter.

'How many times must my heart be broken, Lucy? My son is eighteen years of age, has joined the RAF, and we remain two old widows, something has to be done about our situation, what do you say to a night out at The Stafford?'

'I say yes, indeed, shall we meet at nine o'clock as usual?'

The two friends agreed and then turned their attentions to the customers heading towards them, the new Max Factor range had just come in, and women were flocking into the store to sample the lipsticks and eyeshadows.

That evening, as Gloria made herself up ready for her night out, she stared at her reflection in the mirror. She put on one of the new shades of rich, red lipstick and applied brush on mascara to her already lush eyelashes. With her short bobbed-hair, no one would have suspected she was forty-years-old. Her figure was as slender as ever, and that evening she wore her favourite dusky green beaded evening dress. It had a daring plunging neckline and low waisted gathered skirt, with it, she wore a pair of bronze coloured bar shoes and a simple diamond choker with a teardrop pendant. Gerald had given it to her on her thirtieth birthday, but tonight, like all the jewellery he had bought for her, she wore it because it was beautiful.

She held out her hands to admire the matching red nail polish, looked at her gold wedding band and the exquisite emerald engagement ring on her finger and questioned why she continued to wear them. Was it to keep up appearances when out with her sons? That might have been so whilst Gerald was alive, but she was widowed and single now, in these modern times, no one would bat an eyelid at a woman of her age without rings on her finger. She had not taken off her wedding ring for twenty-two years, perhaps it was time for a new beginning. Holding the thought resolutely in her head, she pulled both rings off her finger, placed them in her jewellery box, and made a mental note to return the emerald engagement ring to Lilian. Such an expensive ring should stay in the Napier family from whence it came.

Inside the box sat the scallop seashell with the little figurine that the boys had bought her from Ramsgate all those summers ago, she picked it up. 'I love you, my beautiful boys, but your old Mama needs more in her life now that you are grown.' She kissed the shell and placed it back on the dressing table, stood up, admired herself in the mirror, picked up her evening bag and fox fur stole and headed out to meet Lucy.

The Stafford was extremely busy that evening, the cocktail bar was full of smoke and people laughing. Gloria and Lucy scoured the room, and eventually, they managed to find a table to sit at and ordered two Singapore Slings.

'Never thought so many people could fit in here,' Lucy exclaimed. The waiter returned, carrying their drinks rather precariously on a tray and placed them on the table. 'Cheers, darling, thank heavens we have no prohibition, those poor Americans.' They raised their glasses and laughed.

The two friends attempted to keep the conversation light despite Gloria feeling sad over David leaving home. He had telephoned to say he had arrived safely and was happily settled into the barracks, reiterating that she must not fret, something she was trying very hard not to do.

'He looked so handsome in his blues, wait until I have the photographs developed, I think you will agree,' Gloria said.

'They are all handsome boys, remember at the time their father was too, he may have turned out to be a rotten husband, but your sons are wonderful because of you, darling,' Lucy replied.

'Thank you, darling. Gabe was a little baby when we first became friends, almost twenty-one years ago, do you remember?'

'How could I forget? I had never been bothered about children until I saw his cute little face and the adoring way he looked at you, but remember Albert and I married for convenience, and he never seemed interested in me in that way. We were good friends, though, and I did miss him very much after he was killed. You know, you never told me the whole story about how you and Gerald met, I think you can spill the beans now after all this time.'

It did not seem to matter to Gloria anymore, so she told Lucy about her being pregnant, the elopement, her miscarriage, how her father had disowned her, and how indebted she was to Marcus. Lucy's eyes widened as her friend revealed her life story and commented that she had often wondered what the real version was.

'I suppose in the end my mother was right, my marriage did flounder, but it was not by my doing though,' Gloria finished.

The two women had not realised how morose they had become until they heard a man's voice beside them. 'I must say, my friend and I have a keen desire to know why two beautiful ladies are looking so gloomy on this wonderful evening.'

Gloria and Lucy looked around to see a man in his early forties holding two gin martinis in his outstretched hands, with a second man loitering behind him. 'Willard Grainger and Roland Butler at your service, I hope you do not think us too presumptuous?' he said, offering them the drinks.

Gloria and Lucy were a little taken aback at his approach, and for a moment were uncertain what to do, then Lucy's eyes lit up with that mischievous glint she often had and replied, 'What the heck, it is 1925, thank you, Willard, I accept,' she said taking the glass from his hand. Gloria remained a little hesitant but decided one drink would not hurt and accepted the glass held out to her.

'Pull up some extra seats, Roland,' Willard called to his friend, who complied, and the two men shuffled the chairs up to the table, placing themselves between Gloria and Lucy. 'Well, ladies, to whom do we have the pleasure?'

'The widows, Lucy and Gloria,' Lucy announced, 'Cheers,' she added, holding her glass up in the air.

'Did not think you were alone by choice, poor things. Now, what can we do to raise a smile on the prettiest faces we have laid eyes on in weeks.' Willard sounded a little drunk, which made Lucy and Gloria suppress a smile to each other.

Then, loudly and brashly, Willard explained that they were both door to door salesmen, selling labour saving devices for the home, such as vacuum cleaners and electric irons. He waxed lyrical about their products, scarcely pausing for breath, Gloria felt sure his friend just carried the bag of samples, as he had not said a word since he sat down. Ten minutes later, Willard eventually stopped talking and asked if the lovely ladies would like another drink.

'Are you sure, Will? I think you may have had a few too many already,' Roland said to his friend.

'Nonsense, Roly, I thought we were set to party with our two delightful companions, I was about to order a bottle to take up to the room,' Willard replied.

Gloria and Lucy shot alarmed looks at each other, this was not what they were expecting.

'Come on, Lucy, Gloria, what do you say to a bit of fun, thought that was what you were up for, two lonely widows and all.' Willard was definitely somewhat worse for wear and was not going to take no for an answer.

'I think not, Mr Grainger, we thank you for the drinks. It is rather late, and we would like to leave,' Gloria said. She stood up, picking up her bag and stole with Lucy following her lead instantly.

'Now, that is no way to treat a gentleman who has bought you a drink,' he said, leering at Gloria as he grabbed her arm. Anger and fear welled up inside her.

'Let go of me,' she hissed, 'or I will call the waiter and have you escorted out of here.'

'Well, aren't you a stuck up madam? Just wanted a little payment for the drink, not that flush, you know,' he slurred.

Gloria pulled her arm away and reached into her purse, she threw enough money on the table to pay for both drinks. 'Here, take it and buy some manners, come on, Lucy, we are leaving.'

They hurriedly left the bar, not daring to look back until they were outside in the street.

'What a diabolical man, if that is the behaviour of men in these modern times, I would prefer to remain a widow, how dare he makes such presumptions.' Gloria was furious.

'I never liked men all that much anyway, and he has just added to my list of reasons why,' Lucy replied, 'rather put the dampers on the evening. I apologise for agreeing for them to sit with us.'

'No apologies required, darling, how were we to know what a rake he was? Maybe we could visit the pictures on our next night out, it might be safer,' Gloria sighed.

The evening out had done nothing to lift her spirits, it had only emphasised her loneliness, the friends bade each other goodnight, and each took a cab home. Granville Square was in darkness except for the hall light, Gloria wearily climbed up the stairs. She tiptoed into Dwight and Julian's bedroom to check on them, they were fast asleep. Across the landing slept Gabe, he would come of age this September, and Gloria wondered what they should all do to celebrate the occasion, reminding herself to discuss it with him tomorrow. She quietly made her way to her room and undressed. As she removed her makeup, the reflection that stared back from the mirror revealed a tired, drawn face. *'You are lonely woman, yes?'* a thick Hungarian voice spoke in her head. *'There will be many men in your life, but you will never find true happiness.'*

Gloria held her face in her hands. 'Yes, I know I have my sons and my father-in-law,' she thought to herself, 'but will I ever love again?' She climbed into bed and fell asleep exhausted.

Gabe celebrated his twenty-first birthday relatively quietly, he told Gloria he did not want to make a big fuss. And so, dinner at Rules was his request, he had heard it was the "in place" for writers and journalists and felt it befitted his new occupation. Gabe escorted his mother to the restaurant, along with Marcus, Lilian, Dwight and Julian. David had sent a telegram to his brother to mark the occasion and wished him all the best for the future as unfortunately, because of his RAF duties, he was unable to attend the dinner.

Gloria had given Gabe a gold and black onyx signet ring with the initial G set in the stone for his birthday, and to complement the signet ring, Marcus presented Gabe with an exquisite pair of onyx and diamond cufflinks set in gold and platinum. His brothers had put some of their allowance money together and purchased a beautiful, rolled gold fountain pen, which Gabe was thrilled with. He raised a toast to his loving family and thanked them numerous times for the generous gifts.

Gloria studied her sons as the dinner progressed and felt immensely proud of them all. She also took notice of how Marcus had aged and wished so desperately that she could support Dwight and Julian and allow Marcus to retire. He had recently spoken of moving back to the coast eventually for some fresh sea air, away from the hustle and bustle of London, but added he was not quite ready for hanging up his stethoscope just yet.

The winter was cold, dull and wet as usual, which added to

Gloria's already melancholy mood, and the new year of 1926 brought further gloom and misery for the coal miners and industrial workers of Britain. Whilst there was great wealth at one end of the scales, the depression of the last few years led to mine owners increasing miner's hours and reducing their pay to such an extent that a general strike was called.

For nine days in May, parts of the country were brought to a standstill as buses and trains stopped running, with demonstrations of thousands of people lining the streets of London. Gloria felt extremely sorry for the working-class people and eternally grateful for her position in society, but equally aware that it could change dramatically if it were not for Marcus's generosity.

Gloria's year carried on very much the same, she loved her job at Selfridges and welcomed the company of the women with whom she worked. They all enjoyed a few evenings at Murray's, especially the new show that came out in March called *Midnight Merriment*. Lucy and Gloria had avoided the Stafford since that uncomfortable night with the salesmen, but with Christmas approaching, they decided to brave it once more.

'Come on, Gloria, a bit of festive cheer will do us a world of good, and I promise not to accept any drinks from strange men this time,' Lucy said.

'Why not, darling, it has always been our favourite place, perhaps we could put a notice on our table saying, *No Men Allowed*, except for the waiter of course,' Gloria said with feigned sincerity, which made Lucy laugh. Therefore, they adorned themselves in their best dresses and shoes and met outside the hotel, it was snowing a little, so they hurried inside.

As they entered the cocktail bar, Gloria and Lucy scanned the room for potential libertines, fortunately, it was mostly couples, with a few younger men and women in small groups.

'I think the coast is clear,' Lucy said, 'there is a quiet table over there in the corner, we should be safe from the attentions of the undesired ones.' They laughed.

The cocktail menu had a few new additions, Gloria decided upon an Aviation Fizz to celebrate David's entry into the RAF, and Lucy opted for a Gibson.

'Mmm… this is delicious,' Gloria said, sipping the purple coloured drink. 'To Acting Flying Officer, David Ralph Phelps, may his flying machine stay up in the air, please.' She spoke the words lightly, but deep down, she prayed for it to be so.

'Do not fret, he will be just fine, the aeroplanes are much safer now than when my Albert went down, and that was during the war remember, we are at peace with the world now, so chin chin, I am in the mood for some fun and people watching.' The friends clinked glasses and prepared to play their '*what do you think they are saying to each other*' game.

Sometime later, they had decided that the serious-looking young couple on the third table away from them were in a fix because she was pregnant. Another couple were obviously recently engaged as they gazed longingly at each other, and the pretty blonde girl kept admiring the ring on her finger. The gentleman who had just sat himself down at the bar and ordered a brandy appeared to have had the worst day of his life. Gloria observed him, and as he turned around to look for a table away from the bar, she felt her heart skip a beat. He was not classically handsome as Gerald had been, but she felt drawn to him somehow.

'I wonder what happened to that poor chap over there, he looks as if he has the weight of the world on his shoulders,' Gloria said, pondering over the possibilities whilst admiring him.

'Lost his fortune at the races, wife walked out on him?' Lucy mused, 'perhaps you should go over and ask him. I can see a look on your face, Gloria Phelps,' she teased.

'Whatever do you mean, Lucy? I have not.' Gloria answered, her cheeks slightly flushed.

'Look, he has a friend,' Lucy observed, as a second man sat down, shaking the first man's hand, 'they are indeed in deep conversation, I am most intrigued.'

They sat and watched the two men for quite some time, Gloria studied the man who had attracted her attention. He looked in his early forties with brown hair combed in a stylish slicked back side parting, he wore a light grey pinstriped suit with his tie loose at his neck as if he had been pulling at the knot. Her gaze must have caught the attention of his friend as he looked directly at her and lent forward to say something to his companion, who turned to see what was happening. Gloria felt embarrassed and looked away.

'Help, we have been spotted,' she said to Lucy, 'they are looking at us, now they are coming over… what are we going to do? We certainly do not want a repeat of our last time here.'

'Stay calm, darling, they look reasonably sober, I think we are the ones who have partaken of a cocktail or two,' Lucy giggled.

'So, why have we caught the attention of two beautiful ladies may I ask?' the friend spoke, 'I have been watching you, watching us for the last twenty minutes.'

Gloria fumbled for words, but Lucy came to the rescue and explained how they enjoy trying to guess people's conversations, apologising if they had made them feel uncomfortable.

'On the contrary, I had already turned Nathan's conversation away from his bad day on to how to approach both of you, we were equally as intrigued. I beg your pardon, we have not introduced ourselves, Harper Jenkins, and this is my friend, Nathan Anslow, from Toronto,' Harper said.

'Lucy Carnegie, and this is my dearest friend, Gloria Elizabeth

Martha Phelps.' Lucy said, introducing Gloria rather grandly.

Looking directly into Gloria's eyes, Nathan replied, 'Well, your parents certainly did not run out of names when you were born. I have seven younger siblings back in Canada, my parents only gave me and Bill second names, they gave up after us.' He had a soft accent and a kind smile, and the foursome felt immediately at ease with each other. 'Would you ladies care for another cocktail?'

'Thank you, but no, we prefer to buy our own drinks,' Gloria hastily said, despite having a tingling feeling inside that made her want to know more about this man.

'Modern women, hey, Harper,' Nathan smiled.

The waiter was beckoned over, drinks were ordered, and an easy dialogue struck up between the four of them. Before long, Gloria found herself telling Nathan about being widowed, her sons and living with her father-in-law, she could not believe how at ease she felt with this man whom she had only just met.

In turn, he explained his earlier dark mood. He too was married, not very contently, he admitted, and a few months ago, his wife just packed a bag and went back to Toronto. She left a letter explaining that she hated London and needed to breathe the clean air of Canada before she suffocated. That was the last Nathan saw of her.

'I have no desire to return to Toronto, I have a very successful dental practice in Fitzrovia, and quite honestly, I cannot stand the snow and bitter cold of the Canadian winters. My mood tonight was brought about by Nora expecting me to ship her possessions back home when it was she who left with just a suitcase.'

Lucy and Harper had also hit it off, they were laughing together about something that lit up Lucy's face with a brightness Gloria had not seen in her before, was their luck turning?

CHAPTER 15

Gloria began to see a great deal of Nathan over the next few weeks, she enjoyed his company immensely, and it was noticed by both Marcus and Lilian that her mood had lifted, remarking that she was more like the Gloria they first knew. Even Julian commented on how she smiled a lot more which pleased him enormously. He was to start Westminster soon and nervous at the thought of following in his brothers' footsteps, worrying that he would not measure up to their standards. When his first day arrived, Gloria took numerous photographs of him in his school uniform, desperately trying to persuade him to smile. He was smaller in stature than his brothers and had an unruly mop of dark brown curls that no amount of pomade could tame. Gloria had always called him her little cherub, loving the way the curls fell over his eyes.

'You will have a style and charm all of your own, Julian,' she told him, 'and I for one think you are a most dashing young man, and I love you very much.'

Being her youngest, she confessed to herself that she had mothered him somewhat and sincerely hoped he would settle in at school and cope with the "new boy" pranks. Seventeen-year-old Dwight had been given strict instructions to look out for his little brother, which he promised to do. He had often pulled Julian out of scrapes at Clerkenwell and was already protective of him.

'Worry not, Mama, I will try and see he comes to no harm, being prefect gives me far more opportunity to deal with any bad behaviour from the other boys. He does need to toughen up a little though if you do not mind me saying so.'

'I know, darling, teach him a few things, will you? I want him to enjoy school like you and your brothers have, he is rather sensitive,' Gloria said.

Julian returned from school that afternoon sporting a black eye and a bloody nose, Gloria was livid. 'Who did this to you, Julian? Did you report it to your master?'

'It matters not, Mama, please do not fuss, Dwight showed me how to defend myself, you should be proud of me. I took the boy by surprise from behind and knocked him down with a rugby tackle that sent him flying, and then ran off before he could get back up. The other boys were too busy laughing at him for being knocked down by a smaller boy, and I survived my first day at Westminster.'

'Well, go and see Grandpapa and ask him to tend to your injuries, I am not very happy, and I sincerely hope this is an isolated incidence.' Gloria was not amused.

Regrettably, it happened twice more in Julian's first week, nevertheless, he held his head high and took the blows with an inner strength that Gloria was unaware of. By the end of his first month at school, he had shown he would not be bullied, and the bully moved on to another poor victim.

'What is it with boys and men that makes them so cruel?' Gloria asked her new lover as they lay in bed together at Nathan's flat.

'Women can be just as cruel, I knew a girl at school who could verbally reduce another to tears with one lash of her tongue, she became a peace officer later, she loved laying down the law to everyone. People are cruel, my darling, Gloria, but not you,' he kissed her, 'you are beautiful, and I am a very fortunate man.'

Their relationship had flourished immediately, and Gloria found herself feeling loved and in love again for the first time since Gerald left her nine years ago. Nathan was so very different, maybe because he was Canadian and not brought up in the strict upper-class system that Gerald had been. She enjoyed Nathan's free way of speaking and his ease in all walks of society, his dental practice was open to rich and poor alike, and he had an excellent reputation.

It was time she thought that he met her sons and asked him if he would like to have dinner with them on Saturday night, he agreed and said it would be a privilege to meet the sons of Gloria Phelps.

She felt slightly nervous as she dressed for dinner, they were to dine at The Ritz with Gabe, Dwight and Julian. Once more, David's RAF duties prevented him from being present. In his last telephone call, he had said he was due some leave soon and promised to come home for a while and meet Nathan then. Gloria had wanted to purchase a new dress for the occasion, but money was a little tighter these days. Therefore, she borrowed Lucy's olive green silk gown, which suited her perfectly, at least Nathan had not seen it before, and even at forty-two years of age, Gloria was the very essence of elegance and beauty.

Gabe was thrilled that his mother had found happiness again with someone and was looking forward to meeting Nathan immensely. 'He must be a decent chap to win your heart, Mama, you deserve it after what father did, and it is certainly time someone took care of you for a change.'

'Thank you, Gabe. Indeed, I was just thinking the same about you, surely there must be a girl you are interested in somewhere,' Gloria asked her son.

'No one special yet, Mama, I would like to concentrate on my writing first before I decide to settle down. I frequent Rules most evenings, listening to the writers and poets' literary discussions, it is great fun and extremely interesting,' Gabe replied.

'More interesting than young ladies then?' Gloria teased.

'Not all of the time, Mama, there are women at Rules too,' he replied with a wink.

Nathan arrived in a cab to take the small party to The Ritz, he told the driver to wait a few moments and rang the doorbell. Polly answered the door, she had remained in service with Marcus and Lilian these past years and was more like a member of the family.

'Good evening, Nathan Anslow,' he introduced himself with a good-natured smile. 'Is everyone ready?'

Lilian was hovering about in the hall as she studied Nathan standing in the doorway. 'No need to be shy, come in and make yourself at home, Mr Anslow. The cab driver will wait a few more minutes whilst we make your acquaintance,' Lilian said with no subtlety whatsoever and ushered Nathan into the sitting-room, where Marcus sat smoking a cigarette. He stood up as Nathan entered the room and put his hand out to greet him, the two men shook hands.

'I am delighted to meet you, Mr Anslow,' Marcus said.

'Nathan, please, no formalities,' he said.

'Well, Nathan, you are most welcome here, Gloria is a changed woman since you met, and we are grateful for you returning the sparkle to her eyes. As I am sure you know, Gloria is like a daughter to me, and I have a great desire to see her happy once more.'

Just then, Gloria came through from the hall wearing a dazzling smile and with Gabe, Dwight and Julian in tow, she walked towards Nathan, who kissed her on the cheek.

'Hello, darling,' she said, 'I see we are all friends. I would like to introduce you to my sons, this is Gabe, my eldest, Dwight, my second youngest and Julian, my youngest.' Nathan shook hands with each son saying how pleased he was to meet them.

'Are you from America?' Julian asked.

'Nope, from the more civilised climes of Toronto, Master Julian, except of course for the snow in winter, mind you Montreal gets it worse,' he replied and pretended to shiver.

Lilian went on to tell Nathan about her sister, who had been matron of the orphanage there for many years. Before long, fifteen minutes of conversation had passed between everyone until Nathan remembered that the cab was still waiting for them outside.

'I do beg everyone's pardon, but our reservation is for half-past seven, so we had better get a move on. A pleasure to meet you, Marcus and Lilian, I hope to see you again soon.'

They left the house in a flurry of goodbyes, have a lovely evening, keep Julian away from the champagne, and they all clambered into the cab.

Dinner was a huge success, Nathan was tremendously easy-going and engaged each of Gabe, Dwight and Julian in conversation, taking an interest in everything they said about themselves. He asked Gabe about his column in the Kensington Post, to which Gabe enthused over how much he enjoyed covering the magistrate's court and inquests. He said it brought together his love of writing and his interest in the law. Dwight revealed his fascination for advertising, especially the artwork for magazines and newspapers. Not too much of a surprise, bearing in mind that Dwight had loved drawing from the moment he had been able to hold a pencil.

'Maybe old Bainbridge will have an opening for you at the Post when you finish Westminster next year, perhaps we could ask Grandfather to put in a good word for you too,' Gabe said.

At thirteen years of age, Julian was undecided what he wanted to do, but even though he was quieter than his brothers, he had always loved the speed of trains and motor cars ever since his first train ride to Ramsgate. He had considered joining the RAF like his brother, as planes flew faster than anything. According to David, a Faery Fox flew at a top speed of over 200 mph, he had told him.

Gloria sincerely hoped Julian would change his mind, she did not think her nerves would take another of her sons in the sky. Taking a sip of her champagne and looking around the table at the men in her life, she had not felt this happy for many years and desperately hoped it would last for many more to come.

Gloria sat next to Nathan in the cab on the way home, she squeezed his hand, he looked into her eyes and smiled.

'Thank you,' Gloria mouthed silently, he took her hand in his and pressed it to his lips.

Harper and Lucy were slowly forming a relationship, he was a civil servant, and part of his job required him to chauffeur foreign diplomats around London. Sometimes, if the Rolls Royce were available, he would drive them all in style either for dinner, drinks or the picture house. Gloria still much preferred the live theatre and persuaded Nathan to take her to watch the *Desert Song* at Drury Lane. It was not his favourite kind of night out, but the fact that the musical made Gloria happy was enough for Nathan, he sat watching her face light up with the songs, dancing and romance.

'You would have loved to have been an actress, I can tell, am I right?' Nathan asked her during the interval.

'In my younger days, I dreamt of it, but my father was so strict, he hated the theatre and forbade me from even thinking about acting, he only just tolerated my going to the theatre,' Gloria said.

Thoughts of her father had not entered her head since he died, neither had she seen her mother for many years. Frances was a recluse now, living with her numerous cats, she was a sad, lonely old woman, Fleur had remarked. This reminded Gloria that she had not seen her sister for ages either and decided it was time for her new-found love to meet her.

Nathan was more than happy to take the trip, and they caught an early Saturday morning train to Ramsgate, where Fleur was waiting to pick them up in her Sunbeam Open Sports Tourer.

'I do not think my sons should see this, Fleur,' Gloria said as they kissed cheeks, 'Gabe and Julian particularly want Marcus to buy a motor car so they can parade around London, thankfully, he keeps saying no.' She grasped Nathan's arm. 'Fleur, I would like you to meet Nathan Anslow, he makes me very happy.'

Fleur could easily see by the look on her sister's face that this was more than true, and like everyone that met Nathan, she took an instant liking to him.

She drove them to her home at breakneck speed, as usual, Gloria and Nathan holding on to their hats and laughing as the wind rushed across their faces, they held hands tightly, and Gloria snuggled up to him very content. They arrived in one piece, much to everyone's relief, and Fleur gave a guided tour around her newly decorated home, it had been completely renovated in the latest Art Deco style. A stunning staircase with a black geometric patterned railing led from the hall, and an enormous crystal chandelier hung from the landing ceiling.

'Come and see the bathroom, darling, it is divine,' Fleur said as they made their way upstairs, she opened the door, and Gloria could hardly believe her eyes. There was a curved bath in the corner of the room with green and black marble tiles on the walls, a shower inside a glass enclosure, alongside a double sink unit.

'One each,' Fleur laughed, 'now Filkes can trim his moustache in his own sink.'

All the rooms were exquisitely decorated, including the bedroom Gloria and Nathan were to have. Fleur insisted they unpack and make themselves comfortable while she went downstairs and asked her maid to make some tea, leaving Gloria and Nathan standing in the middle of the bedroom. Their eyes met a huge walnut bed with a matching wardrobe and a dressing table on which stood a lamp whose design was a bronze figurine of a naked woman holding a glass ball above her head.

'This is so beautiful,' she exclaimed. 'I have only seen these designs in magazines, Fleur has such good taste. Please do not think her frivolous, they were never able to have children, and Filkes can afford it. I would often lend her my boys for the summer when they were younger, they had a wonderful time here and made many happy memories.'

'I never think or judge anyone, darling, your sister is almost as delightful as you are,' Nathan teased, 'and I would want you to have all of this too if I had the money. I do have something to confess, though.'

Her heart thumped. 'What, Nathan, what have I done wrong?'

He took her hands in his and looked lovingly into her emerald eyes, he gently brushed aside a piece of hair from her face. 'Wrong, nothing, how could you possibly do anything wrong? No, my confession is that I have fallen deeply in love with you, Gloria, and if I were free to do so, I would ask you to marry me this instant.'

Looking lovingly into Nathan's eyes, Gloria said, 'I have been longing to hear you say those words because I love you too. I never thought I would ever love again, you have saved me.' He took her in his arms and kissed her passionately.

They dined at home once Filkes returned from the hospital, he was almost sixty years of age, very well respected in the medical world and extremely successful. After dinner, they all retreated to the sitting-room, and whilst Nathan and Filkes discussed the recent advances in dentistry over brandy, Gloria and Fleur chatted quietly in the corner on a luxurious leather sofa.

'I like him very much, Gloria, and I can see you are quite smitten,

I am very happy for you, darling,' Fleur told her sister.

'Yes, life has taken a turn for the better at last, the boys approve, although David has yet to meet him. Gabe is very content at the paper, vying to be editor before his thirtieth birthday, no doubt, Dwight finishes Westminster next year, and Julian finally settled in after a bit of a rough start, as you know.'

Over the course of the evening, they caught up on all their news, and as they talked, Gloria would glance over at Nathan. His hair was tousled from the sea air, and he looked completely comfortable as if he had known Filkes all his life, she had no need to remind herself how lucky she was to find love again at her age. They returned to London on Sunday afternoon, it had been their first weekend away together, and they both whole-heartedly agreed that it should not be their last.

Christmas was approaching fast, and David was finally granted leave for a few days. Lilian decided that the family should have a proper celebration this year, not the half-hearted attempts of previous times. They were more than happy to include Nathan in the festivities, as he had no family of his own in England, and the whole atmosphere on Christmas Day was a heart-warming affair. David cut quite the figure in his RAF blues and announced he would be promoted to flight lieutenant in the new year and transferred to RAF Eastchurch on the Isle of Sheppey. Gloria was nervously proud of him and overcome with relief that he was not to be sent to Iraq.

Everyone took part in decorating the enormous Christmas tree, which now included electric fairy lights. Nathan was introduced to Polly's famous plum pudding, which he thoroughly approved of, flattering Polly by saying his mother could never make one that tasted as good as this.

David also found Nathan's company most agreeable, they sat

together for quite some time discussing the differences in the way of life between Canada and England, concluding that each had its own merits and challenges. For David, hearing about the vast open spaces of land in Canada made him wish he could take his aeroplane up and soar across the country like the huge bald eagles Nathan had spoken of.

'You will have to visit one day. My brother, Bill, has a farm in Toronto and would make you more than welcome in exchange for a hard day's work,' Nathan said light-heartedly.

'I might just take you up on that sometime.' David replied. 'I see you are taking good care of my mother, I have not seen her so happy in a long time, my father broke her heart, you know.'

'Yes, I know, there are no secrets between us, and I promise I will not hurt her, you have my word,' Nathan said with great sincerity.

Just then, the sound of Harry Welchman singing *The Desert Song* could be heard coming from the new electric gramophone Marcus had recently purchased.

David groaned. 'If you love my mother, Nathan, you will have to love her musicals as well, she has sung along to them ever since we were children, we know them all.' Nathan laughed.

Christmas passed as one of the happiest the family had enjoyed in many years, together they all saw in the new year of 1928 and celebrated Julian's fourteenth birthday. As the grandfather clock struck midnight, everyone held crossed hands and sang *Auld Lang Syne*. Nathan turned towards Gloria and kissed her, then he whispered in her ear.

'Move into the flat with me, darling, I do not want to spend another night apart from you.'

Gloria was a little taken aback. 'Nathan, I…'

'Please think about it, I know it is a huge step for you.'

'What about Dwight and Julian, and Gabe for that matter? He

still lives at home. As much as I love you, Nathan, I cannot leave my sons with Marcus and Lilian, it would be too much.' Gloria felt uneasy.

'I am not expecting you to leave them here, we can all live together, the flat has three bedrooms.' He could see the anxious look on Gloria's face. 'Promise me we can talk about it?'

'Yes, tomorrow, but my main priorities are my sons, you know that and I must be certain they will be happy,' she replied.

'Of course, my darling, whatever it takes.'

'Thank you, Nathan, I do love you, you know,' she said and kissed him.

There were lengthy discussions over the next couple of weeks regarding Nathan's proposal. Gloria spoke to Gabe first, and to her surprise, he said one of his friends had wanted help with the rent on his flat for a while now since his previous lodger moved out. He had not mentioned it before, as he had not known how to approach his mother to tell her.

'I will be twenty-four in September, Mama, it is time I flew the nest, and this is the perfect opportunity for both of us. Nathan is a good man, he will take care of you, and besides, Maurie's flat is only a few streets away on Nottingham Place, so I will not be far away if you need me,' he said.

He gave her a big hug and kissed her cheek, and as much as it saddened Gloria that another of her sons was leaving home, she knew Gabe had to make his own life and not feel responsible for her, she had Nathan now. Therefore, within a week, Gabe had packed his belongings, said a cheery adieu to the whole household of Granville Square and took up residence with his friend.

Dwight admitted that it did not matter where he lived as he intended to find a job in advertising and would not be at home much anyway, adding that he too liked Nathan, and it was very kind

191

of him to want to take us all in. On the other hand, Julian did not want to leave his grandfather, and he became quite distraught at the thought of living somewhere strange and ran off upstairs to his room. Gloria could say nothing that would console him, and eventually, she had to concede to Nathan that she must put Julian first at this moment in time. Even though he was disappointed, Nathan understood, and he had no desire to pressure her.

However, it was events over the coming weeks that changed the course of everyone's lives, and it began with the sad news that Marcus's dear friend, Antony, had died of congestive heart failure at the age of seventy-nine. Marcus was devastated, they trained at Guy's Hospital together as young men and had been the best of friends ever since. Gloria was also extremely distressed, Antony had been such a lovely friend to her, so amusing, warm and worldly-wise. She had been able to talk to him about anything, and always had an answer to every question she asked, he would leave a great void in many people's lives.

The weeks following Antony's funeral left Marcus very unsettled, and it was after dinner one evening when he made an announcement that shocked everyone. Marcus cleared his throat.

'I have made a most difficult decision, the result of which will impact on your lives greatly, I am to retire in May, and Lilian and I are going back to live in Somerset. I will be eighty years of age by then, and since dear Antony's death, I have felt my own mortality. I wish to end my days where I started them, in Watchet, where we can breathe that fresh, sweet Somerset air once more.'

Julian burst into tears, pleading with his grandfather not to go away, then begging him to take him to Somerset with them. Marcus attempted to console him, saying he could visit every school holiday, but for that evening, Julian was inconsolable. Between sobs, he blamed Gloria because Nathan wanted them to live with him, she was shocked by the depth of Julian's emotion and not sure how to handle the situation.

'Leave him be, for now, Gloria,' Marcus said, 'he is a sensitive boy, but he will come around. Please do not worry about his schooling, I promised I would always take care of my grandsons, and my retirement does not affect this decision. Now come and partake of a brandy with me, Gloria, and Dwight, I think we can afford you a sherry this evening, young man, let your brother have some peace.'

Eventually, Julian resigned himself to his grandfather moving back to Somerset. In his inimitable, kind, gentle manner, Marcus convinced him that his decision to retire had no bearing on his mother's desire to live with Nathan. It was purely Grandfather's yearning for some peace and quiet after more than fifty years of living in London.

'Watchet is a splendid place, overlooking the sea, I will take you fishing, and you can learn how to ride if you wish, there is nothing quite like galloping across the open fields on a horse if you want to feel speed and power,' Marcus told him.

The two words, speed and power, certainly sparked Julian's interest, therefore, with reluctant resignation, he was obliged to come to terms with moving to Nathan's flat with his mother.

Granville Square was to be sold to a dashing Italian doctor called Riccardo Salvatore Giordano, whom Marcus had known for many years and knew he was more than capable of taking over his practice. After over forty years of service and at sixty-two years of age, Polly left London and went home to Sheffield to live with her sister and brother-in-law. Over the years, Marcus had put aside a generous endowment for Polly, and thus, the lives of the residents of Granville Square were to change forever.

Gloria, Dwight and a somewhat disgruntled Julian moved to

Nathan's flat on Clifton Hill, it was extremely comfortable and spacious, set over two floors. Gloria had very little furniture of her own, most of it belonged to Marcus, except for the bookcase containing her precious photo albums. This was duly delivered by the carriers, along with her numerous records and the electric gramophone. Marcus confessed that, in reality, he had purchased it for her in appreciation of her love of music.

Once Julian saw his bedroom with all of his favourite belongings in place, he cheered up a little. When he unearthed Jip and Prince, his childhood stuffed toy dogs from the trunk, he smiled at how tatty they were now after the immense amount of love and dragging around both had received from him over the years. Gloria had come up to his room to see how he was faring and caught him talking to his two old friends, she listened for a while at the doorway.

'I shall miss Grandpapa so much, it will be an age until the summer holidays when I can see him again, I suppose I will have to get accustomed to Uncle Nathan being my father now, but at least Mama is happy again.'

Gloria felt troubled and immediately went over to her son, 'May I sit with you, darling?' she asked.

'Yes, Mama, of course, look who I found in the trunk,'

'They were your favourite toys when you were small, you never went anywhere without one or the other of them.' She stroked Prince's matted fur and continued to speak. 'I overheard you talking about Nathan as I came in, he is not trying to be your father, darling, but he would like to be your friend. I know how close you are to Grandpapa, and that will never change.'

'I do like Uncle Nathan, honestly, he is very kind and funny, I just find it difficult getting used to things being different.'

'I know, darling, but everything will turn out fine, I promise, now come and give your mother a hug.' Gloria put her arms around her son and kissed his mop of curls, 'I love you.'

'I love you too, Mama.'

The family enjoyed a farewell dinner at The Savoy, and David had been granted an overnight furlough to join them. Everyone dined well, there was much merriment and laughter around the table as they reminisced about the ups and downs of the last twenty-five years of their lives together. Marcus proposed a toast, and the table fell silent.

'To my dear, loving and devoted family, this is not our last dinner together, I expect regular visits, and there is much to see in the surrounding countryside and villages. I may have lost my son prematurely and my dear wife, Edith, begging your pardon Lilian,' she smiled and squeezed Marcus's hand.

'However, I have been blessed with you, Gloria, the daughter I never had and your four fine sons. I am immensely proud of you all, and my heart is filled with love, you make an old man very, very happy. I shall retire content in the knowledge that my work is done, and the Phelps name will be carried through into what hopefully, should be a brighter future, I love you all.'

Glasses clinked around the table, and when Gloria looked over at Marcus, she swore she could see a tear trickling from the corner of his eye, her heart swelled with love and admiration for the man who had been a father to her, and to whom she owed everything. Likewise, a tear welled in Gloria's eye.

CHAPTER 16

It took a while, but eventually, Gloria, Nathan, Dwight and Julian settled into their new lives together at Clifton Hill, whilst Gabe enjoyed a full bachelor life at Maurie's flat.

'He is never at home,' Gloria bemoaned to Nathan one evening, after a fourth attempt that week to call him on the telephone.

'He is doing what all young men do, enjoying life. And you, my gorgeous Gloria, have made me feel young again.' He picked her up by her slender waist, spun her around, threw her into a tango style backdrop and kissed her. 'What I am hoping is that Gabe finds a Gloria of his own and is as captivated and contented as I am.' He swung her back upright, twirled her around and kissed her again.

'My darling, Nathan, what did I do to deserve finding you? I love you so much,' Gloria said.

'My only regret is that we cannot marry, I have people in Toronto trying to track down Nora so I can divorce her, but she seems to have disappeared.'

'It matters not, I am Mrs Anslow in everything but name, and I wear the ring you gave me, so anyone that does not know us will think we are married. Speaking of marriage, Lucy and Harper are very close now, is he the marrying type? I would dearly love to see Lucy happy with someone, I told you all about her marriage to Albert,' Gloria said.

'I have no idea, he was always the bachelor type until Lucy came on the scene, I suppose time will tell, matchmaking are we, Gloria?'

'What me? Perish the thought,' she said, affecting astonishment. 'How about we invite them for dinner on Saturday and find out.'

In answer to Gloria's question, it transpired over the dinner table that Harper was indeed considering moving in with Lucy and "living in sin", following in Gloria and Nathan's footsteps, as certain conditions of the trust Albert left for Lucy stipulated she must not marry again.

'What modern women we have become, Lucy, my Aunt Esther will be turning in her grave,' Gloria declared.

They proposed a toast to modern living, and Gloria served up the strawberry pavlova she had created. Polly had taught her how to cook at Granville Square, and she discovered that it was actually quite enjoyable. However, some of the other household chores were not as much fun, and Gloria was finding it difficult to employ a maid. Eventually, a young girl named Hannah Lucas answered the advertisement and came in each day to clean, shop for groceries and do the laundry, much to Gloria's relief.

The months sped by, the warm weather arrived, and Marcus kept his promise to Julian that he could spend the summer holidays in Somerset with him. Therefore, with his fully laden trunk, Gloria tearfully waved fourteen and a half-year-old Julian off at Paddington station. Making him promise to be very careful about with whom he spoke and keep a watchful eye out for his luggage when he arrived at Taunton. She had purchased a first-class ticket and packed him a picnic lunch to eat on the journey, Marcus and Lilian were to meet him at the other end, with strict instructions to telephone her the minute they arrived home.

Gloria spent the whole day fretting until the telephone rang, and she heard Marcus's voice on the other end, reassuring her that Julian was all in one piece, complete with luggage and already looking forward to his first fishing expedition. It was the first time Gloria had been separated from Julian, and a few days passed before she settled back down and admitted to Nathan that she was probably the last thought in her son's head, he was no doubt having the time of his life with his beloved grandfather.

It had also been Dwight's last term at school, he had turned eighteen years of age in February, and like his brothers, passed the Higher School Certificate with distinction. He also achieved his ambition of entering the advertising world. Gabe had many contacts in the journalism business now and had arranged for the Illustrated London News editor to interview Dwight and look over his portfolio of drawings. Dwight's love of art had never waned since being a small boy, and the editor had to admit how impressed he was and so agreed to take him on a trial basis.

'It is a tough business out there, young man, follow Sebastian closely, do as he tells you and show me what you are made of,' the editor told him.

Thus, Dwight was thrust into the madcap world of advertising, shadowing Seb, the art director, every minute of the day, arriving home each evening worn out but very eager to learn.

'My first solo job is to draw an advertisement for boot polish, the tin and a pair of shoes would you believe. I sincerely hope I can achieve that, Mama,' Dwight said a little indignantly.

'Everyone has to start somewhere, darling, boot polish today, the front cover of Vogue tomorrow,' Gloria teased. 'I would very much like to see your boot polish drawing when it is finished, though, darling.'

As the weeks flew by, Gloria found herself content with the world, she loved Nathan with all her heart and, moreover, trusted him implicitly, a feeling she had never felt with Gerald. She remained working at Selfridges, and Nathan encouraged her desire to keep her independence and appreciated the affection she held toward the women she worked with. Her friendship with Lucy was as strong as the bond with Fleur, and nothing or no-one would stand in its way.

Julian returned home from Somerset with all the appearance of a Romany gypsy boy. His skin was darkly tanned, and he had not had a haircut throughout the summer holidays, which made his dark curls fall into his eyes. He was blissfully happy with numerous tales to tell of his adventures.

'Are your grandfather and Aunt Lilian well?' Gloria asked as soon as she could get a word in edgeways.

'Yes, Mama, they are tremendously well, the air in Somerset is so fresh and clean, not at all like London, Grandfather is very contented. Their house is only small, more like a cottage, but I had the bedroom over-looking the harbour, and I loved watching the boats toing and froing. We went fishing nearly every day, and I learned how to ride a horse, I only fell off a few times, he was a white pony called Misty. It was the most marvellous time ever, Mama, please may I go again next holidays?' he begged.

'If it is alright with your grandfather, then it is alright with me, I am just so delighted to see you happy and smiling, my darling boy,' Gloria replied. 'Mind you, we have to get you to the barbers before school begins.'

'No, not school...... do I have to go back?' Julian groaned.

'Yes, you do, now run along upstairs and help Hannah unpack your trunk, she is unsure as to where everything lives.' Gloria kissed her son on the top of his mass of curls and joyfully watched him run upstairs to his room.

It was unfortunate that out of all her son's Julian was the only one who had not settled at Westminster, and now that Dwight had left, Julian was alone and felt very uneasy at not having his elder brother around to look out for him. There was a fair amount of sulking and dragging of heels on the first day back and even more cajoling from Gloria and Nathan to hurry him along.

'How about if you make it through your first week unscathed, your Mama and I take you to see the amazing mechanical man at the Model Engineering Exhibition on Saturday, would you like that?' Nathan asked.

The idea piqued Julian's interest, he had wanted to see the exhibition after Dwight told him about it. His brother had assisted the artist who drew the robot for an article in the London Illustrated News and had spoken of nothing else on that particular evening.

'I will try my best, Uncle Nathan, I would very much like to see the robot, and I do enjoy learning, but the other boys are so loud and boisterous, and I prefer my own space and my own company,' Julian tried to explain.

'I understand, darling,' Gloria said, 'but you only have one more year until your School Certificate, and we agreed that you need not stay for your Higher if you do not wish to, so come on, chin up, proud thoughts, and we will be watching the robot bow at us before you know it.'

The week went well, and come Saturday afternoon, once Nathan had finished his morning surgery, he accompanied Gloria, Julian and Dwight to the exhibition, and they were very soon marvelling at the robot and the countless other exhibits.

Autumn passed into winter, and Christmas was approaching fast. 'It will be our first proper Christmas together,' Nathan said as they lay in bed wrapped up in each other's arms, 'how would you like to celebrate?'

'All I desire is to be with you, my boys, we could invite Filkes and Fleur, I know they are coming up to London for a conference Filkes is speaking at, and Lucy and Harper, of course.' Gloria said.

'Then dinner for…' he quickly counted up, 'ten it will be, I sincerely hope that Hannah's skills will be much improved by then so she can help you, I heard another crash of broken china from the kitchen the other day.'

'I know, I am sorry, darling, she does try terribly hard, and I do not wish to dismiss her, help is so difficult to find.'

'I am only teasing, she is a sweet girl, just a little clumsy.' Nathan tickled Gloria in the ribs, she began to laugh and tried to pull away. He rolled over on to her and kissed her passionately.

'Again, Nathan, whatever has come over you?'

'Finding the love of my life at long last.'

Christmas was everything Gloria had hoped for, including a surprise guest for the evening festivities. Gabe had asked if he may invite his new girlfriend, Maisie Bloom, for drinks, to which a quizzical Gloria had replied, 'Yes, of course, darling.'

She was secretly dying to inspect the first woman her son had taken an interest in. Naturally, she had notified Lucy immediately, who was equally as intrigued.

Gabe returned later in the evening with Miss Bloom, who nervously entered the room on his arm, looking fearful of what to expect after countless declarations from Gabe that his mother was the most incredible person one could ever wish to meet. The young woman was almost as tall as Gabe and painfully thin, with the waif-like figure that seemed to be fashionable at the moment. Wearing a burgundy coloured dress covered in sequins with a tasselled hem, and with her bleached blonde, Marcel waved hair, adorned by a sparkling beaded and diamante headpiece, she had clearly tried extremely hard to impress.

'Mama, everyone, I would like to introduce you to Miss Maisie Bloom, she is a model,' Gabe said with an enormous smile on his handsome face.

'Good evening, it is very nice to meet you all, Gabe has told me so much about you, I feel I know you already.' Maisie finished her sentence with a high-pitched giggle.

Gloria found herself temporarily lost for words but quickly regained her composure and walked over to Maisie to greet her. 'Good evening to you, Miss Bloom. On the contrary, I have not been informed of you at all, and my what a surprise this is.' She kissed the young girl on the cheek and led her to the drinks table. 'Would you like a martini, dear, or perhaps a Maiden's Prayer?'

'Thank you, I would love a martini, yes please,' Maisie squeaked.

'Nathan, darling, Maisie would like one of your "special" martinis, would you care to do the honours?'

Gabe hastily moved towards his mother. 'What do you think, Mama, quite a peach is she not? Her father is the manager of Morley's stockings, and Maisie always wears them when she is modelling to advertise them, we should get Dwight to draw her.'

Gabe was clearly stricken with the young woman, Gloria had to admit that she was rather pretty, but alas, there was very little happening in the upstairs department, and she sincerely hoped that Miss Bloom would be a passing fancy. Unfortunately, she seemed to have the power to reduce young men into simpering idiots. Gloria sat with Lucy sipping their own martinis, and they watched as Gabe, David, Dwight and even Julian, to a lesser extent, laugh at her awful jokes and tales of the catwalk.

'I feel old, Lucy, is this really what young women of today are made of?' Gloria sighed.

'We still have our charms, darling, I mean, look at you and Nathan, you positively glow around him, and Harper has at last decided to move into the house with me, not bad for two old widows, I say. Cheers.' Lucy smiled triumphantly.

Another high-pitched giggle came from the other side of the

room. 'Nathan, darling, make Miss Bloom another of your extra special martinis please, maybe she will pass out soon.'

It took until almost midnight before Miss Bloom decided she felt unwell and asked Gabe to take her home. It was too late to call for a taxi, so Harper, who had the Rolls over Christmas, kindly offered to drive them to Gabe's flat. He returned twenty minutes later, reporting that the couple had happily tripped up the steps to the flat and were now safely indoors.

'Mmm... that made for an interesting evening, did it not?' Gloria said to Nathan as they lay in bed.

'It will not last, darling, Gabe is far too intelligent to fall for the likes of Miss Bloom, I promise you, it will be over by the end of January.'

True to Nathan's word, Gabe telephoned a few weeks later to inform Gloria that he had moved on from Miss Bloom, as he had met someone whose conversation was more interesting, and would she like to join them for lunch next week.

'Is this what it is going to be like, Nathan? An endless stream of lunch dates until Gabe finds the perfect match, it was so much easier when they were small boys,' Gloria lamented.

1929 turned out to be quite eventful. Dwight successfully passed his probation at the Illustrated London News and impressed the editor enough with his design and artwork to be offered a full-time position. On the other hand, Gabe found himself tired of covering the courts for the Post and realised that he had more of a flair for publicity than writing. His good looks and easy manner endeared him to everyone he met, and when Dwight told him there was a position for a publicist at the News, Gabe jumped at the chance. He sweet-talked the editor into a trial period, and before one could bat an eyelid, the Phelps brothers were working together and making a tremendous job of it.

David had now served four years in the RAF and was already made flight lieutenant. He came home on leave as often as possible, relaying numerous stories of his flying escapades to Julian, who seemed in awe of his brother, and again began to speak of joining the RAF himself once he left school, much to Gloria's alarm.

Come the summer holidays, she packed her youngest son off to Watchet and his grandfather once more, with sincere hopes Marcus would talk some sense into Julian and persuade him that there were safer ways of making a living. Gloria sometimes pondered over the fact that none of her sons had expressed a desire to go into medicine, Gabe had changed his mind after Gerald deserted them, and indeed she realised that none of them even spoke of their father.

Another Christmas arrived at Clifton Hill, and the new year heralded a brand-new decade, it was 1930, Julian's sixteenth birthday and four years of bliss together for Gloria and Nathan. However, in late February, a sadness clouded their little world when Gloria received a phone call from a tearful Fleur with the news that their mother had passed away. Evidently, Mrs Smedley had been concerned at not seeing Frances for a few days, which was not unusual in itself, but her cats were wandering around the garden, mewing loudly to be let into the house. She called round and observed Frances lying on the living room floor through the French door windows, the poor woman had suffered a heart attack and died instantly.

Gloria felt numb, there was no feeling of grief or loss, in fact, she was unsure how to feel. Fleur was by far the more upset as she had not been subject to the rejection Gloria received all those years ago, in the end, Gloria just felt sad that her mother had died alone and un-noticed for days.

'She could have had so much more in her life, but she chose solitude, I gave up many moons ago attempting to build a bridge with her. I suppose we will have to make some arrangements,' Gloria said to her sister flatly.

Thus, a small funeral took place at the village church near the family home in Cambridgeshire, only Gloria, Fleur and Mrs Smedley stood around the grave as Frances's coffin was lowered in. The vicar spoke the words. *'Ashes to ashes, dust to dust...'* and they each threw in a handful of earth.

The house was sold at a loss due to its run-down condition, and the sisters shared the profits. Thus, a chapter of their lives closed, and Gloria deposited her share of the money in the Finsbury and City of London Savings Bank for a rainy day.

The end of summer term approached for Julian, and even though he passed his School Certificate with distinction, he was adamant he had no desire to return to Westminster to study for his Higher. True to her word Gloria did not insist, instead she spoke to Harper, who was now happily ensconced at Lucy's house and asked if he could help Julian find a position in the Civil Service as a junior clerk or such like.

'Alas, he is yet to find his vocation other than joining the RAF, and after much discussion, the matter ended in a compromise that if he were still resolute when he reached eighteen, I would reconsider,' she said to Harper. 'So, if you can, something to keep him occupied and provide some experience of working life would indeed be most gratefully received.'

Within a few weeks, Julian sat behind a desk in the Home Office wearing a splendid new suit and slightly unsure of what to expect. Harper left him in the care of Mrs Lawson, the office supervisor, who took Julian under her wing and led him towards the filing cabinet. His narrative over dinner that evening included a detailed explanation of how one files in alphabetical order and how Mrs Lawson very kindly made him a cup of tea at lunchtime, finishing with, 'And I have to go to night school and learn how to touch type.' He then asked if he could have some more potatoes, please.

'It is all good experience, Julian, you will be typing sixty-words a minute before you know it,' Gloria said, trying to be serious.

Her youngest son ate his dinner utterly unfazed by his first day at work, he had enjoyed the relative peace and quiet of the office and, moreover, relieved not to be at school. To encourage Julian with his typing course, Gloria purchased a brand-new Remington typewriter to practice on at home. With very little encouragement required, within three months, his typing speed was almost as fast as the other clerks in his office. He genuinely appeared far more content, which pleased Gloria immensely.

Christmas and New Year's Day were once more seen at Clifton Hill, Gloria had never felt so at peace with herself or the world, and her sons were enjoying their lives to the full. Dwight had moved into the flat with Gabe and Maurie, they both worked hard and played hard and appeared to have a new girlfriend on their arm every time they took Gloria out for lunch or dinner.

She remembered what a shame and embarrassment she had been to her father for becoming pregnant and eloping with Gerald and contemplated how much times had changed, nowadays it just seemed to be live and let live. She was happy for them living without the restraints her generation endured, still, she sincerely hoped that one day at least one of her sons would settle down and get married.

It was the 15th of May 1931, and spring flowers were blooming in the garden, deep red peonies, purple pansies, Gloria admired them through the window before she made her way to work. She gaily walked through the staff entrance of Selfridges humming *Dancing on the Ceiling* from the show *Evergreen* that she and Nathan had watched a few weeks ago at the Adelphi. Also in her mind was a plan for them to have a weekend away, maybe Brighton or Hastings, she pondered.

'Good morning, ladies, how are we all on this fine and beautiful day, ready to greet our customers with our inimitable charm and grace, I hope,' Gloria said to the group of women standing at their counters.

'Good morning, Mrs Anslow.' The women chorused back.

'Then let the day begin, remember eyes and smiles.' It was the usual morning ritual.

'Yes, Mrs Anslow.'

The doorman unlocked the front doors, and customers gradually began to filter through.

'You are very perky this morning,' Lucy said to her friend.

'I am, Lucy, we are very fortunate women you and I to have found two wonderful men at our age, you and Harper are perfect together and my Nathan… I wish I had met him at sixteen years of age,' Gloria sighed.

'Shall we have lunch on the rooftop today? I think the weather will stay fine.'

'Yes, that would be marvellous, shall we say one o'clock?'

'Perfect. I say, look who has just walked in, Desiree Ellinger, she always spends well, let me see what I can persuade her to purchase today.' Lucy winked at Gloria and subtly swooped in towards the famous actress.

The morning sales were excellent, as was lunch, Gloria and Lucy returned to the shop floor to continue the afternoon. It was almost three o'clock when a young girl came up to Gloria informing her that there was an urgent telephone call for her in the office. 'Thank you, Elsie, I will just let Lucy know.' Gloria then followed the girl through the side door.

Gloria picked up the receiver from the table. 'Mrs Anslow

speaking, how may I help?'

A woman, on the other end, spoke with a trembling voice. 'Mrs Anslow, this is Connie, Nathan's secretary, I.. I ..' She could not speak.

'Connie, what is it, what has happened?' Gloria replied, panic-stricken.

'Come quickly, Mrs Anslow, Nathan is... he has....'

'Connie, what has happened? Tell me!' Gloria almost shouted.

'He has been taken terribly ill at the office, please come now.......'

Gloria dropped the telephone as her knees buckled underneath her, Elsie caught her just in time before she fell. Between gasps for breath, Gloria told Elsie to fetch Lucy and hail a cab outside the store. This only took a few minutes, by which time the taxi was weaving its way through the traffic towards Devonshire Street, where Nathan's office was situated, it was less than a mile away. The journey seemed to take forever, with Gloria and Lucy sitting in silence, holding hands tightly. Eventually, the cab pulled up, Lucy paid the fare, and they hurried as fast as they could to the office.

Gloria knocked on the door, and Connie opened it, she was a small, neat woman in her twenties with short-cropped blond hair.

'Where is he? Is he alright?' Gloria said, hurriedly pushing her way past Connie. 'The doctor is with him now. Mrs Anslow, it was terrible, he was treating a patient and suddenly clutched his head and fell to the floor.'

Nathan was laying on a sofa in the reception with Dr Giordano, from Marcus's old practice bending over him, listening intently to his chest through his stethoscope and feeling for a pulse. As Gloria entered the room, Dr Giordano stopped his examination and turned to look at her.

'Signora Anslow, Gloria,' he spoke with a lilting Italian accent,

'I am so sorry to tell you, Nathan, he suffer a catastrophic brain aneurysm, I am afraid he is dead, there was nothing I could do to save him.'

'NATHAN!......' Gloria screamed and collapsed in shock.

CHAPTER 17

Gloria awoke to find herself at home in bed, she felt woozy and light-headed, she massaged her forehead. Then reality hit her like a sledgehammer, Nathan was dead, her darling, funny, wonderful Nathan. She dragged herself up to a sitting position, mumbling incoherently to herself.

'No, no, not Nathan, please let it not be true, Nathan, NATHAN....' she was becoming hysterical.

'Gloria, darling, try and calm yourself.' It was Lucy. She had sat beside her friend for hours after Dr Giordano had administered Gloria with a heavy dose of barbiturates at Nathan's office to sedate her. Harper had driven her home in the car and carried her upstairs, laying her gently on the bed. Lucy telephoned Gabe and Dwight at the paper, and they both came home immediately, she had also left word at David's RAF base for him once he returned from his flight. Gabe took a cab to the office where Julian worked to tell him the terrible news in person. His brother's words were an immense shock, but somehow, he held his composure until they were sat in the back of the cab.

'But it is not fair, Mama was so happy with Nathan, he was such good fun, poor Mama,' Julian said once he had calmed down.

'She is distraught and heart-broken, I honestly do not know how she will recover from this, losing Nathan has hit her far, far worse than what Papa did to her or when he died,' Gabe said sadly.

Gloria was crying uncontrollably with Lucy sat on the bed at her side, holding her like a child, rocking her back and forth in an attempt to soothe her grief-stricken friend.

'Why, Lucy, why my Nathan,' she sobbed. 'he never hurt anyone, I loved him with all my heart and soul, am I such a wicked person that I am being punished for having been happy?'

Tears fell like waterfalls from her red blood-shot eyes, make-up streaked down her face, there was no consoling her. Lucy had no words, what could she say to someone whose life had just been ripped apart by a cruel fate of nature.

Gloria did not leave her room for two days, Lucy stayed with her constantly, whilst Hannah made numerous cups of tea, none of which Gloria would drink. Lucy eventually managed to persuade her to sip some water before she fell back to sleep, comatose by the sedatives Riccardo had left for her.

Julian was terribly upset at seeing his mother in such a dreadful state, he too had become very attached to Nathan, they had developed a strong bond over the last five years, and Julian grieved intensely. Gabe took control of the arrangements, he telephoned Marcus, who was devastated for Gloria and immediately began to make plans to come up to London. Regrettably, Fleur and Filkes were away in Paris.

'Thank goodness, Mama has Lucy,' Gabe thought to himself. He then realised he had no way of contacting Nathan's family in Canada. The only solution he had thought of was telegraphing the Toronto Star and placing a notice announcing Nathan's death, hoping word might reach his brother at the farm.

The funeral was arranged for Wednesday at two o'clock, it was cold, with thick black cloud covering the sky, and it rained all morning persistently, it was as if the weather chose to add to everyone's misery. The day before, with much persuasion and coercion, Gloria had eventually managed to rouse herself from her bed and taken a long hot bath, she wrapped herself in a thick robe and sat at her dressing table. The woman who stared back from the mirror shocked her, she was so drawn and pale, with dark purple circles under her eyes. Lines seemed to have appeared overnight, and with her wet hair pulled back from her face, Gloria barely recognised herself, she held her head in her hands in anguish and began to cry again.

'Why have you left me, Nathan, why, why…. how am I to go on without you?' she sobbed.

There was a tap on the bedroom door. 'Mama, may I come in.' It was Gabe.

There was no answer.

'Mama,' Gabe repeated and slowly opened the door peering around to look for his mother, he saw her, head down on the dressing table, crying and breaking her heart for the thousandth time. He went over and gently put his arms around her shoulders. Sitting on the stool next to her, he pulled her towards him, holding her while she wept.

When the sobs finally subsided, Gabe took his mother's face in his hands and looked deeply into her eyes. 'I know how much you loved him, Mama, I have never seen you so happy in all the years of my life that I can recall as you were with Nathan, and it was plain to see that he felt the same about you. Try to hold fast to the few special years you shared together and know that they far outweigh the years of solitude and misery you endured because of Father.'

'I know all of that, Gabe, but why could I not have more, why could we not grow old together? I am broken, and I do not think I will ever mend.'

Gabe held her hands in his, not knowing what else to say.

On the morning of the funeral, Lucy came over to Clifton Hill to help Gloria dress and apply her makeup, neither of which Gloria felt like doing.

'Come on, darling, let me paint you on a face, we must not let the side down and appear undone, must we now?' Lucy said, attempting to raise a glimmer of something in her friend. She carefully applied just the right amount of everything to Gloria's beautiful, forlorn face, brushed her hair and kissed her cheek, 'Perfect. Now, where is your dress?'

'Laid out on the chaise-longue with my wrap coat and shoes, thank you, Lucy, thank you for everything,' Gloria said, looking at her dear friend, Lucy gave her a small smile.

Gloria had the ability to look attractive in anything she wore, and despite her drawn appearance, today was no exception, the final touch to her outfit was a black wool hat with a small net veil to cover her eyes. Together they went downstairs, where the others were gathered.

'I need a brandy, Lucy, my hands are shaking,' Gloria said.

Lucy poured the drink and passed it to Gloria, who swallowed it down in one. She turned to face her family, the one constant in her life, her boys. All four were dressed impeccably in black suits and ties, with sadness and concern written all over their faces. Even the overwhelming love she felt for them could not fill the hole ripped in her own heart for the loss of the only man she had truly loved.

The car arrived to convey Gloria and her sons to St Mark's church on Hamilton Terrace, it followed slowly behind the hearse bearing Nathan's coffin. Almost fifty people had gathered to pay their respects, many of his patients, friends and colleagues from amongst the dental fraternity, his secretary Connie, and neighbours from Clifton Hill. All of whom knew Nathan as one of the most affable and easy-going people they had ever encountered.

Gloria held on to Gabe's arm tightly with her head held high, staring into nothingness as the family slowly walked into the church and made their way to the front pews. The people seated turned their heads as they passed, many of the women holding handkerchiefs to their noses. Marcus and Lilian were already seated, Gabe sat down next to them with Gloria at his side and Julian, David and Dwight beside her. She scarcely heard a word the minister said and could not sing a note of any of the hymns, she felt totally and utterly numb.

The service finally came to a close, and as Nathan had always wished to be cremated, Gloria, her boys, Marcus, Lilian, Lucy, Harper and a few of his closest friends and colleagues travelled on to the City of London crematorium. Another short service was held before Nathan's coffin disappeared behind a red velvet curtain, and he was gone from Gloria's life forever.

A small number of people gathered back at Clifton Hill, where Hannah had prepared a light buffet and set it out in the dining room. Gloria had barely said a word to anyone, she was too scared that if she did, her emotions would get the better of her, and she would break down once more. All she could do at this moment in time was sit on the sofa with a large glass of Nathan's favourite claret and listen to what everyone was saying about her dearest, perfect, Nathan.

Marcus tried his utmost to engage her in some sort of conversation, but even his attempts made no impression on Gloria whatsoever, he felt grieved and terribly anxious about her. He stayed for an hour or so, but he was an old man now, and the journey and emotional upheaval left him exhausted, therefore, he and Lilian returned to their hotel, promising to come back and visit the next morning.

Others stayed for a couple of hours before they began to filter away, somehow Gloria went through the motions required on these occasions until only her sons, Lucy and Harper, and Nathan's solicitor, who had the will ready to read out, remained. Gloria poured herself another large glass of wine and sat next to Gabe on the sofa. The solicitor cleared his throat before he began to speak, and Gloria recalled the occasion of hearing Gerald's will read. She let out a small, bitter laugh, much to everyone's surprise, eyes turned towards her, but nobody dared ask.

'This is the last will and testament of I, Nathan Matthew Anslow, of 6 Clifton Hill, London, dental surgeon, I hereby declare this to be my last will and testament. I give to my dear, Gloria Elizabeth Martha Phelps, the total value of my real and personal estate to be valued upon my decease.....'

The solicitor read out the remainder of the short will, folded the piece of paper back up, returned it to its envelope, and passed it to Gloria. Her emotions welled up inside her, Nathan had made certain she would be well taken care of, he truly did love her and clutching the envelope in her hands, as tears rolled on to her cheeks, she mouthed the words, 'Thank you, darling.'

Needless to say, what she wanted more desperately than anything else in the world, was Nathan alive, walking through the door at any moment, with his beaming smile and a bunch of flowers in his hand. Knowing that would never happen, she was stricken by an overwhelming feeling of complete and utter anguish.

The days dragged by, and Gloria slid into a deep depression, Julian went to stay with Gabe and Dwight as he was unable to bear witnessing his mother's grief. She drank herself to sleep every night, took up smoking, would not get out of bed in the mornings, barely ate a morsel, even though Hannah went in every day and attempted to feed her and tidy up. Lucy also called in each morning, having handed in her notice at Selfridges after Nathan's death. Gloria was quickly replaced by one of the other women in the store. Not that she cared one iota, she had no intention of working there anymore. Indeed, she cared about nothing, until after four weeks, her gaunt appearance scared Gabe into taking it upon himself to telephone Dr Giordano and ask him to call on his mother. Gabe made sure he would be at Clifton Hill when the doctor arrived and let him in.

'Thank you so much for coming, Dr Giordano,' he said.

'Please, call me Riccardo, I knew your grandfather well, there is no need for formalities.'

'Riccardo, my mother is in her room, and I am terribly worried about her, my youngest brother misses her and wants to come home. I cannot think it good for him seeing Mama like this. Please can you talk to her, give her something, anything to pull her out of the dark hole she has buried herself in,' Gabe pleaded.

'Grief is a terrible thing, it never really goes away, life just gets different, believe me, I know, but I will talk to her, I will try,' Riccardo replied.

He made his way up to Gloria's bedroom and gently knocked on the door. 'Gloria, it is I, Riccardo Giordano, may I come in and speak with you?'

'If you must,' came the reply from inside the room.

The doctor quietly entered to find Gloria sat in her armchair, smoking a cigarette, she had the appearance of a ghost. Despite it being eleven o'clock in the morning, the curtains were closed, and Gloria was still wearing her nightclothes.

Riccardo walked over to the window and made to draw the curtain back a little. 'May I?' he asked. Gloria just waved her hand in the air in a gesture that she did not care what he did.

A beam of sunlight entered the room in which particles of dust hovered in the air, the brightness hurt Gloria's eyes, she squinted and looked away. The room was untidy with clothes and dirty wine glasses everywhere and an ashtray piled high with cigarette ends.

'I suppose my son sent you to talk some sense into me,' she said, 'well, it will not work, I have no desire to go back outside without Nathan, I have no life without him.'

'You have your sons, Julian is desperate to come home, he misses you and shares some of your grief,' Riccardo replied.

The mention of Julian stirred a brief moment of guilt for neglecting her son, but he was seventeen years of age now and safe with his brothers, what did he need her for?

'May I sit with you?' Riccardo asked.

Gloria gestured to the other chair in her room and drew deeply on her cigarette. Riccardo began to speak, his soft lilting accent had a calming effect. He said that he understood how every person's grief is different, and he could not possibly know exactly how she felt. He then related the story of his own personal tragedy twenty years ago when he lived in Italy.

'I was married to the most beautiful girl in Rome, her name was Sofia Francesca, we had been together for four years. I worked at a hospital in Rome as an obstetrician, we were so happy together, like you and Nathan, and when we learned we were expecting our first child, we thought our life was *perfetto.* When her time came, the labour was long and very painful, I knew something was wrong.

'The baby had not turned, and after twenty-four hours, Sofia was exhausted. She gave one final push, and I pulled the baby from her, the cord had wrapped around his neck and strangled him, he was dead. I passed the child to a nurse and turned my attention back to Sofia, her temperature was dangerously high, and she suddenly haemorrhaged, the blood poured from her, it was impossible to stem the flow. She died in my arms, and my life was shattered.' Riccardo wiped a tear from his eye.

'I too drank myself into a stupor every night, I began to miss shifts at the hospital and eventually I was dismissed, I did not hurt

217

anyone, but I was not to be trusted. That is when I decided to come to England and start a new life. When I met Marcus, he helped me set up a practice in London for which I am eternally grateful, he turned my life around. You have the rest of your life to live, you have four fine sons and grandchildren one day, grieve for Nathan, yes, but do not let that grief destroy your life, you still have much to live for.'

Gloria had sat in silence throughout Riccardo's tragic story, and afterwards asked if he had ever married again, he told her no, as no other could have taken her place in his heart.

'Summer is with us, Gloria, and I am told it is your favourite season, venture out I beg of you, let your son come home, he is distraught, and he needs you, it will take time, but you will feel better I promise. Now, I have said enough, it is your choice, I will call on you next week and see how you are bearing up. Goodbye, mio caro.' He stood up and left the room quietly, leaving Gloria to ponder over all he had said.

His words reminded Gloria that she was not the only person in the world who had suffered a catastrophic loss and survived, and deep down inside of her she knew, somehow, she would have to find the strength to go on. The mention of poor Julian, her most sensitive son, made her feel a little ashamed. She walked over to the window and pulled the curtains back, the sunlight blinded her for a moment, and she blinked. Then, as her eyes gradually accustomed themselves to the light, she noticed roses growing in the garden and a fledgeling blackbird attempting time after time to fly back up to its nest. Eventually, the bird succeeded, which prompted Gloria to think long and hard about her life, she made her way to the bathroom and ran a hot bath.

While she soaked, she reminisced about Nathan and the things they had done together, smiling to herself about the day he had borrowed a car and driven them to Southend-on-Sea for a day trip, only to run out of petrol halfway home. They had to take a bumpy ride in a trailer on the back of a tractor to the nearest village for a can of petrol and walk the five miles back to the car. Her poor feet were bleeding and covered in blisters, and once they arrived back in London, Nathan had tended her sore toes and heels and massaged her feet as she lay on the sofa.

'I miss you so dreadfully, darling,' she said to herself, however, for the first time in weeks, thinking about him had not reduced her to a flood of tears.

Her reflection in the mirror had a haunted expression, and her skin looked exceptionally sallow. With trembling hands, she applied some powder, lipstick and a little mascara, and a slightly brighter Gloria stared back. She dried her hair, which desperately required a cut and put on a pretty floral dress, one that Nathan always loved. It hung off her shoulders, so she pulled the sash belt in tightly, surprised at the amount of weight she had lost.

Taking a deep breath, she picked up the telephone and dialled Gabe's number, he answered, 'Gabe Phelps speaking, what can I do for you?'

With a shaky voice, Gloria said, 'Gabe, darling, can you bring Julian home tonight, please? Indeed, can you all come home and have dinner with me? I am in dire need of my boys' company.'

As her sons entered the flat, Julian rushed to his mother and threw his arms around her shoulders. 'Mama, I have missed you so much, we have all been so worried about you.'

Dwight had not seen her for a while and was terribly shocked by her gaunt appearance, whilst Gabe realised just how much effort it must have taken to pull herself together to dress and make-up. He was equally aware of how strong his mother was and felt maybe this was indeed the beginning of her return to the land of the living.

Over the next few weeks, Gloria began to take walks in the park with Lucy, go for tea and do a little shopping. Riccardo visited her each week and was tremendously pleased with her progress, one matter he insisted on most strongly was that she stop smoking.

'It does not become you, Gloria,' he chastised. 'My next prescription is for two weeks at your sister's home and a daily dose of sea air and beachcombing.'

After much protesting, Gloria agreed, Fleur pampered and fed her sister, and on her return to London, a healthier-looking Gloria unlocked the door of 6 Clifton Hill.

It was the end of August, three months since Nathan died, Gloria still felt bereft, but with the help and love from her sons, Lucy and Fleur, the days began to pass a little less painfully. The summer weather had been unpredictable this year, and today it brought rain. The day also delivered a visit from a most unexpected and unwelcome visitor. Hannah answered the doorbell to a woman she had never seen before, asking for a Gloria Phelps, she spoke with a strong Canadian accent.

'I think you must be mistaken, Mrs Gloria Anslow lives here,' Hannah replied.

'No, it's you who are mistaken, Miss, I am Mrs Anslow, Mrs Nora Anslow, and I believe this is now my flat.'

Gloria heard the voices in the hallway and came through to see who it was. Nora pushed by Hannah and strode towards Gloria.

'How dare you pretend to be Nathan's wife, my dear departed Nathan. As soon as I found out about his passing, I came all the way from Canada, heard it from his brother who saw a notice in the Toronto Star put in by a Gabriel Phelps, whoever the hell he is.'

Nora was loud and brash, she made Gloria feel extremely apprehensive. 'Your Nathan, how dare you, you left him, walked

220

out on him months before he and I met, get out of my home, you have no right to be here.' Gloria almost screamed at her.

'I have every right, I am Nathan's widow on paper, and he owes me all of this,' Nora said with a sneer. 'I like what you've done with the place, should fetch a pretty penny.'

Gloria was shaking with anger and bordering on hysteria, her grief being too raw to deal with this dreadful woman. 'I shall not ask you again, now get out before I telephone the police.'

'A right high and mighty madam ain't ya, don't worry I'm leaving, but I'll be back,' Nora said and walked out of the front door, her heels clicking loudly on the parquet flooring.

Gloria was incensed, the whole episode had only lasted a few minutes, but she felt dizzy and unwell, she quickly made her way to the sitting-room and poured herself a brandy, and despite not having had a drink in a while, this one was needed. She sat down and sipped the warm brown liquid, her hands were shaking, and it helped calm her shattered nerves a little. 'The audacity of the woman,' Gloria thought to herself and decided that the best course of action would be to telephone her solicitor. Surely Nora could not contest Nathan's will, it was legally written, she could not possibly have any claim, Gloria's heart sank.

A telephone call was made to Mr Westwood, the solicitor who dealt with Nathan's will, relaying all the sordid details of Nora's visit and pleading with him to assure her that the woman had no legal claim on Nathan's estate. He had bequeathed everything to Gloria in the name of Phelps, not Anslow, so there was no fraudulent misuse of names.

'I will look over the documents with a fine-tooth comb and get back to you shortly,' he said, 'in the meantime if she returns, I must insist you not say anything unless I am present. Try not to worry, everything will be alright.'

True to his word, he returned Gloria's telephone call an hour later with the excellent news that Nathan's will was entirely legal, and although Nora might attempt to contest it, he promised there were no grounds for her to win. She replaced the handset, extremely relieved.

Much to Gloria's dismay, Nora returned the following morning, once more barging her way in and demanding to look around the flat for any of her belongings. 'The miser never sent me the rest of my clothes and jewellery when I asked him to, I suppose you've been wearing my best pearl earrings and necklace, they belonged to my mother, you know,' she drawled.

Gloria was better prepared for her this time. 'I have never seen your precious pearls, and what on earth makes you think I would want to wear them? I have my own. Anything you left behind I suspect Nathan disposed of the minute you walked out of the door, and now I have met you, I cannot for the life of me imagine why Nathan ever married you.'

Nora looked Gloria up and down contemptuously. 'We were happy on the farm with Bill, then Nathan gets ideas above his station, decides he wants to be a dentist, next thing I know he wants to come to England, says there's more chances for work here. He dragged me all the way across the Atlantic to this hellhole called London and expected me to like it. Well, I didn't, so I went home, and now I want some reward for my misery.'

The way Nora told her story did not make Gloria believe there had ever been much love between them, particularly on Nora's side. Gloria knew she would need to tread very carefully with this vindictive woman, studying Nora's appearance as she spoke. She was in her mid-forties, with curly auburn hair cut short with a side parting and a freckly complexion. Her figure was trim, but her dress probably came from a cheap department store and was the same one she wore the day before, the woman clearly had very little money. What was Gloria to do? She was not a vengeful person herself and wondered how much she would have to pay Nora to go back to Canada. The last thing Gloria could cope with at this moment in time was an ugly scene with a woman determined not to go home empty-handed. So, instead of retaliating to Nora's attack, Gloria said, 'How much do you want?'

'I told you, I want this place, or rather what it's worth, I ain't staying in London a minute longer than I have to,' Nora replied.

Immediately, Gloria realised that Nora was unaware of the total of Nathan's effects, he had left almost £3000, she only wanted the value of the flat, which was about £300. With her mother's nest egg and the remainder of Nathan's effects, Gloria could easily afford to give Nora what she asked for, and then she would be out of her life.

'Come back tomorrow, I will speak to my solicitor,' Gloria said, 'now please, leave.'

There was a hard look in Nora's eyes as she turned away from Gloria and left the flat. 'Tomorrow at half-past ten, I'll be back, and you had better have what I want or else….'

'Goodbye,' Gloria said and almost pushed her out of the door.

Mr Westwood chastised Gloria for making such a rash promise to a stranger. How did she know that Nora was whom she said she was, he had asked. Gloria reassured him that she felt absolutely certain Nora was indeed who she said she was, and could he just prepare a bank draft for £300.

'£290 will be quite sufficient,' Mr Westwood said, 'and I will call on you tomorrow at ten o'clock and hand it to the woman myself.'

Gabe had also admonished his mother, saying that she was far too noble for her own good and once that money was spent, Nora would probably be back for more.

'She could have it all, Gabe, if I thought it would bring Nathan back, and to be honest, I was thinking of selling the flat anyway, it has far too many painful memories. I think a fresh start is required, somewhere new, somewhere that is mine,' Gloria told him.

Mr Westwood arrived promptly at ten o'clock with the bank draft, and when Nora arrived, he gave it to her. He insisted she sign a document declaring that she would never ask for any additional amounts during her lifetime.

'Won't need it with this tidy sum, much more than I expected, should get the farm up and running again, oh yeah, I didn't tell you that me and Bill are together now. Always liked him better than Nathan, to be honest, only he had a wife at the time, she's dead now and Bill's mine.' Nora said. 'Won't be seeing you again or this miserable country. Bye.'

She turned around and walked out of the flat, waving the bank draft in the air as she left, leaving Gloria and Mr Westwood standing in the hallway speechless.

Over the next few months, Gloria's health improved, although moments of despair and loneliness overwhelmed her frequently. Still, with Riccardo's encouragement, she drew upon her inner strength, and the pursuit of a new flat for her and Julian to live occupied much of her time. Not wanting to be too far away from her sons, nor Lucy for that matter, numerous places in Marylebone and Fitzrovia were explored until she finally took a lease on an elegant two-bedroomed second floor flat on St George's Terrace. It overlooked a beautiful park where she could take daily walks and attempt to restore something of her well-being.

There were two bedrooms, two reception rooms, a kitchen and a large bathroom. Not at all on the scale of Fleur's, but it had a white cast iron skirted bath with chrome taps and a matching sink. The tiles were white with a black border around the middle of the walls. Those on the shower floor were laid in the style of a Roman mosaic,

Gloria loved it. The front room was to be her sitting-room from where she could view the park, and her bedroom was adjacent via a connecting door. The second reception room would be the dining room, and Julian could take the other bedroom. It was smaller than anywhere she had lived before, but then she was on her own now. Even Julian came and went more frequently than before, often staying with his brothers now he felt his mother was more settled.

She brought her favourite furniture from Clifton Hill, including her bookcase containing the precious photograph albums. There was far too much to fit in her new flat, anything left behind had gone to auction. The whole process had been harrowing, it almost felt as if she were betraying Nathan, but he had never been sentimental about household items, and she hoped he would not mind. One thing she could not bear to part with was their huge brass bed, it rattled a great deal, and that had always made them laugh whenever they were trying to be quiet and not wake Julian.

'I miss you so much, Nathan,' Gloria said out loud on her first night at St George's Terrace. As she lay wrapped in the covers, she imagined Nathan's arms around her, holding her and kissing her lips….. she felt tears roll down her face.

CHAPTER 18

For a while, the solitude suited Gloria, she regained her physical strength walking in the park. In the evenings, she would listen to the wireless and her records, read and look through the dozens of photo albums she had put together ever since Gabe was born. Her sons visited her as often as their busy lives allowed, and various new girlfriends were brought back for tea or a pre-dinner drink by Gabe and Dwight, all very pretty and mostly empty-headed.

What was Gloria going to do with her flirtatious sons? At least Julian had not joined in his brothers' quest to court every young woman in London just yet. She wrote weekly letters to Marcus and Lilian, keeping them up to date with all the comings and goings of the family, and they wrote back with tranquil tales of their quiet life in Somerset. They were forever asking her to visit them, as was Fleur, however, Gloria did not feel up to travelling and kept making excuses. Lucy and Harper came over for dinner once a week, but eventually, she began to wonder if this were it, is this how the rest of her life would remain? What was she to do with herself? A dark cloud began to descend over her once more.

Gabe observed that she was becoming distant, so he telephoned Riccardo to ask his advice.

'I think, Signora Gloria, requires a little excitement, leave it with me, Gabriel, I think I know just what the doctor should prescribe this time. The rolling ball in the spinning wheel soon takes your mind from its worries, and the food and wine are *eccellente.* Tell her I will pick her up on Saturday evening in her most becoming gown, and I promise she will not be disappointed.'

'Gabe, what have you done? I really do not feel up to being escorted out anywhere, how ever delightful Riccardo's company is,' Gloria bemoaned to her son.

'He insisted and said it was just what the doctor ordered, and you are to wear your best dress,' Gabe replied.

Gloria groaned. 'I no longer have a best dress, I do not even have a dress that is in fashion.'

At that, Gabe telephoned Lucy and more or less ordered her to take his mother out shopping tomorrow, thus, it was arranged for them to meet outside Harrods at eleven o'clock. A disgruntled Gloria arrived and greeted her friend with a kiss on the cheek.

'I look a fright, Lucy, I will need more than a new dress to come up to Riccardo's expectations,' Gloria said.

'A visit to the salon will soon have you spruced up, now come on, I feel the urge to shop, we have not done this for ages,' Lucy smiled at her friend and linked her arm in hers. 'This way, darling, in case you have forgotten.'

The friends spent hours in the store, Gloria tried on numerous evening dresses that all suited her splendidly. She finally settled for a beautiful long, black, silk charmeuse dress cut on the bias with a low cowl back, she looked every bit the elegant film star. Lucy gasped with delight when Gloria came out of the dressing room.

'How do you do it, darling? you still look thirty years of age, I find it harder and harder to keep my figure these days, but you, darling, you are perfect.'

'It is rather gorgeous, I must admit,' Gloria said and smiled at herself in the full-length mirror. She had not felt like dressing up for an occasion since Nathan died and hoped he would not mind her being escorted by Riccardo, he had become a very good friend over the last few months and was always exceptionally charming.

Gloria wore her diamond teardrop necklace and earrings, which added the final perfect touch to her ensemble. The hairdressing salon had done wonders with her hair, styling it into a waved bob and painting a little colour over her few greys. She heard the doorbell ring, picked up her black beaded evening bag and made her way to the door. Riccardo was waiting outside with a cab, and his face lit up with delight when he saw Gloria.

'Molto bellisomo,' he exclaimed, 'you will turn every head at the casino, mio caro, I am a very fortunate man tonight,' he said.

'So, that is where we are going, I have heard all manner of rumours about it. Antony once told me it was a place where one could lose one's fortune and one's camis all in one night, his words, not mine I hasten to add,' Gloria replied.

'Well, you will lose neither with me tonight, mio caro, I assure you.' He smiled and led her to the cab.

They arrived outside the club, where the uniformed doorman opened the cab door and took Gloria's hand to help her out, Riccardo came around, and she took his arm, taking a deep breath as they entered the club.

'I feel quite apprehensive, Riccardo, are you sure I will fit in here? I have never been anywhere like this before.'

'We will have dinner first and some fine champagne, then afterwards, my only desire is for you to be my good luck charm at the roulette table.' Riccardo spoke reassuringly.

Dinner was far more sumptuous and delicious than Gloria had anticipated, there was an oyster cocktail, followed by a filet mignon with mushrooms, a stuffed French endive salad and for dessert, fresh strawberry parfait. She had not felt so pampered in a long time and enjoyed the feeling far too much, then when Nathan came into her head, she felt a pang of guilt and wondered what he would think of her in a casino.

Riccardo must have read her mind. 'Nathan would not want your beauty to remain hidden from the world, you are far too young and beautiful to stay cooped up in your flat alone.'

'I am not young anymore, you flatter me, and I certainly do not want any more men in my life, I am destined to be alone from now on.' Gloria told him the story of Madame Burton's prediction all those years ago, which made Riccardo laugh heartily, chastising her for believing the absurd words of a gypsy woman.

'Someone is waiting for you, Gloria, believe my prediction, and when the time is right, you will welcome him,' Riccardo said.

Gloria shrugged her shoulders. 'That will remain to be seen,' she declared and changed the subject. 'Thank you for a wonderful dinner, now tell me what happens next?'

Riccardo led her to the gaming room, the clientele was from the upper classes of society, and membership to the club was very exclusive. A waiter in a black tuxedo made his way towards them, 'Good evening, Count Giordano, your usual place, I presume?'

Gloria felt her eyes widen, although she said nothing, and followed the man towards the roulette table where he pulled back a luxurious red velvet-covered chair for Riccardo to sit down and gestured for Gloria to stand slightly behind him. She quietly obeyed, having no understanding of what the etiquette was in a gambling club, but mostly she was intrigued as to why Riccardo had been addressed as count.

He had a pile of tokens in front of him, and she silently observed the other people seated around the table. Everyone was dressed impeccably, and Gloria was extremely relieved that her dress was of the correct couture, making her feel comfortable in that area at least. The gamblers were mostly men, some alone, others with a woman companion, but most of all, Gloria noticed how little conversation passed between anyone, it seemed to be all eyes on the table. The atmosphere was charged as the croupier began to spin the roulette wheel.

'Ladies and gentlemen, please place your bets,' he said. There was a calm movement of hands as tokens were pushed into position, Gloria vaguely knew the rules and watched intently. The ball rattled around the spinning wheel and eventually settled.

'Black thirteen,' the croupier called. Riccardo had won, he turned around and smiled at Gloria, his eyes twinkling.

He carried on playing for two hours, during which time another waiter walked around with a tray asking quietly who would like a drink. Gloria ordered a gin martini and a whiskey and soda for Riccardo, whose pile of tokens was growing. Alas, the pile in front of the man opposite was dwindling, much to his despair judging by the expression on his face. Riccardo played one more game and then politely gathered up his tokens and bowed.

'Good evening, ladies and gentlemen, grazie,' he said.

He led Gloria to the bar, and they sat together, talking. 'Are you really a count?' Gloria asked.

Riccardo put his finger to his lips and said, 'Shush, mio caro, that would be telling.' He winked.

'Why did you not carry on playing while you were winning?'

Riccardo explained that he always limited himself to two hours whether he was winning or losing, that way, he could stay in control. For him, it was about the calculated risk of either outcome, not about trying to win a fortune, continuing to play on is mostly when fortunes are lost.

'Do you play any of the other games?'

'I like the Pontoon, a game that I think you must try, come, we will invest some of tonight's winnings on the Blackjack,'

A delighted Gloria added further additions to Riccardo's winnings for the evening, and by two o'clock in the morning, a relieved Gloria still had her fortune and underwear intact, just as Riccardo had promised. She was rather tired though and asked if he minded taking her home. The cab arrived at St George's Terrace, and Riccardo walked Gloria to her door, she thanked him for a most fascinating evening.

'It was not at all how I expected it to be,' she said.

'Then you must accompany me on my next visit, I return regularly just once a month, it helps keep up my mystique.' Riccardo kissed Gloria's hand and wished her good night.

True to his word, Riccardo picked her up every first Saturday night of the month and took her to the casino. She began to enjoy the atmosphere at the club, it was like a secret place, away from the harshness of reality, where most people were anonymous, and she could almost pretend she was Riccardo's countess, no one asked any questions. When playing roulette, she took Riccardo's advice and never played for longer than a couple of hours. The different interactions between the guests were intriguing. Gloria witnessed gentlemen lose and win their fortunes whilst women were escorted to private rooms, just as Antony had revealed. Watching the comings and goings of the clientele all added to the fascination.

Gloria's daytime life floated along, and on the year anniversary of Nathan's death, she cried all day, feeling like her heart would never heal. Nevertheless, she survived, and two more weeks passed by when she received a telephone call from Gabe, who said he had something to tell her and could they meet for dinner at Rules the following evening.

There was always something happening in Gabe's life, and she wondered what antics her eldest son had been involved in this time. She arrived at the restaurant to discover Gabe sitting at the table deeply engrossed in conversation with an attractive young woman, whom Gloria thought she may have already been introduced to at some point in the past but could not be sure.

'Mama, over here.' Gabe waved at his mother when he spotted her in the doorway, Gloria smiled and made her way to the table, whilst a feeling of curiosity came over her as to what Gabe's announcement was going to be.

Gabe stood up and kissed her on the cheek. 'Hello, Mama, you remember Miriam Miller? She has been over for drinks at the flat a few times.'

Miriam stood up to shake Gloria's hand, all very modern, and she greeted her with a broad, genuine smile. 'Hello, Mrs Anslow, I am very pleased to meet you again.'

Gloria's brain ran through a sort of filing system she had stored containing the names of Gabe's and Dwight's numerous girlfriends that she had been introduced to. Fortunately, Miriam's name was amongst them.

'Good evening, Miriam, likewise,' Gloria said, shaking her hand.

'What would you like to drink, Mama?' Gabe asked.

She quickly browsed the cocktail menu and chose a Singapore Sling, one of her favourites, Gabe beckoned the waiter over, ordered the drink and whispered in his ear.

Gloria was busy scrutinising Miriam, she was about twenty-one years of age and had a pretty face with large brown eyes, her bob length brown hair styled in a sweeping side parting with soft waves, much like her own. She wore false eyelashes emphasising her eyes under the thin arched eyebrows, her lips were painted a rich red, and she wore a lovely green and white floral chiffon dress, the overall impression was most pleasant.

'So, Miriam, tell me how you two met?' Gloria asked.

'We work together, I am a secretary at the publishing agency,

Dwight goes out with my friend Dolores sometimes, we have such fun, do we not, darling?' she said, turning to Gabe.

She gazed adoringly at him, and Gloria hoped that Gabe would be announcing their engagement. It was actually rather exciting the thought of one of her sons settling down at last, perhaps a grandchild might be just the tonic she required. Gabe was twenty-eight years old and well established in the world of publicity, he and Dwight made a marvellous team. They were in demand from numerous magazines and newspapers for their talents, a wife and family would most certainly complement Gabe's success.

They ordered dinner and chatted amiably amongst themselves, Gloria learned that Miriam's family came from Croydon, where her parents owned a hardware shop. Wanting to "better herself", as she put it, Miriam went to secretarial school and headed to the bright lights and glamour of the city.

'At least she is being honest,' Gloria thought to herself as Miriam spoke, finding her quite a steady girl and certainly not unlikeable.

Dessert had been ordered, and Gabe was still to make his announcement, Gloria began to wonder if he had forgotten why he had invited her for dinner when the waiter brought a bottle of Moet et Chandon over to the table. He pulled the cork and placed the bottle in an ice bucket. Gabe poured each of them a glass and then spoke. 'Dearest Mama, we wanted you to be the first to know... Miriam and I are married.'

Gloria stopped in her tracks, this was not quite the scenario she had conjured up, already married. Then it dawned on her, the reason was obvious, it was like history repeating itself.

'Am I to congratulate you on two accounts?' she asked.

Miriam's cheeks flushed, and Gabe stuttered. 'Wh..Why, Mama, what on earth do you mean?'

'I was not born yesterday, and believe me, I have the utmost understanding of your predicament. I wish you had told me I would have entirely understood and already married, how could you? Now you have not allowed me the opportunity to purchase a new hat,' she admonished with a smile.

'Mama, you really are the most wonderful person in the world,' Gabe said. He took her hand in his and kissed it. 'Thank you.'

Gloria remembered her own situation some thirty-years ago with all the guilt and shame, her father banishing her. She wondered if times had changed sufficiently for Miriam not to suffer the same fate if indeed she had even told her parents. This was Gloria's next question.

'No….. my father would kill me, please, he must not know, that is why we married so quickly, the baby can be early then. Please, do not tell him, Mrs Anslow,' Miriam begged.

'It is not my place to tell him and believe me, it is the last thing I would do, and please call me Gloria,' she said, thinking of that dreadful day when she and Gerald had revealed their elopement. No, she had only just met Miriam, and she would certainly not do anything that would cause her to possibly suffer the same humiliation that she had been subjected to. 'When will you tell your parents?' she asked.

'I do not know how to tell them, I have not been home for months. I have told them about Gabe though, and how wonderful he is, maybe when they see the baby…..' her voice trailed off.

Gloria looked at her son and the young girl he had married and could only hope that their situation worked out better than her own had all those years ago.

They took a flat together on Brechin Place, a bachelor flat with Dwight and Maurie was now out of the question, and much to Gloria's dismay, Julian told her he wished to live with Dwight at the flat on the pretext it was closer to his workplace. She was more than sure that was not the only reason as he was hardly ever at home with her nowadays. Her sons were grown men, with lives of their own, each with their own paths to tread, and Gloria hoped that she had prepared them sufficiently.

David came home for a week during August, tremendously excited that he was to be stationed in Cairo and was to take part in an aerial pageant before King Fuad. The RAF suited David well, he valued the camaraderie of his fellow airmen, whilst the order and discipline of the ranks gave him something to aspire to, and he often spoke of his ambition to become a wing commander one day. Egypt was thousands of miles away, and David's news had rocked Gloria somewhat, she had never been more than a hundred miles or so away from any of her sons since they were born. This was a huge event to come to terms with, and she floundered for a while. If it were not for her casino nights with Riccardo and the loyalty of dear Lucy, a dark cloud might have descended upon her once more.

Summer and autumn passed, and winter set in, although there were quite a few sunny days during the beginning of December, but also some cold and misty ones. Gabe and Miriam's baby was due, and on the 19th of December 1932, Ruby Gloria Phelps came into the world, she was healthy and beautiful. Riccardo attended Miriam during her labour ensuring it went as smoothly as possible, and Gloria stayed by her side throughout, as Miriam was yet to tell her parents that she was married or having a baby. It was far from an ideal situation, and Gloria felt she was in no position to interfere in her daughter-in-law's family relationships. Remembering her own dilemma all those years ago, she understood Miriam's reluctance and thought it best to leave her to tell her parents when she felt the time was right.

Baby Ruby was just the tonic Gloria required, her love of children had not waned, and Miriam welcomed her words of advice on the subject of motherhood, which Gloria was happy to impart. Gabe adored his baby daughter, even if he was a little unsure of what to do with her. He was nervous about dropping her or breaking her somehow, and the worried expression on his face was immortalised in the first photographs that Gloria took of the latest addition to the family. Gabe and Miriam appeared very happy together, much to her relief, as she had become quite fond of her daughter-in-law.

Gloria sent photographs of Ruby through the post to Marcus, he was immensely proud to be a great-grandfather and pleaded with Gabe to bring his new family to meet him in the spring.

'I am an old man, Gabe, and I wish to see all of you once more before I die,' he said over the telephone one evening.

'We must make an effort, Gabe,' Gloria said, 'we owe everything to your grandfather, I know that David cannot be with us, but we can all go. I feel rather ashamed that I have not visited before now, we could go during the Easter break, surely you and Dwight can arrange a few days off work.'

Thus, a family trip was organised, first-class tickets purchased for the train to Taunton, and rooms booked at the local hotel in Watchet. The reunion with Marcus and Lilian was full of hugs and smiles, and whilst Miriam looked on holding baby Ruby in her arms, she wished so much that her own family were as devoted. Having been accepted into Gabe's family so readily made her decide to tell her parents about their marriage and Ruby when they returned to London, it was time they knew, and to hell with the consequences.

They had a wonderful three days, Julian had the opportunity to ride Misty once more, and despite the chilly spring weather, he went fishing with Marcus as they had always done during the summer holidays. Ruby was the centre of attention as she lay gurgling in her rattan crib. Marcus and Lilian were besotted with her, and Miriam gratefully accepted the intricate lace shawl Lilian had knitted. Gabe and Dwight entertained their grandfather with outrageous stories from the publishing world.

'It is not all about the fun and entertaining of clients though,' Dwight said, 'I spend hours drawing, sometimes to have them tossed in the bin, and Gabe has to sweet talk the clients into believing that our advertisements will convince people to buy their product. There is far more to it than meets the eye.'

'If you say so, my boys,' Marcus said with a twinkle in his eyes.

He also had a long talk with Gloria regarding how she was coping after Nathan's death. The pain had lessened, she told him, and Ruby's arrival had helped immensely, although a great sadness came over her knowing that Nathan was not here to see her. She admitted suffering a turmoil of emotion at times, and Marcus, as usual, had all the right words to say in his calm and gentle manner. He approved of Miriam and was delighted that at least one of his grandsons had settled down at last.

'Fine men they have grown into, Gloria, their father did not know his own mind back then, I am sure of it. You have taught them well, you are quite a woman,' he said.

'No, Marcus, if it were not for you, we would have been destitute, you are their shining light, and you know how much they love you, as do I,' Gloria replied.

The departure was as equally emotional as their arrival, and the train journey back to London was filled with reminisces of their childhoods, to which Miriam listened intently. It was much akin to Gloria hearing tales of Gerald's early years, and she sincerely hoped that Miriam and Gabe's marriage would be a long and happy one.

CHAPTER 19

Within the blink of an eye, it was New Year's Day 1935, and Julian celebrated his twenty-first birthday with a splendid dinner at Claridge's to mark the special occasion. With Julian was a young woman named Audrey Swann, with whom he appeared to be totally besotted. Gloria had invited Riccardo, and Gabe and Miriam were able to be there as their neighbour, Mrs Van der Sprenkel, had kindly offered to sit with Ruby for the evening. Dwight was accompanied by his latest flame, a pretty redhead, Lucy and Harper came, and even Fleur and Filkes had travelled up to London to be with them. It was a marvellous night, marred only by David's absence. He was home from Cairo and been promoted to squadron leader following his transfer to the new base at RAF Mildenhall in Suffolk, but this year was only granted leave for Christmas Day.

Gloria presented Julian with a beautiful rose gold Rolex watch engraved with his initials J. P. H., she purposely left off the P for Phelps as Julian had for quite some time started going by the name of Julian Piers Huxley. He told Gloria that having never really known his father, he preferred to have his own identity, and as Huxley was his mother's favourite grandmother's name, he much preferred it. Gloria was very touched. On the other hand, she was not too sure that she agreed with Julian's next announcement a few weeks after his birthday.

'Audrey and I are going to live together, Audrey thought this would be a good idea, she is so modern,' he said.

Gloria was yet to formally meet Miss Audrey Swann and felt a little concerned that her youngest son was being influenced by this woman. But rather than express her doubts, she first asked Julian to arrange for them all to have drinks together one evening so that Gloria could learn more about Miss Swann.

They arranged to meet at Rules, which seemed to be the centre of the world for her sons, and Gloria arrived to find them already deep in an animated conversation. Moving closer, she could see it was more like Audrey holding court, talking at Julian. It took Gloria to stand by their table for a couple of minutes before her son noticed she was there.

'Mama, there you are, come and sit down, what would you like to drink? Audrey was just telling me about the latest goings-on in Germany and that Hitler chap, did you know he has declared that Jews are second class citizens? Audrey is so knowledgeable about these things.' He hastily beckoned the waiter over.

Gloria ordered a gin martini with the feeling she was going to need it. The young woman was very confident and sharp, she had short blond hair and a slim figure, not overly attractive, but with piercing blue eyes, and one felt as if she could read your very soul. Audrey was twenty-three years old and wrote short stories for Woman's Weekly, with a driving ambition to break into Fleet Street and have her own news column in one of the broadsheets. They had met at one of Gabe and Dwight's publishing soirées, where Audrey had announced that in her opinion - 'Men think they are the only human beings capable of doing anything properly. Well, I intend to change all of that one way or another.'

Julian was fascinated by her, and Audrey being very flirtatious by nature, encouraged his attentions.

The evening was exhausting, it was not that Gloria disliked

Audrey, she was a very intelligent woman. She came from a poor background, her father had been blinded by mustard gas in the war and became an alcoholic, he died when Audrey and her sister were young, leaving their mother to bring them up single-handed with very little money. Last year she had died of TB, worn out with life at forty-five years of age, it made Gloria realise just how privileged her life was, and she did feel a pang of sorrow for Audrey.

Nevertheless, her early years had not affected her ambition and zest for life, and if Gloria was honest with herself, them living together first was probably not a bad thing, as suddenly her own mother's words came into her head. *'A hasty marriage never has the foundation required to build a strong relationship, one way or another it will flounder.'* She had been right in the end, so Gloria felt she was in no position to judge and thought to herself that at least Julian's life would certainly not be dull with Miss Swann around. Within two weeks, they found themselves a one bedroomed flat to rent on Birchington Road and moved in together.

For a while Gloria was settled, her life tended to revolve around Ruby, who was now almost two and a half years old. She toddled around, always smiling and saying, 'Gramma, Gramma,' she was delightful.

However, it always seemed as if Gloria was destined for sorrow in her life. It was an evening in March when the telephone rang, Gloria answered to hear Marcus's voice.

'Gloria, dear, I have some terrible news to impart,' he said, sounding very upset, 'Lilian has suffered a stroke, I, I... was unable to save her, it was dreadful. My housekeeper is here, but I have no one else to turn to. Gloria, please can you come down to Watchet? I desperately need your help.'

'Dearest Marcus, I am so dreadfully sorry, of course, I can come,

I will catch the train tomorrow morning, I should be with you by tea-time,' Gloria said.

They talked on the telephone for a little while longer until Marcus admitted that he was rather tired and thought it best he retire to bed.

'Goodnight, Marcus, try to rest, and I will see you tomorrow.'

Gloria was thrown into somewhat of an emotional state herself, despite not being as close to Lilian as she had been to Edith, still, Marcus and Lilian had been happy together these last years, and he sounded broken. The train departed at half-past ten in the morning, and Gloria had packed herself a small case. She attempted to sleep, which was impossible with all manner of emotions running through her head and boarded the train the next day bleary-eyed.

She arrived at Taunton station and took a cab to Marcus's house, where she found him talking to the vicar about arrangements for the funeral. Marcus was almost eighty-eight years of age and finding Lilian's death too much to bear. His voice cracked as he spoke, and he broke down. Gloria sat next to him and took his hand, all she felt she could do at this moment in time was attempt to comfort him and take over the funeral arrangements. None of this was easy for her, nevertheless, she dug deep and summoned up the strength to take control of the painful situation.

The funeral took place two days later at St Decumen's church, many of the town's people came to pay their respects, some of the older residents having known the Phelpses when they had lived locally. Marcus and Lilian had been very well-liked since his retirement to Watchet. Gloria was saddened to see Marcus so wretched and feared for his health, she even tried to persuade him to come back to London with her, but he refused, saying that Somerset was his birthplace and that is where he wished to die.

Thus, a weary Gloria boarded the train, closed her eyes, and slept for most of the journey. When she arrived back at her flat, she lay down on the bed, and it was then that her tears flowed. So many people she had loved and cared for were gone, her grief welled up in her heart, and it felt as if it would burst. 'Nathan, my darling, Nathan, will my heart ever truly mend? It is too much….' Gloria sobbed for an hour and was left feeling desolate.

Six weeks later, Marcus passed away quietly in his bed, his housekeeper found him when she arrived in the morning, which was a terrible shock for her. Gloria was devastated, and when she broke the news to her sons, they were utterly heartbroken. Riccardo stepped in and gallantly made all the required arrangements. Marcus's death was significantly felt by the medical fraternity, and an outstanding obituary appeared in the British Medical Journal, praising his work over his many years as a doctor, paying him the utmost respect in what was written.

David was granted special leave, and the whole family attended Marcus's funeral at St Decumen's, it was a sombre and moving service. And even though the vicar said the most touching words about Marcus, they were of no comfort to Gabe, David, Dwight or Julian, they had lost their beloved grandfather and Gloria, the man who had been her father in every way except blood.

Marcus was buried beside Lilian in the church graveyard, and the following morning, a solemn party returned to London to congregate at Gloria's flat. The family grieved deeply for their loss, nevertheless, as they each remembered their favourite things about him, there was even some laughter.

Gloria pulled down some of the oldest photograph albums from her bookcase, and each one was eagerly looked through, it was a wonderful tribute to a special man who was loved by all who knew him. He was the kindest and most just man Gloria had ever known, and even his will reflected his generosity. The estate was to be shared equally between all of his grandchildren, including Justine, Gerald's illegitimate child. It was right and fitting, and no one thought anything of it, only of what a truly wonderful man, Dr Marcus Phelps, had been.

It took a few weeks for everyone to stop reeling over the loss of Marcus, but gradually as is the nature of things, their lives went on, and they each settled back into their routines. Gloria had been entirely bereft, and both Gabe and Riccardo kept a watchful eye over her. However, she was stronger now and managed to pull herself from falling into a depression.

A year passed, and the summer of 1936 arrived, and Gloria decided it was time that young Ruby, now three and a half years old, should follow in the family tradition and spent the summer at the seaside with her grandmother and great Aunt Fleur. Miriam was hesitant at giving up her daughter for four weeks, and it took some convincing by Gabe that Ruby was in the very best of hands and that running wild at Aunt Fleur's was all part of growing up in their family.

Miriam tearfully waved her little girl off at the train station, who had gone off with Gloria quite contently and barely turned around to wave goodbye to her mother. Gabe stood with Miriam, his arm around her waist, watching his mother holding his daughter's hand. It was as if he were seeing himself at Ruby's age, running along beside his mother, trying to keep up with her steps as they boarded the train together for his first time to Ramsgate.

'She will have the time of her life, do not fret, mark my words, Ruby will return fit and well,' he said to his wife as she wiped the tears from her cheeks.

Fleur was so excited about having Ruby come to stay, she had redecorated one of the bedrooms her nephews used to sleep in and transformed it with a fabulous pink and white décor. She also purchased a magnificent dolls house complete with a miniature family for Ruby to play with. The little girl was awe-struck and unsure at first whether she was allowed to touch it. Before long, with some gentle persuasion, Ruby was soon opening the tiny doors and admiring the dolls furniture and was delighted when she saw that one of the little bedrooms had the same colour scheme as her own.

'It is so good to see you, darling,' Fleur said to her sister, 'Filkes has become rather crotchety in his old age, and I was thrilled when you asked if you could come to stay. She is a beauty, is she not,' Fleur added, looking at her grandniece.

'All dark hair and curls, just like her uncle Julian was at that age, I adore her. I am also very fond of Miriam too, she and Gabe seem very happy together despite their having to marry in a hurry. I am sure they will last, Gabe is not like his father at all,' Gloria said.

It was as if time had frozen, the two sisters took Ruby for long walks along the beach, watching her run around in the sand, her hair blowing free in the wind shouting, 'Grandma, Aunt Fleur, look at me.' They spread the big old blanket on the sand and picnicked just as they had done many years ago when the boys were young.

'Look at us, Fleur, I shall be fifty-one-years-old this year, and what are you now, fifty-six?' Where did all the years go, I wonder,' Gloria sighed?

'Do you still miss him, darling?' Fleur asked.

'All the time, it has been six years, and I cannot lose the ache in my heart. I am grateful for the years we did have together, they were the happiest of my life. For now, I am content watching my granddaughter grow up and my sons make their way in life, they make me proud. What about you, Fleur, any regrets?'

'Just not having children of my own, but sadly, it is nature's way, and I have everything I need here. I have some dear friends, I enjoy my charity work, and there is clean, fresh air to breathe every day. I can never understand why you love London so much.'

They sat on the blanket together and reminisced as they watched Ruby build a sandcastle and cover it with the shells she had collected in a little blue bucket.

The four weeks flew by, and before they knew it, Fleur was driving Gloria and Ruby to the train station in her new MG motor car to return to London. There were tears as they said farewell, and even Ruby held on to her aunt tightly, giving her a big wet kiss on the lips.

'Goodbye, Aunt Fleur, may I come again next year?' she asked.

'Of course, my darling, if your mother will allow it. Have you put her gift safely in Grandma's handbag?'

'Yes, Aunt Fleur.'

Gloria lifted Ruby up, and the little girl wrapped her legs around Gloria's waist, holding closely around her neck. 'Goodbye, Fleur, come up to London soon, please,' Gloria said.

They waved through the carriage window, the porter blew the whistle, and the train chugged slowly out of the station.

Miriam was waiting anxiously at St Pancras, she had missed her daughter dreadfully and ran towards her as they stepped down from the train.

'Mummy, Mummy,' Ruby squealed when she saw Miriam, who picked her up and squeezed her tightly.

They took a cab home to Brechin Place and went inside, Miriam made tea for both herself and Gloria, and they sat down with Ruby between them. Gloria delved into her handbag and passed the little girl a package to give to her mother, it was wrapped in pink and white striped paper.

'For you, Mummy, from the seaside,' she said.

Inside was a small china vase painted with purple and orange crocuses and the words *A Present from Ramsgate.*

'Darling, it is lovely, thank you, I will treasure it always,' Miriam said and kissed her daughter.

It was a precious moment, and for Gloria, brought back the memory of when Julian gave her the shell with the little figurine inside it, which she still kept in her jewellery box.

A surprising but welcome announcement came from Dwight in the summer of 1937, he became engaged to a young woman he had been seeing for over a year. Her name was Rebecca Marchbank, eldest daughter of the editor of one of the newspapers Dwight freelanced for. Gloria had met her on quite a few occasions and liked her very much, she was relieved that Dwight had found a girl he seemed settled with at last. Rebecca was a classic beauty, blonde with a perfect English rose complexion, well-educated and from a good family.

A friendly dinner at Rules was arranged where Gloria could meet Rebecca's parents, Elias and Victoria. The evening definitely required a new outfit, and Gloria and Lucy had shopped for hours to find a suitable ensemble. She chose a burgundy crepe two-piece dinner suit, the long skirt had a belt that enhanced Gloria's forever slim figure, with it she wore a pearl necklace and earrings, and the overall effect was one of tasteful elegance.

Elias had an overly assertive manner, one could tell he was used to being in charge and demanding the highest standard of work from his staff, this aside, he was not unlikeable. He was tall, with balding grey hair and a pencil moustache and an air of respect surrounding him. On the other hand, his wife, Vicky, was a quiet, nervous woman, she barely said a word, just agreeing with everything her husband announced. It was difficult for Gloria to form an opinion of her. Too many years of being overshadowed by her larger than life husband, Gloria thought, perhaps if she could speak to her alone, she might open up a little.

The evening passed pleasantly enough, and they agreed that an engagement announcement should be placed in The Times for the following Saturday.

'Actually, can we just hold back on that for another week, please,' Dwight said, 'there is something I have to do first.'

'How mysterious, darling,' Rebecca said, 'you are not thinking of changing your mind, are you?'

'No, silly, just my name, I have an appointment with a solicitor next Wednesday, I wish to change it by deed-poll to Anslow like my mother, Nathan was so good to us all, and I think it the right thing to do, to keep his name in the family. It will go in The Gazette, and then we can formally announce our engagement,' Dwight said.

Gloria felt her heart lurch, she was speechless, it was a purely selfless thing to do, and she was incredibly touched.

And so, it was done, both announcements were printed, and the wedding was arranged for Saturday the 23rd of April 1938, at St Augustine's on Queen's Gate.

It was a gorgeous spring day, the sun shone, and Rebecca looked exquisite in her wedding gown made from a heavy crepe Romain, embroidered with pearls and diamante. The fullness of the skirt fell back into a pointed train, and she carried a bouquet of red and white roses. Her two younger sisters were bridesmaids, they wore pale mauve lace dresses and looked very striking. Gloria had chosen her outfit with great care, it was a stone and pink metallic cloquè two-piece, and with it, she wore a Panama hat adorned with a ribbon made from her dress fabric. She wished to look her best but did not want to overshadow Vicky, who wore a most stylish rust silk two-piece with a spray of white carnations.

Dwight had asked Gabe to be his best man, David and Julian

were ushers, Gloria looked at her four sons, they were all so dark and handsome dressed in their grey morning suits, and her heart swelled with love. There were about sixty guests, and Gloria was grateful that Riccardo had escorted her so she would not be alone. The wedding breakfast took place at the Savoy, and a marvellous time was had by everyone, all in all, it was a wonderful day.

'At last, a proper wedding,' Gloria said to Lucy as they sipped on their champagne.

'What do you mean, darling? A proper wedding.'

'I mean, they became engaged, it was properly organised, the bride is not pregnant, well at least I am not aware that she is, they are going on a honeymoon, and I was able to purchase a new hat,' Gloria said, and the two old friends laughed.

The bride and groom were waved off as they headed for a two-week honeymoon in Paris, and all the guests retired extremely happy. Peace reigned in Gloria's family, and she was content.

However, it was at Gloria and Riccardo's November casino night that she overheard a disturbing conversation in the bar between two gentlemen. All through her life, Gloria had never taken too much interest in politics, but they were discussing Adolf Hitler and how he was becoming a serious threat to world peace, she heard enough to make her feel quite alarmed. Thus, she broached the subject with Riccardo, who also expressed his concerns over Benito Mussolini.

'They speak of living in peace, but I fear they are warmongers, let us say I have no desire to return to Italy,' he said.

'Do you think there will be another war?' Gloria asked.

'Let us hope not, mio caro, there is certainly a great deal of unrest on the continent, but you must not fret, I am sure the British Government will not allow it.'

'It would be the most appalling thing, the thought of my sons having to be part of a war like their father is too much to bear. David is already in the RAF, you know Lucy's husband was killed in his plane, it must not happen, too many people remember the first time.' Gloria was becoming quite distressed, and Riccardo tried his utmost to allay her fears.

'Come, let us have one more spin of the roulette wheel, perhaps our luck will change.' Riccardo led her to the table, and they placed a square bet, the croupier spun the wheel, and the ball stopped on black twenty-nine. 'Well done, mio caro,' Riccardo whispered in Gloria's ear, 'we have just won eight to one on our two-pound bet.'

They shared the winnings between them as usual, and Gloria arrived home in a much happier frame of mind, she had rather taken to the casino, calling it her "little escape."

Christmas 1938: Gloria insisted the whole family have dinner at her flat, Gabe, Miriam and Ruby, David, who still had no sweetheart in tow, Dwight and Rebecca, along with Julian and Audrey. Gloria observed her youngest son's girlfriend and was not too sure how long it would last. As far as she could see, Audrey openly flirted with every man she talked to, and when she mentioned it delicately to Julian, he laughed it off saying it was just her way, it meant nothing.

Dinner was a combined effort from Gloria, Miriam and Rebecca, Audrey's excuse was that cooking was not her forte, they usually ate out or went around to friends for dinner. Nevertheless, the turkey and trimmings were delicious, and Gloria made her best attempt at resurrecting the recipe for the plum pudding Polly used to make when the boys were young. It was more for Ruby's sake, and Gloria made sure that her grand-daughter had the slice containing the silver sixpence, much to her delight.

Plenty of wine flowed, they played songs and jazz tunes on Gloria's gramophone, and the party were extremely happy and content. Miriam had made an enormous pass the parcel, which

Gabe won in the end, much to everyone's exasperation and shouts of "cheat", particularly as the present was a small mohair teddy bear obviously destined for Ruby. Gabe held it just out of his daughter's reach while she tried to grasp it from him, teasing her until Miriam intervened before tears started.

'Gabe, how many times have I told you not to tease her so much? She is not old enough to understand, you really are incorrigible,' she scolded.

Riccardo joined them later in the evening, he had a prior dinner engagement with a colleague, Dr Rudolph Von der Braun and his wife. When Gloria answered the door to let him in, she thought he appeared somewhat fraught despite him insisting he was fine, but Gloria knew him too well.

'Is something wrong, Riccardo?' she asked.

Not at all, I am just a little disturbed by a subject of conversation at dinner today, but it is nothing for you to worry about, mio caro.' He kissed her cheek and walked through to the sitting-room, and the others gathered therein.

They partied for another hour or so until Ruby fell asleep on her mother's lap, she carried her gently to the spare bedroom and lay her on the bed, covering the little girl with an eiderdown.

'Goodnight, my sweet girl, sleep tight,' Miriam said and kissed her daughter on the forehead.

She returned to the living room and re-joined the family, her own parents had mellowed since the day she told them about Ruby and being married. There had been an initial outburst, but when they met Gabe, it was difficult for them not to like him, and of course, Ruby melted their hearts immediately. There was not a vast amount of contact as they could not leave the shop, nonetheless, Miriam took Ruby once a month on a Sunday to visit them and stayed for tea, it was steady and comfortable.

Miriam sat by Gabe and sipped the glass of wine he had poured for her, the conversation had as always amongst the men and Audrey, of course, turned to the latest news about Hitler, and the terrible goings-on abroad. It was during their discussion that Riccardo revealed his distress from earlier today.

'It is a sad fact that my friend Rudy, who was born in Munich, is sensing a change in people's attitude towards him, many of his patients have made excuses and moved to other practices, and I myself have lost a few because I am Italian. I despise Mussolini as much as any Englishman, and Rudy feels the same about Hitler, just because we were born in those countries does not mean that we are allied to them.'

Gloria, Miriam and Rebecca listened in until Gloria could stand it no longer. 'Please stop,' she said, 'I cannot bear anymore, it is Christmas Day, we have lived through one war, I do not wish to contemplate there being another, we all have too much to lose. Save your debates for another day, I beg of you and put a record on, *Anything Goes,* please, I wish to hear some happy songs, not your doom and gloom talk.'

It was of no use, the mood of everyone had darkened, and even the musical songs could not shake off a feeling of foreboding.

The news reports over concerns about Hitler worsened as 1939 developed, the RAFVR was training up its volunteers to provide a reserve aircrew in the event of war. As both Julian and Gabe were already volunteers, they were involved in the preparations. Dwight, on the other hand, had never volunteered as he had a fear of heights, but confessed that if a war did break out, he would prefer the Royal Navy, where at least his feet would be on the ground, albeit the ship would be floating on water, he would feel safer.

Julian and Audrey married hastily as soon as Julian's change of name deed was announced in The Gazette. Despite having been using Huxley as his surname for a number of years, like his brother, he wished to make it legal for the marriage certificate.

Gloria was extremely uneasy over the whole affair, a feeling of doom spread over her, and as she watched her eldest and youngest sons don their uniforms, she had a terrible sensation of déjà vu.

Political events deteriorated in Europe and when Germany invaded Poland on the 1st of September, Britain and France were not convinced that it was a defensive act as Hitler had announced. And, on Sunday the 3rd of September 1939, they declared war against Germany.

CHAPTER 20

'I have to sign up, Mama, it is my duty to King and country, Gabe and Julian are doing their bit in the reserves, David is already a squadron leader. I must do something, and the Royal Navy is where I wish to be,' Dwight firmly told Gloria a month after war had been declared.

'But nothing is happening yet, darling, please wait until absolutely necessary, think of Rebecca.' Gloria was beside herself.

'I understand your worries, Mama, but it has to be done, I can enlist as a petty officer and begin training. I have talked it through with Rebecca, and she is on my side, Elias was in the Royal Naval Reserves in the first war, and I have spoken with him at great lengths about it, my mind is made up,' Dwight said.

Gloria fully appreciated that most mothers in the country would be having the same conversations with their own sons, but it brought back such dreadful memories of how the war changed Gerald, and she feared for her daughters-in-law suffering the same fate that she had experienced. Nevertheless, Dwight was adamant, the necessary paperwork was signed, and he was posted to the Royal Naval Barracks at Plymouth to commence his training.

The family had the chance for a farewell dinner before he left, but it was a subdued affair, their lives were once again to be filled with danger and fear. David being away had become an accepted part of Gloria's life, however, Dwight had never been further than a few streets away, a quick telephone call if she needed him. Now he would be over two-hundred miles away and then being sent who knows where. She realised how selfish her feelings were when she realised that Rebecca, as his wife, must be experiencing the same dread that she had felt the day that Gerald went off to France.

'Damn politicians and warmongers, I loathe and despise them all, let them all rot in hell,' Gloria said to Lucy when they were having tea at their favourite Lyons. 'Look at us having to carry these wretched gas masks around with us, the streets piled high with sandbags, blackout curtains at every window, the world is insane.'

'I know, darling, it brings back the most frightful memories, we have to hope that nothing comes of it this time and those in power come to their senses. Harper has been driving various diplomats, even Mr Chamberlain, around London at all hours, I never know when he will be home, it is all too much,' Lucy replied.

'You know, Audrey is now the foreign correspondent for The Telegraph, she has no fear and totally believes she is the best journalist in London. Julian is besotted with her, and I have an awful premonition their marriage will end badly, she enjoys the control she has over him, and Julian is not strong enough to keep her. My poor, sweet Julian, he was always the quietest of my boys, and this woman has taken him over. Why he could not have found himself an agreeable girl like Miriam and Rebecca, I do not know,' Gloria said.

'It took us time to find our men….. I am so sorry, darling, that was thoughtless of me,' Lucy said.

'There is no need to apologise, I have my memories, please do not fret,' Gloria said to her friend and lightly squeezed her hand. 'What is it they say? It is better to have loved and lost than to have never loved at all, that is how I cope now.'

They talked, drank tea, and sampled the array of delicious cakes on the stand in the centre of the table until the clock struck five, after which they each made their own way home.

'Telephone soon, darling,' Lucy said and kissed Gloria's cheek.

Even though David and Dwight were already away, Gabe and Julian were waiting for the time when they would be required. Both were trained pilots but had very little flying experience at present. Very soon, that was to change and not in a pleasant way.

Gabe became extremely concerned that Miriam and Ruby would be isolated at their flat on Brechin Street if he were called up for duty. He felt equally worried for his mother living alone, therefore, he offered the proposal that they should all move to the flats at Endsleigh Court, with the added bonus that Ruby could attend his old school at Clerkenwell, only a mile away.

'Please, Mama, I beg of you,' Gabe pleaded, 'we must stick together, the flats there are lovely, they have all the latest mod cons, you will be very comfortable. The building is portered, and your granddaughter will be close by, I need you to take care of my family if I am called up. Rebecca has returned home to live with her parents now that Dwight is at sea, it makes sense we stay close to each other. As for Julian, he is so wrapped up in Audrey's life I doubt he would even notice where we live.'

After much thought, Gloria agreed, and within a few weeks, her new abode was 135 Endsleigh Court, a modern two-bedroomed flat with Gabe, Miriam and Ruby at number 335, two floors above. Gloria had to admit she was very comfortable and had already charmed the desk porter Daniel, a Canadian man in his sixties. He had fought in the first war and lived in Toronto at the same time Nathan was studying there, so they had plenty to talk about.

May 1940 arrived, and the newspapers and wireless broadcasts were filled with reports of the French invasion, of Winston Churchill becoming prime minister, the Dunkirk rescue operation, and the terrible loss of 68,000 lives. By the middle of June, France had surrendered to the Germans and was now an occupied country. Gloria wept as she listened to her wireless, remembering the catastrophic loss of life during the first war and knew that history was about to repeat itself.

Come July, terrible reports came in that British ships in the Channel were being bombed by the Luftwaffe. They attacked airfields and harbours, aircraft factories, and radar stations. Gloria was petrified for her sons' lives. David had telephoned briefly to tell her that they were being transferred here, there and everywhere as squadrons lost planes and pilots, he had already been promoted to wing commander, his present squadron being based at Gravesend.

'It is hell, Mama, I have taken over the day after Shorty was shot down and killed, but at least I have a Hurricane, poor old Shorty was in one of those wretched Gladiators, they have no chance against the Henckels and Messerschmitts.' Gloria could hear a siren wailing in the background. 'Sorry, Mama, I have to go, I love you and everyone.'

The telephone went dead, and Gloria was left petrified. As for communication from Dwight, she would just have to wait.

Only days later, Gabe and Julian were called up from the reserves, the desperate shortage of pilots meant that more or less any man who could fly a plane was drafted in. Due to his colour blindness, Julian was to be trained as a navigator on bombers.

Having an I.Q. of 140, Gabe was chosen for intelligence training at Bletchley Park rather than flying, and both Gloria and Miriam felt as if they were living in a nightmare.

Then the air raids began.......

'Gloria, Gloria,' Miriam shouted as she hammered on Gloria's door, 'hurry, the siren is going, can you not hear it? We need to get to the underground.'

Miriam put her ear to the door and heard Gloria calling back that she was on her way, she opened the door and came out of her flat carrying a bag containing biscuits, cakes, a flask of tea, and a blanket draped over her arm.

'Good heavens, Gloria, we are not going on a picnic,' Miriam exclaimed.

'I know that, dear, but we have no idea how long we will be trapped down there, do you want Ruby to go hungry?' Gloria said.

Somehow, she had found herself in a trance-like state, unconsciously packing supplies in a bag, preparing for the worst, she remembered the Zeppelin air raids when her boys were young and instinctively felt that this was going to be much, much worse.

They hurried to the underground entrance at Euston station, it took them about five or six minutes, masses of people were crowding down the steps, desperate to shelter from the oncoming attack. The noise from the sirens was tremendous and terrifying, eight-year-old Ruby was clinging on to her mother's hand for dear life as they found themselves a spot to settle down on the platform of the station. Hundreds of people were packed together, some sleeping on the escalators, others had slung hammocks across the rails, and the stench of people relieving themselves in the tunnels was dreadful. Someone in the distance from where Gloria, Miriam and Ruby sat began to sing *Roll out the Barrel*, and other people started to join in, no-one knew what devastation they would face when the all-clear sounded a few hours later.

Night after night the German bombers flew over London dropping bombs, and fires lit up the sky a fiery red. The drone of the aircraft engines was deafening, and every night the tube station became home for Gloria, Miriam and Ruby, alongside almost every Londoner who had not already lost their home or their lives in the utter carnage happening above them. No-one knew what they would face when they emerged from their subterranean shelters, whether their homes would still be standing or if they would be spending their next night at a rest centre. Death and devastation surrounded the frightened, bewildered population, never had war come so close to home, to innocent civilians, women and children blown up or buried in the rubble of what was once London.

Ruby was offered the chance to be evacuated to the countryside for safety, but she chose to stay with her mother and grandmother, saying she felt safer with them than anyone else. Each morning workers returned to their jobs, children went to school, and every night the Luftwaffe returned.

'I have to do something to help,' Miriam said as she and Gloria sat having a cup of tea. 'You did your bit in the first war, you told me how you, Lucy and your friend Dorothy worked at the Civil Service office. Gabe has suggested I volunteer for the WAAF.'

'I know, Lucy and I feel the same way, the women in our group have all decided to become fire wardens, I am to manage the stirrup pump outside the flats. Fleur telephoned the other night and told me that despite Filkes's age, he works flat out at the hospital, and she is doing her bit with the W.I., we must all do our utmost to carry on, it is the only way we will survive this hell,' Gloria replied.

And so, Miriam began her training at West Drayton, and there being no regular pattern as to when Gabe was home from Bletchley, Ruby moved to Gloria's flat while her mother was away.

Thus, another new chapter of their lives began, with death, tragedy and heartbreak.

It was a rainy Thursday afternoon, there was very little to do, so Gloria sat in her armchair reading the latest Poirot mystery, *Evil*

Under The Sun. She was totally absorbed in the story when her telephone rang. 'I wonder who that can be?' she thought to herself as she picked up the receiver. 'Bloomsbury, 246.'

Through a crackling line at the other end, she heard a voice saying, 'Mrs Anslow, is that you?'

'Yes, who is this please, I can barely hear you.'

'Hello, this is Mrs Drake from next door to Mrs Allen, I am afraid I have some terrible news for you,' the distant voice said.

Gloria went cold, icy fingers crept up her spine, knowing with dread the words she was about to hear.

'There was an air raid last night, I do not know how to tell you this…' Mrs Drake's voice trailed off.

'Is she dead?' Gloria asked in an emotionless tone.

'They both are, I am so terribly sorry. Dr Allen was called out to help the injured, and of course, Mrs Allen drove him there, they were hit as they were making their way to the hospital. I really am so dreadfully sorry.'

The telephone receiver slipped out of Gloria's hand and slid down her chest, she was frozen, her eyes fixed on the wall in front of her, and then she wailed. 'NO, NO, NO…'

She held her head in her hands and sobbed. 'Not Fleur, not my darling sister….. Filkes, they have never harmed anyone, how can life be so cruel.' Her heart broke for what felt like the thousandth time in her life, and as she contemplated all the despair that surrounded her, she wished the ground would open up and swallow her whole.

For hours she sat while darkness fell until the wail of the air raid siren roused her, but she remained motionless. This time she cared not whether she lived or died, nothing mattered anymore. She heard her doorbell ringing and Gabe, who was home on leave, shouting her to hurry up, but even so, she sat in the blackness. A key turned in the lock, and Gabe entered, they each had keys for each other's flats, he had Ruby with him and their bag of shelter supplies for the night. He turned the light switch on and saw his mother in the chair.

'Mama, come on, what is the matter? Where are your things?'

She did not move. 'Go without me, Fleur and Filkes are dead, I cannot take anymore,' she said.

Gabe was stunned, it took a moment for what his mother had said to sink in, but there was no time to think, he had to get them all to the underground as quickly as possible, they could talk there. He knew where Gloria kept her bag, so he grabbed it, along with her coat and ushered her out of the door. Leading Gloria with one hand whilst his daughter was clinging to the other, he pulled the door behind him and steered his distraught mother outside. The sharp evening air and noise of the sirens roused Gloria from her shock, and she managed to take a grip of herself, Ruby kept calling, 'Grandma, hurry up the planes are coming.'

They made it to the tube entrance just as the first bombs of that night's onslaught could be seen exploding into flames in the distance. They found their spot, there was a ticket system now so that everyone had their own place and spread their blankets and pillows down for the night. As they huddled together for warmth, Gloria told Gabe about her sister and Filkes, she cried on her son's shoulder as he held her close. Above them, the faint bang, bang of bombs dropping could be heard, regardless of the tunnel's depth from the surface.

A hasty funeral was arranged for Fleur and Filkes, to which only Gloria and Gabe could attend from the family, the rest of the mourners were made up of Fleur's friends and Filkes's colleagues from the hospital. It was a sad, sorry affair that followed and preceded services for the other people killed on the same night.

Ramsgate had been decimated, although by some miracle Fleur's house had survived, however, Gloria could not face staying there, she was grief-stricken. So, they waited at the station and caught a late train home, returning to London in silence, there was nothing that could be said to ease the pain of their loss.

A few days later, Filkes's solicitor telephoned and informed Gloria of the contents of his will. As they had no children of their own, they had expressed that the estate was to be shared equally between Gloria, Gabe, David, Dwight and Julian after both of their decease. The solicitor advised that probate was likely to take some time, nevertheless, he promised to keep her informed.

Eventually, the air raids lessened as the Luftwaffe changed tactics and began bombing other industrial cities. And at last, David was granted some long overdue leave, how he had survived the ferocity of the aerial combat that had taken place over Britain had been nothing short of a miracle. He arrived at Gloria's flat one afternoon in May 1941. It was chilly and raining, and she opened the door to her second eldest son, whom she had not seen for almost a year, and found, to her surprise, that he was accompanied by a young woman holding a baby about six months of age.

'Hello, Mama, it is so good to see you,' David said, kissing her on the cheek. 'May I introduce Amelia Marriott, Shorty's widow and their son Robert.'

'Yes, of course, how do you do? Please come in, forgive me I was not expecting company, come in and sit down,' Gloria said.

David's appearance was alarming, he was dreadfully thin, and his face was pinched and drawn, Gloria could not help noticing the slight tremor in his hands and the involuntary twitch in her son's eye as he spoke to her. Amelia looked in her early twenties and was dressed in a brown tweed two-piece suit. She had light brown hair pinned back in a roll that enhanced her pretty hazel eyes. An air of sadness surrounded her, and she held on to baby Robert as if his life depended on her never letting him go.

She sat next to David and glanced at him as if prompting him to say something, at last, he spoke. 'Mama, Amelia and I are to be married while I am on leave, I promised Shorty that if anything happened to him, I would take care of her and Robert, and I intend to honour that vow,' David said.

Gloria was quite taken aback. 'Do you love each other?'

'Love has very little to do with it, Mama, us single chaps all promised the married ones we would care for their widows in the event of the inevitable, it was the right and proper thing to do. Amelia and I get on just fine, and at least Robert will grow up with a father, Shorty never lived to see his son,' David explained.

There was very little Gloria could say, the world had gone mad, she sat looking at the couple in front of her and wondered what would happen next in this bizarre life they were all living. Robert began to stir and cry softly,

'May I warm him some milk please, Mrs Anslow?' Amelia asked.

'Of course, my dear, and please, call me Gloria. Come with me, I will show you the kitchen,' she replied.

Gloria placed a pan of milk on the stove as Amelia fumbled in her bag for the baby's bottle, trying to open it with one hand while holding Robert.

'May I hold him for you?' Gloria asked.

'I can manage, thank you,' Amelia replied, struggling with the fastener.

Gloria looked on at the poor young mother and so desperately wanted to help her, she moved towards Amelia, holding out her arms towards the baby. 'Please, let me hold him, I would like to see my new grandson properly if that is alright,' she said, smiling.

The younger woman looked into Gloria's emerald eyes,

searching them for any sign that she might harm her child, but she saw none, only a kind and beautiful woman offering to help.

'I am sorry, Gloria, of course, you may hold him, I have been so used to managing on my own since Shorty went that I find it hard to accept help. I did not want Crocky to honour his word at first, I told him I would manage, but he insisted, and Crocky being Crocky is hard to resist. Please, believe me, I am very fond of him, he will make a good husband and father.'

'Crocky?' Gloria enquired.

'Sorry, yes, the chaps call him that after Davy Crockett, they all have names for each other, Shorty was such because he was the shortest, as simple as that,' Amelia replied.

Gloria held the baby who was wrapped in a knitted shawl, he was a sweet little thing with pink cheeks and blue eyes, she rocked him gently, having had four sons of her own, babies were second nature to her, and Robert settled immediately. Thus, Gloria gained a step-grandson and another daughter-in-law.

David and Amelia married at the register office two days later, Gloria and one of David's friends were witnesses. Afterwards, they had lunch at the Hotel Russel, one of the few hotels that had not been commandeered by the war office. The next day David, Amelia and Robert returned to RAF Debden, where he was to resume his command. Gloria saw them off at the station and returned to her flat in a state of bewilderment, the turn of events over the last few days had left her feeling quite dazed. She poured herself a large glass of sherry, thankfully that was not in short supply, she thought to herself and sat down, imagining what could possibly happen next that could surprise her.

Some good news came Gloria's way a few weeks later, Dwight had been granted a couple of days shore leave, not that she saw much of him as he spent the majority of his time with Rebecca at her parents' home. It was understandable, Gloria attempted to convince herself, she worried about her sons endlessly. Dwight had taken to life at sea extremely well and fortunately had escaped many close combat situations so far. When Gloria heard the news that he was to be sent out to the Mediterranean and the Middle East, it unnerved her immensely. It could be months or even years if this wretched war continued before Dwight would return home.

Riccardo had talked to Gloria about U boats and attempted to explain the campaigns that were taking place. However, her brain either could not or did not want to take the information in, to her, it only meant death and tragedy, more years of futile loss of life like the ones she had experienced during the first war. Outwardly, she displayed the strength and resistance that every Londoner presented but inwardly, fearing for her family and everyone she loved or had acquaintance with. Having already lost her beloved sister, she could not contemplate another loss.

Before Dwight returned to Plymouth, Gloria had dinner at the Marchbankses, they lived in a stylish townhouse overlooking what was left of Eaton Square Gardens following the air raids. Dwight picked Gloria up from the flat in Elias's car, and they drove through the devastation of London. They had to weave in and out along the back streets to bypass the huge craters in the roads, everywhere you looked, there were piles of rubble, bricks, and metal, and the bizarre sight of rows of houses where some stood intact, while others were reduced to ruins. It was about six o'clock in the evening, and people were returning home from work, picking their way through the debris of the streets. Gloria marvelled at how quickly human beings adapt to their surroundings, and equally, immense anger flared inside of her against the atrocities that they could also inflict upon each other.

Dwight was dressed in a beautifully tailored doe skin suit, he called it his tiddly suit. 'I had it made up for walking out, lots of us have, so we look our best on shore leave, the tailor I found even managed to put silk linings in, rather dapper is it not, Mama?'

It brought a smile to Gloria's face, and she replied, 'I would expect nothing less from any of my boys, Dwight.'

'Elias and Vicky are looking forward to meeting you again, Rebecca is having a bit of a time with her mother, her nerves are bad. Both her sisters are V.A.D's at Devonport hospital, and in between volunteering at the canteen, Rebecca is left holding the fort at home as Elias is so busy at the newspaper,' Dwight said.

Gloria did not want to think ill of Vicky Marchbank, but she had found the poor woman somewhat downtrodden when they first met, and the air raids must have torn her nerves to shreds.

They arrived at Eaton Square, and Dwight parked up, went around and opened the passenger door to help his mother out. She was wearing a knee-length navy and yellow pin-striped silk dress and wore an angora bolero around her shoulders. At fifty-five years of age, her face was unravaged by the years, and Riccardo had recently commented upon this fact, his theory being that her beauty radiated from within and would never fade. How Gloria wished he could have accompanied her tonight, they were the best of friends, however, as most doctors were, he was required day and night at the hospital tending the sick and wounded. People seemed to have forgiven him for being Italian for the time being, as doctors were so desperately needed everywhere.

Gloria entered the hallway and immediately noticed the long, wide crack in the wall caused by a bomb blast a few weeks ago, it was a stark reminder of the terrors they had all endured. Dwight led his mother to the sitting-room where Rebecca and her parents were sat chatting and sipping gin and tonics. Elias immediately stood up to welcome Gloria with his booming voice, offering her a seat and asking what she would like to drink.

'Thank you, Elias, I will have what everyone else is drinking, a gin and tonic is fine,' Gloria said. Inside her head, she thought that tonight was probably going to be a long one.

The conversation over dinner was loud and mostly one-sided, Elias led the subjects, which were mainly about the war and politics, with Dwight adding his opinions when he could. No wonder Vicky was like a nervous mouse, there was literally no room for her. Fortunately, Rebecca was possessed of a naturally sunny character, and her father's manners washed over her without any bother.

Rebecca had prepared an excellent dinner despite the shortage of many commodities. As they settled down after a remarkably good bread and butter pudding, the conversation finally turned around to Dwight's departure the following day. Elias was full of words of wisdom and advice on keeping one's sea legs on a long voyage, and there was an overall air of concern for Dwight's safety with a desperate hope for his safe return.

There were smiles and the kissing of cheeks as Gloria said her goodbyes, she climbed gratefully into the passenger seat of the car, sank back and let her son drive her home.

'I know, Mama, there is no need to say anything, the main thing is that Rebecca is safe with her father while I am away, I would imagine Elias could command a bomb to not drop on his house if needs be.' Dwight looked at his mother and laughed when he saw the expression on her face, she looked as if all the life had been sucked from her.

'Please, be careful, my darling,' she said to her son, 'no-one knows what terrors lay await, but if the first war is anything to go by, I feel certain there will be many.'

They hugged in the hallway of the flats, and Gloria fought back the tears as Dwight blew her a kiss, turned around and walked out of the door, she watched him climb into the car and drive away, hoping beyond all hope that one day she would see him again. Her heels clicked on the marble floor, and she passed by the porter sitting at the desk, he wished her goodnight.

'Good night, Daniel,' she replied.

'He'll be back, Missus Anslow, he has a spirit guardian at his shoulder,' Daniel said.

'How do you know? Can you see it?' she asked, rather amazed.

'Not all the time, but she was there, just then, an old lady, she calls herself Lizzie.'

Gloria went cold. 'My grandmama, her name was Lizzie, and she was a medium.'

'I have seen her next to all of your sons and you, Missus Anslow, she takes care of you all,' Daniel said.

'She was my favourite grandmother, I loved her with all my heart. Thank you, Daniel.'

Scarcely holding back her tears, Gloria wished Daniel goodnight once more, hastened to the lift and went up to her flat. Once inside, she threw down her bolero, poured herself a large brandy, sank into the armchair and let her tears fall.

She woke the next morning with a dull throb in her head, but then remembered that she was having lunch with Lucy that day, the thought of seeing her dearest friend cheered her somewhat, and so she arose and went to the kitchen to put the kettle on the stove to make some tea. It was just before nine o'clock as she settled down at her chrome kitchen table in one of the red leather chairs when the doorbell rang, it made her jump and spill her tea.

'Who on earth can that be at this time in the morning?' she thought to herself as she mopped the spilt tea with a cloth. The bell rang again. 'All right, just a moment,' she called out.

Tying her robe tightly around her waist, she peered through the peephole, and to her surprise, saw Julian standing there. She hurriedly unlocked the door and took off the chain. 'Julian, darling, what are you doing here? Look at you all dishevelled, what on earth has happened?'

'How could she do this to me, Mama? I thought she loved me.' He was distraught.

'Who, what, Julian, what is going on? Come in and tell me, what on earth has happened?' Gloria said.

'I was granted two days leave after all the raids we have been on, and I arrived home late last night to find Audrey......' he choked on the words, 'to find Audrey in bed with another man. How could she do this to me, with that weaselly little journalist Aurelius Trent?

'It has been going on for weeks, all the time I have been away, risking my life every night, she has been with him in our bed. We argued all night after the swine scuttled out of the door, and Audrey told me straight that she had bigger plans than me, she said Trent was going to take her to Europe to cover the war. Our marriage is over, she made that perfectly clear.'

Gloria was actually not all that shocked, more surprised that it had taken this long for Audrey to cheat on him if indeed this was the first time. Understandably, this was not what her youngest son wanted to hear, and so, she sat him down at the table and poured him a cup of tea.

'My poor, darling, Julian, this war is making people do the most extraordinary things, look at your brother, marrying his friend's widow just because he promised to look after her. Audrey was always ambitious, you knew that, although I did not take her for being quite so ruthless. There is a saying about every dog getting its day, I think Audrey will get hers in some way or another, in the meantime, you have to try and stay strong, you cannot afford to make any mistakes up there, are you listening to me, darling?'

Julian nodded his head, he was exhausted from lack of sleep and hours of night bombing raids. 'I need sleep, Mama, can I stay here, please?'

'You do not have to ask. Now drink your tea and climb into the spare bed, we will talk later. I am truly sorry, darling, you did not deserve any of that.'

Julian drank his tea, undressed and was asleep the moment his head hit the pillow. Gloria left a note telling him that she was out with Lucy, and on her return in the afternoon, she found him still sleeping. Watching her son as he lay in the bed that Ruby usually slept in, she smiled at his dark unruly curls, even Brylcreem could not tame them. How young he looked, indeed, how young all the airmen were who lost their lives daily in this ghastly war.

'Please let it be over soon, I cannot, I will not lose a son.'

Julian awoke much refreshed, he had slept solidly for eighteen hours, he showered, shaved and dressed in the uniform that Gloria had brushed up, she had washed and pressed his shirt and laid everything out for him on the bedroom chair. She cooked him breakfast from her own rations, preferring her son to have a decent meal rather than herself.

'Thank you, Mama, you know Audrey never did anything like that for me, she was always too busy writing and talking on the telephone, maybe when this war is all over, I might find myself a woman just like you, and I can spend my time with my feet up reading the newspaper.' He laughed at the thought and at the look of feigned horror on his mother's face.

'My leave is up, Mama, I have to return to Waddington, thank you for everything. Audrey already told me that she wants a divorce so she can marry this Trent chap, I cannot believe she could be so heartless, but they say love is blind, and I did love her,' Julian said with a dejected look on his handsome face.

'I know, darling, but you will survive, you have to. May I come to the station with you and see you off? It might be the last time we see each other for a while.'

'Of course, if the last face I see is that of my beautiful mother, then I will be a happy man.'

'Please do not say such things not even in jest, now get your bag and walk your old mother to the station.'

She took his arm, and they made their way to Euston, Gloria held her son for an age until he broke away. 'I have to go now, I will try and telephone, but it is not easy. I love you, Mama, take care of yourself,' he said.

'I love you too, my darling son, come home soon.' Gloria wiped tears from her face as she waved him off.

The next communication she received concerning her son was that he had been shot down over Germany and taken a prisoner of war, it was July 1941.

Through his contacts, Gabe established that Julian had been taken to Dulag Luft near Frankfurt. There were rumours of some prisoners there being tortured under interrogation, which severely added to Gloria's distress.

'Mama, please calm yourself, try and think of it in the way of Julian now being out of it,' Gabe said. 'He will not be shot down again, and provided he keeps his head down at the camp and does not do anything stupid, he will spend the rest of the war as a prisoner, yes, but out of immediate danger. He can write to us, and the Red Cross is arranging parcels to be sent out to all British prisoners of war, he will survive.'

'When will this wretched war ever end? At least you are safe on the ground, and I know you cannot talk about your work, but I am certain that with you as part of it, you will succeed,' she said. 'Have you any idea when Miriam is next home on leave?'

Miriam had been trained as a special duties clerk and worked as a plotter in the command room at RAF Uxbridge, she only came home for one week every three months, and so Ruby lived most of the time with Gloria, returning to her own flat when either of her parents came home. It did not seem to bother the little girl, the lives of all the children had been turned upside down, they seemed to take it in their stride, more so than some adults. Ruby felt loved all of the time, and that seemed to be enough for her.

Almost a year had passed since Fleur and Filkes were killed, and Gloria's telephone rang one afternoon. She picked up the receiver to hear a man's voice asking if she was Mrs Anslow.

'Yes, this is she,' Gloria replied.

'Hello, this is Mr Murton, your late brother-in-law's solicitor, I have news regarding his estate. Mr Allen's personal estate has gone through probate and amounts to just under £9000,' he said.

Gloria was quite taken aback for a moment, it was much more than she imagined. 'I see, thank you, Mr Murton.' Not that it will ever bring my beloved Fleur and Filkes back, she thought to herself.

The solicitor continued. 'The money will be sent by wire transfer to your bank, after which your solicitor can arrange to have it shared out according to Mr Allen's wishes between yourself and your four sons. Would you like to try and sell the house?'

'I do not know what to do, with this terrible war going on, who will want to buy a house like Fleur's? I suggest we leave it for now, we have to hope the war might end soon, do we not?'

'One can only hope, Mrs Anslow.'

'Thank you for your telephone call. Goodbye.'

Gloria replaced the receiver and sat down in her armchair, she thought of her sister and all the blissful times they had at the house in Ramsgate and contemplated whether she could ever face going there again. Tears rolled gently down her face, and she wondered if she were indeed cursed when she thought about the amount of death that seemed to surround her. Gerald, Lavinia, Dorothy, Edith, Lilian, Marcus, her mother and father, her adorable Nathan, Fleur, Filkes, who else will be added to the list if this vile war did not come to an end.

She contacted her solicitor and booked an appointment to make the necessary arrangements for the money transfers. None of it seemed important at this time with the world at war, she just instructed Mr Westwood to deposit the money in her sons' and her accounts and leave it alone.

Rationing and making do became the norm, and everyday life somehow continued. Musicals began to be played at the theatres once more, films were shown at the cinemas daily, and even Gloria, whose love of the theatre had never waned, became entranced with the glamour of the Hollywood film stars. She especially enjoyed the love stories, *Rebecca* being a particular favourite, and the musical comedies such as *Holiday Inn*, she was in awe of Fred Astaire's dancing. Even though she was heading for sixty years of age, Gloria was an old romantic at heart, and the films reminded her of her love for Nathan, her one true love.

'You know, Lucy, I still feel like a young woman inside, it is the mirror that tells the truth,' Gloria said on the night they had watched *Casablanca* and shed tears, 'I am sure I once looked like Ingrid Bergman.'

Lucy laughed. 'I know just how you feel, darling, I sometimes wonder how Harper can bear to look at me in the mornings. I look so frightful these days.'

'I am so glad that you have found happiness with him, he is a wonderful man. How is it for him at the war office?' Gloria asked.

'Honestly, he is telephoned at all hours to chauffeur ministers about to meetings and everywhere, as Staff Sergeant he gets to drive the Humber that Mr Churchill prefers, it has been bullet-proofed, you know,' Lucy said.

They wandered home together arm in arm, talking about their lives and what they thought the future held for them, coming to the conclusion that as long as they all survived this damned war, anything else would be a bonus.

CHAPTER 21

The newspapers were full of the invasion of Normandy by the Allied Forces, they were calling it D-Day, France was liberated, and the allies pressed on through Europe. Dwight's ship was part of the landing craft fleet taking the soldiers across the English Channel, after which many were converted to hospital ships ferrying the wounded back to England. He had been home on leave just before the invasion, and two months later, Rebecca announced that she was pregnant. The news lifted Gloria's heart, and she hoped beyond all hope that Dwight would survive to see his child born, unlike Shorty, Amelia's first husband.

David had been fortunate enough to have been transferred to Intelligence on his return to RAF Debden, he flew his last mission and was awarded the DFC for his tremendous bravery and leadership skills. Gloria attended his investiture at Buckingham Palace, it had been a proud but poignant day, with her overriding emotion being one of relief, knowing that he would now be safely on the ground and not flying again.

Julian was moved to Stalag Luft I, and from his letters, he appeared to be coping reasonably well. The camaraderie of the officers and other prisoners was tremendous, and although they were cold and hungry a lot of the time, they were treated reasonably well. He discovered he had a talent for singing and acting, maybe growing up listening to his mother's musicals had rubbed off as

Julian played leading roles in the theatrical productions that regularly took place in the camp. The chaps always made him play the leading lady, joking with him that he looked more like a girl with his dark curls and handsome face. Again, Gloria's feeling of relief that Julian was alive was overwhelming, but she also felt guilt when she thought of all the mothers who had lost their sons and daughters, and there were millions of them.

The months dragged on, and it was incredible how people adapted, London was a city of death and demolition. They travelled to work each day, shops opened with the meagre supplies they had to sell to the housewives that queued with ration books at their registered shop. What was not available legally could be obtained on the black-market if one were willing to take the risk or indeed had the money to pay the inflated prices the spivs charged.

A glimmer of joy came into Gloria's life with the arrival of Milton John Anslow in March 1945, he was small but healthy and made a welcome diversion to the horrors of the war. Rebecca had a difficult time with the birth, but with Gloria's insistence she be in Riccardo's expert hands, little Milton came safely into the world.

Elias, of course, placed a full announcement in the Times of the arrival of his grandson. And to Gloria's surprise, Vicky came out of her shell and fairly blossomed as she stepped into grandmother mode, it really was a pleasure to witness.

Victory in Europe came at last, on the 8th of May 1945, Hitler had committed suicide, and the Germans surrendered. Huge crowds gathered outside Buckingham Palace to celebrate and wait for the Royal Family to appear on the balcony. Gloria and Ruby stood with Lucy as the crowds cheered and waved, people were singing *Land of Hope and Glory* at the top of their voices, the atmosphere was one of immense relief and joy.

Gloria had to raise her voice to be heard as she said, 'It is rather a feeling of déjà vu, do you not think, Lucy?'

'Yes, darling, I remember that day clearly, we stood with Dorothy, bless her soul, and the boys, Julian was only about four years old, was he not?'

'Yes, he was, who would have known then that there would be another war? I do so hope that Julian will be home soon, surely they will all be released now, and Dwight has to make it all the way back from Singapore. I want my sons home and safe before anything else happens, I have lost my darling sister and brother-in-law to this nightmare war, I will not lose anyone else,' Gloria said defiantly.

Lucy slipped her hand through her friend's arm and squeezed it gently. 'They will, Gloria, I can feel it.'

Gloria felt a tug on her cardigan sleeve. 'Grandma, will Mummy and Daddy be at home together again now?' Ruby asked.

'There is no reason for them not to be, my darling, I am sure they will be back as soon as they can,' Gloria told her now twelve-year-old granddaughter. She was growing into a pretty girl, albeit a bit thin as were most people, but she had endured the war with incredible resolve, as had all the children that Gloria was acquainted with in their neighbourhood. 'Let us hope this is the end of it all,' she added quietly to herself.

Soon, reports of the extermination of over a million Jewish people in the concentration camps at Auschwitz began to filter through. The harrowing images on the Pathé news of the starved, skeletal prisoners in the forced labour camps were impossible to absorb, how human beings could do this to each other, Gloria could not comprehend.

Stalag Luft I had been liberated by Russian troops at the end of April, and the prisoners were evacuated. By May, Julian and the rest of the British airmen were flown home. Gloria wept tears of joy when news reached her that Julian was back on English soil. However, due to the years of imprisonment and hardships he and the rest of the POW's had endured, he could not return home immediately. They were in dire need of rehabilitation at one of the personal reception centres before they were deemed fit to go back to their families.

The war did not stop in the Pacific until two atomic bombs were dropped on Hiroshima and Nagasaki, the horror and devastation of which the world had never witnessed before. On the 15th of August 1945, the Japanese surrendered, and the war was finally over.

Once again, tens of thousands congregated in London's streets, crowds of smiling, happy faces, couples dancing and kissing, servicemen and civilians alike, everyone celebrating the end of six years of death and destruction worldwide, it was a glorious day for all. But for Gloria, her happiest moment came when her doorbell rang, and she unlocked the door to discover Julian standing in the passageway. She held her hands over her mouth as she gasped with relief at seeing her son.

'Come here, and give your old Mama a hug,' she said, not bothering to fight back her tears.

They stood in the doorway, holding each other tightly until, eventually, Julian pulled away. 'Shall we go inside, Mama? I need a drink,' he said.

He dropped his kit bag on the floor and sank into Gloria's armchair, he was exhausted from the train journey having had to stand for most of the way. The carriages were packed with ex-servicemen making their way home and civilians travelling to be reunited with loved ones from whom they had been separated during the long war years.

Gloria came through from the kitchen with a bottle of Dom Perignon that Riccardo had generously given to her a while ago.

'Save it for a special day, mio caro, you will know when that moment arrives,' he had told her, and this was that moment, the evening when her youngest son returned home after four years imprisonment, she could think of no better reason. She popped the cork and poured each of them a glass.

'Welcome home, darling.'

The conversation began rather stilted, neither of them knowing what to say until the champagne gradually worked its magic, and they began to relax. Julian told her some of what life in the camp had been like, but she felt convinced he glossed over the worst of it.

'But you know, Mama, we got off lightly compared to those poor chaps from Stalag Luft III, they were forced to march through freezing snow for miles and miles, hundreds of them died on the way before they were liberated, it was the most diabolical thing,' he told her. 'I also heard a rumour about Trent, that journalist Audrey went off with, he joined the army and was taken prisoner also, seems she was bad luck for both of us.'

'I know, darling, I did hear about it along the grapevine, she came back to England and resumed her job at the Telegraph, I understand from Dwight's father-in-law that she is actually very well respected in her field. Not something I expect you want to hear, but it is a fact, she achieved what she set out to do, I am just sorry that you had to be hurt along the way,' Gloria said.

'It matters not, Mama, there was plenty of time to think about all of that in the camp, I was a fool, you tried to warn me, but I thought I knew best, should have listened to my wise old mother.' He raised a wry smile and lifted his glass in the air, they were rather tipsy now. 'To better times ahead, I shall never take life for granted again, I feel that those of us that survived this hell has been given a second crack at it, and I, for one, am not going to waste a moment more of my life. Cheers, Mama.'

Gabe, Miriam and Ruby were soon back together as a family in their flat, and it did not take long before Gabe was able to return to his old job as publicity manager at the News. On the other hand, Miriam was expected to pick up where she left off as a mother and housewife, something that did not sit right after her responsibilities during the war, she desperately wanted more. She argued bitterly with Gabe about her situation, but the stark reality was that many of the jobs women had done during the war were handed back to men. Alas, the women were expected to return to domestic duties much as they had done after the first war.

'But I can do so much more, Gabe, please try and find me something to do at the paper, there must be something, I am going out of my mind,' Miriam had bemoaned for the umpteenth time.

'We need someone to make the tea.' Gabe had meant for it to be a joke, the vase that flew across the sitting-room aimed at his head made him suspect that his jest had not been taken in good spirit. Miriam let out an exasperated groan as she left the flat, slamming the door so loudly behind her Gabe swore his mother would have heard it two floors below.

In the meantime, David and Amelia visited with young Robert, who was now five years old, with a mop of blonde hair and blue-grey eyes, he was very quiet and clung to his mother.

Gloria wondered if Amelia had overprotected him, perhaps understandable given his circumstances. Nevertheless, David was the only father the boy knew, and Gloria was certain he treated him as if he were his own son. They had gone out for afternoon tea at Lyons and were sat with a pot of tea and scones whilst Robert enjoyed a raspberry sundae.

'We have some good news for you, Mama, two bits actually,' David said. Gloria raised an eyebrow, wondering what they would be. 'I am buying a house in Elmdon with the money that Aunt Fleur

279

left me, and I think she would have approved, it is a lovely village just a few miles from the base, the thing is, we are going to need some space for our growing family, Amelia is expecting.'

'Well, that is good news, I must say, my congratulations to you, my dear,' Gloria said to Amelia.

'Thank you, we hoped you would be pleased,' she replied.

'I do not want a brother or sister, I like it just Mummy and me, it is not fair,' Robert piped up, his mouth all sticky and covered in ice-cream and raspberry sauce.

Gloria was taken aback at the boy's words, and furthermore, surprised by Amelia not chastising her son for his rudeness, but she said nothing and kept her expression neutral.

'Now then, Robby, you know we have talked about this, your father and I want a baby of our own, it will still be your brother or sister.' Amelia said.

'But he is not my real father, you told me so, how can your new baby be my brother or sister? I do not understand.' Robby scowled.

Once again, Gloria bit her tongue, but in her mind, she wondered why they had chosen to confuse the boy by telling him at such a young age that David was not his real father. 'They must have their reasons,' Gloria thought to herself, she appreciated it was none of her business but could foresee difficulties ahead if Robert continued to feel this way.

Amelia managed to calm Robert, and they discussed plans for Gloria to visit Elmdon once the new baby had arrived, with David trying his utmost to persuade his mother that the countryside was a beautiful, quiet and calm place to live. Gloria was not in the slightest bit convinced, she had loved London from the first time she visited in 1901. It seemed like a century ago, how times had changed since then. As she sipped her tea, her life began to play out like a movie before her eyes until she heard David's voice break through her daydream.

'Mama, where on earth are you? We have to go, we promised Robby we would take him to see Dumbo at the pictures, he has never seen a film before.'

'I am terribly sorry, what was that? Dumbo? Yes, you will enjoy it, Robby, very much, I am certain.' Gloria reached into her purse and gave the boy sixpence to buy a drink or another ice-cream at the picture house.

'Thank you, Grandma Anslow.' Robby said.

At least he acknowledged her as his grandmother, Gloria thought to herself, which was good to hear.

They said their farewells, and Gloria watched her son walk away with his family, she hoped he was happy as he had an air of melancholy about him. The last time they spoke on the telephone, he said that many of the chaps who had fought so bravely during the war were being transferred here, there and everywhere to train on new aircraft. It felt as if the solidarity they had experienced during those terrible years had been taken from them. David admitted he felt quite bereft of his comrades' company at times.

He was now group captain and commander of his station, a rank he had earned through years of dedication and tremendous bravery during his twenty-years as an officer in the RAF.

Moving into the new house at Elmdon seemed to do David a power of good, and as the weeks grew near to the birth of the baby, Gloria sensed an improvement in David's manner. Then in early March 1946, Amelia gave birth to another son, whom they named Jeremy David.

So, Gloria promised to visit very soon despite her aversion to the countryside, as she was desperate to see her fourth grandchild, always careful to include Robby as if he were one of her own.

Dwight finally returned home in the spring of 1946, he had been drafted to barracks in Singapore after the war ended, and it had taken months of organisation to bring the sailors home. He was de-mobbed at Plymouth and caught the first train possible back to London, he had a son to meet, and he could not wait. He briefly called in on Gloria before heading off to Eaton Square to be reunited with his wife and son.

'You will at least stay for a cup of tea, Dwight, please,' Gloria said. Her son stood in his de-mob suit, sun-tanned from his time in the far east, and looked the healthiest out of each of her sons. For Gloria, the relief that they had all survived the war physically uninjured felt like nothing short of a miracle, and she welcomed her son with open arms, squeezing him so tightly, he begged to come up for air from her shoulder.

'It is so good to see you, darling. At last, all my boys are back home, I have missed you all so much,' she said. 'How was life at sea?'

'There is a huge world out there, Mama,' Dwight said. 'I visited places one has only seen on a map, I hope one day to be able to show my family some of them. Singapore is such a wonderful place, it might rain a lot as it does in England, but it is welcoming as it is so hot and humid. Overall though, we were very fortunate not to have suffered any great damage or loss of life, I feel very humbled when I think of all those souls that perished at sea, and I will be eternally grateful to have returned in one piece.'

They talked for a while longer about Dwight's plans now he was home, he also wanted to return to his job at the paper with Gabe and find a place to live with Rebecca and Milton. All too soon, he was kissing Gloria on the cheek and saying goodbye.

'I really must go, Mama, I am sorry, but I am desperate to see my wife and son, come over for dinner tomorrow night, please,' he said.

With all four sons home and safe, Gloria sat down in her armchair and heaved a huge sigh of relief, but what the future held for them and the rest of the country, no one really knew. England would have to rise out of the devastation the war had caused, and the new prime minister, Mr Attlee, was already promising a welfare state. Everyone would be looked after from the cradle to the grave, it was to be the dawn of a new Britain, but it also heralded the drawing of an "iron curtain", as Mr Churchill had described it, between eastern and western Europe.

With Riccardo's help and much to Gabe's relief, Miriam found herself a job at Guy's Hospital as a records clerk. Her organisational skills, honed by her work during the war, were exceptional, and she soon had the office running like clockwork.

As for Ruby, a row flared up with the announcement that she wanted to leave school and start work like many of her friends had.

'Rosemary Spencer is learning how to be a telephonist, and I would really like to work in an office and learn how to type,' Ruby told her parents. 'I could become a secretary eventually, to someone important like Daddy, it would be wonderful.'

Despite pleas from Gabe and Miriam that she should stay on for the higher certificate, the truth was, her education had suffered because of the war. She reminded Gloria of herself at that age, headstrong and independent, and doubted that Gabe would have any influence over Ruby's decision, advising him that if he wanted to keep an eye on her, he had better find her a job at the paper.

'I will see what I can do once she has finished what is left of her education, I take it she can actually read and write?' Gabe had said only half-joking.

His daughter was hardly ever at home, she was always out at some friend or another's house, Ruby was a very popular girl, attractive and witty. A boy rang the doorbell of the flat a couple of weeks ago, he was sent packing immediately, much to Ruby's disdain, and yet another argument ensued.

Gloria laughed when Gabe related the story. 'She is young and finding her feet, please do not come down so hard on her, I beg of you. I hated my father most of the time while growing up, and you know how that story transpired. Guide her, but leave her space to grow, she will be just fine.'

'What a wise old woman you have become, Mama,' Gabe teased.

'The cheek, less of the old, thank you,' Gloria replied and managed to flick her head, in much the same manner she had done as a young woman, to which Gabe burst out laughing and remarked it was like seeing Ruby's double.

Dwight was able to pick up his old job at the paper, Rebecca managed to find them a two bedroomed flat on Abbey Gardens despite the shortage of housing, and with the announcement of a second child due next January, their life, for now, was complete.

Julian, on the other hand, maintained his yearning for flying, and as an experienced navigator, he secured himself a position with BOAC. He was very excited, as the first flight from London to New York had recently taken place in July that year, and with their procurement of five Constellation planes, the company were in dire need of good crews. The glamour and appeal of transatlantic flight were in their infancy, which Julian was thrilled to be a part of. Besides, having learned of Audrey's marriage to Aurelius Trent after his release, Julian was happy to leave north London for a while, he had no desire to see them about town or read their newspaper columns.

'I will bring you back a souvenir from New York, Mama,' he said as he left Gloria's flat and headed for his new life.

CHAPTER 22

Thus, the war had ended, Gloria's family were settled once more into their respective lives, which left one thing she knew she must do, brave the countryside and visit David. Baby Jeremy was already six months old, so she could no longer put the journey off. It was a straightforward train ride, there was no excuse, even the September weather was warm and sunny. So, she packed a small suitcase for a few days stay and took a taxi to Kings Cross station. Everyone had been too busy to come with her, but she did not mind and settled herself down in the first-class carriage, looking out of the window as it pulled out of the station.

'Here goes, old girl, hopefully, the cows will be too far away from David's house to smell them, and heaven forbid there be any wretched cockerels waking me at the crack of dawn. 'David, why could you not have come back up to London?' she thought to herself as the train passed through the countryside.

It was harvest time, and she could see haystacks in the fields, with sheep and cattle dotted about grazing. Here and there were huge Shire horses pulling wagons piled high with hay as it was moved to barns in readiness for the winter.

Amelia was at Saffron Wilden station to meet her in the car, it was a red Triumph Roadster and very sleek, Gloria thought it would certainly have been the model of car Fleur would have purchased, and the thought made her feel sad. She had grieved deeply over the loss of her sister, and her house in Ramsgate was now being rented by two families as housing was in such short supply after the war, requiring those with larger homes to take in lodgers. 'What times we live in.' Gloria had thought.

It was Friday, and Robby was at school until four o'clock. Amelia had left Jeremy with a neighbour so she could pick Gloria up, greeting her with a handshake, not a kiss on the cheek. This made Gloria realise how very little she knew of her daughter-in-law, something she felt she must make amends towards.

'How was the train?' Amelia asked.

'It was fine, thank you, dear, scarcely anyone aboard actually,' Gloria replied.

She hoisted her suitcase into the boot of the car and sat in the passenger seat next to Amelia, it took them about twenty minutes to drive the five or six miles to Elmdon. Amelia handled the car with confidence, and they chatted politely along the way about how Jeremy was coming along and if Robby was enjoying school.

They pulled up outside *Field View,* it was a delightful, detached house with a thatched roof and a blue painted front door. Gloria was rather disturbed to see cows in the field opposite the house and very much hoped they would be moved elsewhere later. Amelia parked the car at the side of the house, and they both climbed out.

'Mmm, the smell of the countryside, there is nothing quite like it, do you not think, Gloria?' Amelia said.

'You are quite right there, dear, there is definitely nothing quite like it,' Gloria replied. She was trying not to make it evident that the smell of cow dung was not at the top of the list of odours she wished to inhale, it was actually making her feel a little queasy.

Amelia unlocked the front door, and Gloria followed her inside. There was a coat stand in the corner of the hallway with three pairs of gumboots around it and various sized raincoats hanging up,

Amelia spied Gloria looking slightly aghast at them.

'It gets rather muddy when it rains, they are essential items out here. I have a spare pair you can borrow, but fear not, there is no rain forecast this week, I think you will be fine.'

'Thank you, that is very good to hear,' Gloria said in a relieved tone and horrified at the thought of wearing gumboots.

Amelia showed Gloria to her room, which was actually quite pleasant, decorated in pink chintz wallpaper. A brass bedstead stood against the wall, similar to her one at home, the sheets were crisp and white, and there was a bedspread made from multi-coloured crocheted squares draped over it. A small mahogany dressing table sat under the window, out of which the view was fields of green grass and sheep.

'I will leave you to unpack while I go and put the kettle on to make some tea, Robby will be home from school soon, and I will just nip next door and fetch Jeremy, he will be ready for his tea,' Amelia said.

'Thank you, dear, you are very kind.'

Amelia went back downstairs, leaving Gloria to take in her surroundings, it was not quite her cup of tea, but she sat on the bed, which felt comfortable, this made her feel hopeful that she would get some sleep tonight. She hung up her clothes in the wardrobe, which was more akin to a walk-in cupboard, placed her night things and underwear in the chest of drawers at the side of the bed, her toiletries on the dressing table and sat for a while looking out of the window, waiting for Amelia to return.

She gazed at the nothingness on the horizon, it was a sight that was not familiar to her, the skyline of London was full of buildings, hardly anywhere had space except for the parks, Gloria was just not used to seeing nothing, and found it very strange.

After a few minutes, she heard the front door open and Amelia returning, so she made her way downstairs, very eager to meet baby Jeremy. Her face lit up when she saw him in his mother's arms, he was pink and chubby with a head of fine, light brown hair, he had Amelia's colouring as opposed to David's dark hair and eyes.

'Jeremy, say hello to your grandmother,' Amelia said and lifted up his little arm to wave it at Gloria.

'He is delightful, look at him, please may I hold him?' Gloria asked, with a huge smile on her face.

Amelia passed him over to Gloria, who had the gift of holding a baby in a way that made them feel secure. She looked at him and said, 'Hello, Jeremy, I am your Grandmama Anslow, and I am very pleased to meet you.' To her utmost delight, he smiled.

Amelia led them through to the kitchen, it was quite basic with an oak table and chairs in the centre and a range on which the kettle sat, it was singing loudly, letting them know the water had boiled. Just as they had sat down to drink their tea, they heard the front door open, it was Robby.

'Mummy, I am home,' he shouted.

'We are in the kitchen, darling, Grandma Anslow has arrived, come and say hello,' Amelia called.

He was almost six years old now, and he ran through from the hallway to greet his mother but stopped in his tracks when he saw Gloria holding Jeremy.

'Have you come to see my brother?' he said with a sulky look on his face.

'I have come to visit both of you, Robby, now come here and let me have a look at you,' Gloria said. 'My goodness, you have grown since the last time I saw you, and becoming a very handsome young man, I am very pleased to see you again.'

'Where are your manners, Robby? Say hello,' Amelia said.

The little boy spoke. 'Hello, Grandma, how are you today?'

'I am very well, thank you, have you enjoyed school?'

'Yes, thank you, we have been doing sums, reading and writing, Miss Pemberton is very nice.'

Amelia told him to go and wash his hands before tea, and he dutifully went off to do so. He came back a few minutes later and sat at the table where Amelia had placed a glass of milk and a doorstep of bread and homemade blackberry jam for him. He tucked in and cleared his plate with remarkable speed.

'May I go outside to play now, please?' he asked.

'Yes, run along, why not take your kite out on to the field? There is sufficient breeze today, I think,' Amelia said.

With Jeremy perched on Gloria's lap, happily sucking on a finger of bread and jam, the two women began to chat and become acquainted with each other. Amelia spoke about her early childhood in Norfolk, where her parents had a small farm, she was an only child, and tragically, her father died in a farming accident when she was four years old. It was impossible for her mother to keep the farm on her own, so they moved to London, where she found work waitressing. Within a year, she married again to a bank clerk, he was an older man and was very kind to them both.

'Where do they live now?' Gloria asked while passing Jeremy another bread and jam finger, he was decidedly sticky and very content.

'My step-father died just before the war started and left my mother quite comfortable, and when I married Shorty, she moved back to Norfolk to be near her sister. Unfortunately, I have not managed to see her because of the war, I really must do something about it,' Amelia said.

Jeremy had fallen asleep in Gloria's arms after his tea and milk, and Amelia was just boiling the kettle again to make another pot of tea when the front door opened, and a voice called out.

'Did you get her, darling?' It was David.

'Yes, darling, all present and correct,' Amelia replied.

David was smiling as he swooped into the kitchen and went over to kiss both his mother and wife on their respective cheeks.

'Someone looks very happy,' he said, looking at his baby son.

'He is adorable, darling,' Gloria said. 'How are you, David? you look well.'

'I have the country air to thank for it, Mama, you should move into the village to be near us,' he teased, knowing full well his mother would never leave London.

They continued to banter between each other until the front door burst open again, and Robby returned with his kite.

'It flew Father and went very high today,' the little boy said.

'Well done, old chap, I told you it would with the right wind.'

The smell of cows wafted in with Robby as he came and sat at the table, and Gloria wondered how on earth they could stand it. However, each to their own, she thought to herself and conceded that apart from detecting a little jealousy by Robby over his baby brother, they all looked happy and content, which for Gloria was more than enough.

She had planned to stay for the weekend, and it passed by quite pleasantly once ground rules were laid down, that she would not be traipsing across muddy fields, so please would they drive her around to see the little villages and the countryside. It was very picturesque, although Gloria thought she would probably die of boredom living in a small village.

On the other hand, when it was time to go home, she was very sorry to leave her little family. Robby had warmed to her, and she adored Jeremy, who cried when she handed him back to Amelia, with whom she had made a great deal of headway in forming a friendship. As for David, it was a relief to see him more relaxed than when they were up in London, despite continuing to talk about how the tremendous loss of life during the war affected him and some of the other men at the base.

David drove his mother to the station on Monday morning on his way to work and saw her safely on the train.

'Goodbye, darling,' Gloria said as he gave her a big hug and kiss. 'Amelia is lovely, and so are the boys, you must be very proud, please come up to see me when you can, I miss you, I always do.'

'Goodbye, Mama, thank you for everything you have always done for all of us, I love you,' David replied.

'I love you too, darling, goodbye.'

She climbed up the step on to the train and looked back towards her son, the look on her face was priceless as she spotted cows being herded onto cattle trucks on the other line, ready to be taken to market. David laughed out loud and wished he could have captured her expression on film but knew it would stay immortalised in his memory forever.

Following her countryside adventure, which was described to Lucy in minute detail over lunch, they planned a few evenings at the pictures and the theatre, even so, Gloria felt unsettled.

'Perhaps our age has something to do with it, Lucy, do you feel the same? As if life might pass by without us noticing, and all too soon, it will be over.'

'Perhaps the difference is that I have Harper, and I do not wish to upset you, darling, but have you ever thought of meeting someone else for companionship? I know you have Riccardo, but he is not with you every day,' Lucy said.

'Who would want an old girl like me, for goodness sake, I am far to set in my ways, I am just feeling melancholy, I should be grateful that most of my family survived this ghastly war and be done with it,' Gloria replied.

'Why not come over for dinner tonight and ask Riccardo if he is free? Harper has some supplies stashed away, I will ask him to find the cocktail shaker, and we can have some fun like the old days, what do you say?' Lucy said.

'What a marvellous idea, what time do you want us?'

'Seven o'clock?'

'Perfect.'

Riccardo was free, and the evening went as planned, the cocktail shaker was dusted down, and for the first time since the war ended, the four friends enjoyed themselves without fear of what the following day might bring. What the following morning did bring were dull heads, but also a sense of freedom at last from the war years and one of hope for the future.

Gloria and Riccardo had decided during the cocktail evening that it was time to re-establish their casino nights.

'We had such fun before the wretched war started, do you think it will be much changed?' Gloria asked Riccardo as they alighted from the taxicab outside the casino.

'Let us find out, mio caro, but I can say that one thing has not changed, and that is your beauty, look at you.' He took her hand and spun her around. 'Bella donna.'

Gloria was wearing a new Grecian style gown made from black silk, ruched in at the waist with a low v neckline front and back, which showed off her stunning diamond necklace perfectly. Even at sixty-one years of age, she had preserved her figure, and her waist had only slightly thickened. Although her hair had turned a silvery-white, her beautiful emerald green eyes still sparkled as if she were twenty.

At sixty years of age, Riccardo had also maintained his swarthy looks. He was dressed in an immaculate black tuxedo, his slick-backed hair had silvered at the temples, but his olive, Mediterranean skin had remained smooth with only a few crow's feet around his eyes. Together they were quite remarkable and turned heads as they entered the casino arm in arm.

'Good evening, Count Giordano, Mrs Anslow, it is a pleasure to see you here again after the last few terrible years,' the Maître D said as he led them to a table in the restaurant.

'Good evening, Emmanuel, it is good to be back,' Riccardo said.

They took their seats and studied the menu, and even though rationing remained, non-rationed foods such as grouse and pheasant were an available luxury and were on the menu that evening. Riccardo ordered them both a daiquiri, and over dinner they began to talk about plans for Christmas, which was only a few weeks away.

'I do wish the whole family could come together, my sons, daughters-in-law and my adorable grandchildren, and you, of course, my dearest Riccardo, it would be so marvellous,' Gloria said.

'Well, if that is what the beautiful lady desires, then we must make it happen, but first, we must see if our luck still holds at the roulette table, come take my arm, and let us make our way.'

They had an enjoyable and lucrative night, after which Riccardo walked Gloria into the lobby of her flat building and then waltzed her across the marble floor passed Daniel, who was on night duty at the desk. He smiled to himself but said nothing as he watched them, he could see the spirit of Lizzie at Gloria's side, smiling as if she knew something no-one else did.

Christmas 1946 was everything that Gloria had wished for, indeed, it had been Riccardo's and Lucy's doing that the whole family, including a heavily pregnant Rebecca, were to have dinner at Lucy's house. With the large party expected, she was the only one with a dining room spacious enough to accommodate everyone. Riccardo had long since moved his practice to rooms on Harley

Street and had a flat nearby, as a bachelor, Marcus's old house at Granville Square had been far too large for him.

Gloria's eyes travelled around the dinner table at her family and friends. Riccardo sat on her right, and to her left were Gabe, Miriam and a rather glamourous looking Ruby, wearing a green satin, shirred cocktail dress with a sweetheart neckline. She was only just fifteen-years-old and already very attractive.

Next to them sat David and Amelia with Robby and Jeremy in his highchair, he was sitting up beautifully on his own now and trying his very best to feed himself, although he missed his mouth with the spoon more often than not.

Then were Dwight, Rebecca and twenty-one month old Milton, who looked incredibly adorable in his little shorts and matching blue jacket with a white-collar. He was every bit his father's son in looks and just as lively, judging by how much he was wriggling to get down from the table.

Julian managed to make it in time after his return flight from Rio de Janeiro, which had landed earlier that morning at London airport. He arrived at Lucy's house in a taxicab, still wearing his BOAC uniform in which Gloria could not help thinking how debonair he looked. She desperately hoped that one day the right woman would walk into his life to help make up for his disastrous relationship with Audrey. She was unsure whether to tell him that her marriage to Aurelius Trent was already floundering. Within a year, he had been recruited by the Secret Intelligence Service and spirited away to an unknown location, very soon after, Audrey had been seen out with another man.

'It could only end badly once more,' Gloria had thought to herself, as Gabe relayed the information to her a few weeks ago. No, today was not the day for gossip, despite looking tired, Julian was very content with his work, enthralled with the countries he flew to and always managed to bring Gloria a souvenir from each one he visited. After his first flight to New York, he had returned with a miniature Statue of Liberty, and the smile on his face as he gave it to her brought back memories of when he was a little boy and the shell figurine he had given her. Julian could always melt her heart, and that had been one of those occasions.

A space for him had been saved by the side of Lucy, her oldest and dearest friend, Harper sat next to her, and Gloria thought about Nathan and the night they met, her eyes misted over, it was sixteen years since he died, and she would always love him. She was able to remember their years together with a warm feeling in her heart now, rather than bitterness that he was taken too soon.

'Mama, where are you?' David's voice broke into her thoughts, and she shook her head slightly as if to clear it.

'Sorry, I was miles away, darling, what is it?' Gloria said.

'Robby wants to pull a Christmas cracker with you.'

'Well, you had better come around here, young man, and bring your cracker with you.'

Robby moved to the other side of the table and held out his Embassy cracker to Gloria, who took the other end and said, 'Alright, Robby, pull.'

Gloria did a gentle tug-o-war with the cracker and made sure that Robby won, he almost fell over when it snapped. He regained his balance and hastily looked to see what was inside. There was a hat, a joke and a brass lapel badge in the shape of an aeroplane with which he was thrilled.

'Look, Grandma, it is just like Uncle Julian's, I want to be a pilot when I grow up like my real Daddy.'

His words created a momentary uncomfortable silence until Gloria rescued the situation by offering to pin his badge on the lapel of his jacket.

'Which side shall we put it, Robby, left or right?'

'This one,' he said, pointing to his left lapel.

'And which side is that?

'My left, of course.'

'Clever boy,' Gloria said and pinned the badge in place, she made a mental note to remind her to speak to David and make sure everything was well at home.

Christmas Day continued with music, of course, singing, cards and charades, then they all gathered around the wireless to listen to the king's speech, the national anthem played, and the king began.

'This Christmas Day, surrounded by our family circle in our own home, the Queen and I are thinking of that world-wide family of the British Commonwealth and Empire.

To each member of that family, the young and old, composed of so many races dwelling in so many climes, we send our heartfelt and affectionate greetings wherever you are....

We have survived the greatest upheaval in human history. Our hard-won liberties and our democratic institutions are unimpaired, our Commonwealth and Empire, though subject to the changes that time must bring, have not been disrupted by the stress and peril of war. We are celebrating Christmas as free men and in peace.

Christmas is the season in which we count our mercies.....

We are back, most of us, with those we love. The guns have ceased to kill, and the bombs have ceased to fall. Better days lie ahead. We must not concentrate too much on the difficulties of the present – they will pass – so let us rather think of the possibilities that the future may hold for us.'

The room sat in silence as they took in the words being spoken, and the king concluded his speech by saying,

'And now, my dear people, I wish you well. May the new year be full of blessing for each one of you. Welcome it when it comes with

hope and courage and greet the unseen with a cheer.'

There was much clinking of glasses and wishes of a Merry Christmas from everyone. Gloria sat on the sofa with Jeremy on her lap and observed her family and friends smile and cheer, it was a wonderfully happy atmosphere. It brought a feeling of peace and tranquillity to her heart, something she had not sensed for many, many years.

CHAPTER 23

And so, 1947 found Julian spending his thirty-third birthday in Buenos Aires, and Dwight and Rebecca's second son, Stephen Miles Anslow, came into the world towards the end of January, much to everyone's delight. Rebecca recovered from the birth quickly, and Gloria was, of course, immensely proud of her latest grandchild. As she watched Ruby blossom into womanhood and the younger children grow, her life revolved around her family and friends.

Come 1948, Riccardo was very excited regarding the founding of the new National Health Service, despite huge opposition from many doctors who were against having their private incomes taken away. Riccardo was one of the few that welcomed free healthcare for all, both rich and poor. He had witnessed far too much sickness and disease brought about by extreme poverty in his years. For him, it was only about being a doctor, and now he would be able to treat all of his patients, not just those who could afford it.

'I see a new world coming, Gloria, we cannot allow such things as the wars to happen again. I wish to see equality between men and women, with everyone given the same opportunities, it would be the most wonderful thing,' Riccardo said over dinner at their latest casino night.

'I do hope so, I would very much like my grandchildren to live in a peaceful world, we of our generation have lived through two ghastly wars, I agree it must never happen again,' Gloria replied.

They proposed a toast to peace and good times and made their way to the roulette table. Even though it was not one of their most fortuitous evenings, they did break-even and returned to their homes happy.

It was a glorious August morning in 1949 when Gloria received a rather mysterious telephone call from Gabe, asking her to meet him for coffee at the café around the corner from the office, as he had something to show her. His tone piqued her interest, so she picked up her bag, caught the tube and within an hour of replacing the telephone receiver, she was with her son.

Gabe greeted his mother with a kiss on the cheek and pulled out a chair for her to sit down. He had chosen a small table in the corner of the café, with a red and white gingham check tablecloth and a vase of pinks in the centre. The waitress came over, and he ordered coffee for them both.

'Well, what is so important that I have dashed all the way over here for, I am not as young as I used to be, you know,' she said, pretending to be out of breath.

Gabe knew full well she was teasing him and that she was in perfect health and furthermore could never resist a mystery, besides which, even though they lived in the same flats, he had not seen her for a few days. His promotion to business manager recently kept him extremely busy, nevertheless, he enjoyed his new job tremendously. Dwight had been quite peeved, and Gabe had sensed a restlessness in his brother recently.

Gabe pulled out the day's Times and showed his mother an announcement. It had been placed by a firm of solicitors in Bridgwater. It read, "*PHELPS – If Gerald, David, Dwight and Julian Phelps, believed to be the children of Lilian Phelps, late of Watchet, Somerset, would please communicate with Messrs Squibbs,*

Champeney and Mordecai, solicitors of Westminster Bank Chambers, Bridgwater, they will hear something to their advantage. Bridgwater, 2795."

'What do you think this is all about, Mama?' Gabe asked.

'I have absolutely no idea, darling, and why would anyone think that Aunt Lilian was your mother?' Gloria replied, 'I am most intrigued.'

'I thought I ought to show you first to see if you could shed any light on the matter.'

'Unfortunately, I cannot, I think we must telephone Messrs Squibbs.... who are the others?'

'Champeney and Mordecai.'

'Honestly, why do these men have such names?' Gloria said with exasperation. 'I could do with a little excitement, can you telephone from the office?'

'Yes, of course, we will go back as soon as we have finished our coffee.'

As they sipped their drinks, Gabe talked to his mother about Ruby and how headstrong she was, it was as if her son were talking about herself at sixteen years of age, and she suppressed a smile, he had absolutely no idea how to handle her, and Miriam despaired. He told her how Ruby was out every Friday and Saturday night dancing at the town hall, or wherever there was a venue, and not returning home until after midnight, often with a boy loitering about outside the flats. Whenever he asked Ruby who he was, she became very defensive, saying that he was just a boy. More often than not, any further questioning led to an argument that resulted in Ruby slamming her bedroom door and playing her jazz records as loud as possible.

'I assume Miriam has explained the birds and bees to her.'

'I have no idea, I leave all that womanly talk to women, perhaps you could talk to her?' Gabe replied.

'Leave her to me, darling, I will invite her out for tea. Now, drink up, I am dying to find out about this mysterious announcement.'

They finished their coffee and walked arm in arm around the corner to Gabe's office, he had a new sign on the door - Mr Gabe Phelps, Business Manager, and Gloria could not help feeling very proud of her son. Having forsaken his ambition of becoming a doctor or lawyer due to his father's scandalous doings, Gabe had found a niche that suited him well and made it succeed.

He showed Gloria through the door, and they sat down, Gabe picked up his telephone and dialled the operator.

'Bridgwater 2795, please,' he said.

He waited a few moments, heard the click of the connection and then a crisp woman's voice at the other end said, 'Squibbs, Champeney and Mordecai, how may I help?'

Gabe explained the reason for his telephone call and was transferred to Mr Squibbs.

'Yes, good morning, thank you for contacting us so swiftly, Mr Phelps.'

The solicitor explained that he had been instructed by Miss Mabel Jessop's executor that as Gabe and his brothers were her only living relatives, she had bequeathed her entire estate to them. They would, of course, be required to visit his office with the necessary proof of their identity, then he could read the will and inform them of the sum of their inheritance, after which they could sign the relevant documents.

Gabe had a puzzled expression on his face throughout the entire conversation as he had no idea who Mabel Jessop was. He went through the motions of replying by means of the correct responses and finished with, 'Yes, thank you, Mr Squibbs, I will contact you again to make an appointment once I can ascertain when my brothers and I can be available at the same time. Goodbye.'

He put down the telephone and looked at the expression on his mother's face, he could see she was desperate to find out what the solicitor had said, as all through his conversation, she had been silently mouthing, 'Who is it?'

'Well, come on, darling, divulge,' Gloria said.

'Who is Mabel Jessop?' he asked.

For a moment, Gloria was as mystified as her son, and then it dawned on her.

'My goodness, I remember now, she is Aunt Lilian's sister from Montreal, how odd she should think that you were all Lilian's sons, perhaps she was never told the full story about what your father did. That matters not now, we must inform your brothers and attempt to get you all together, how exciting,' Gloria said.

It took six weeks before David could take leave that coincided with Julian's flight plans, but the day arrived and Gloria, escorted by her handsome quartet of sons, boarded the train to Bridgwater. It was a long journey, but it provided them with a much overdue chance to catch up with each other's lives and reminisce about times gone by.

Gloria was rather tired when they arrived at the Royal Clarence hotel that evening, she was feeling her age a little more these days. At sixty-four, she was remarkable, nonetheless, after dinner and a brandy nightcap, she retired to bed, leaving her sons to enjoy the rest of the evening. Her room was comfortable, a little old fashioned in its décor and furniture, but it was clean, and after her long tiring day, Gloria was more than content to wash, undress and climb into bed, she fell asleep the moment her head touched the pillow.

Their appointment with Mr Squibbs was at ten o'clock the following morning, so the family had time for breakfast. Most foods continued to be rationed, but there were eggs and bacon, kippers or fishcakes and plenty of toast as bread was now out of rationing at last. Gloria felt quite sprightly after her refreshing night's sleep, although she noticed that her sons were a little more subdued and suspected a few too many nightcaps might have been consumed the previous night. They confessed this to be the case but argued it was the first time they had been together for years and had a great deal to catch up on.

Gloria glanced at her watch, it was already half-past nine.

'Come on, boys,' they would always be her boys to Gloria, 'time is marching on, and we do not want to miss our appointment with Mr Squibbs, do we now?'

The four brothers looked at each other and smiled, they adored their mother, she had been their rock throughout their lives. Always at their side during every adventure, every disappointment, every crossroad, and here she was now, more excited than any of them to find out what the solicitor had to reveal.

It was about a ten-minute walk to Squibbs, Champeney and Mordecai, the air was warm for mid-September which made the walk very pleasant. They found the office on High Street, it was an unusually shaped building with a round-shaped frontage situated at the end of the street where the road circled back on itself. They all entered through the door and were greeted by the receptionist. When she said good morning, Gabe recognised her voice as the woman he had spoken to on the telephone.

'Yes, Mr Squibbs is expecting you, his office is on the first floor, you may go up.'

The small party went up the gloomily lit, dingy staircase, and at the top of the landing were three black painted doors with brass nameplates on them, Mr C Champeney, Mr D Mordecai and Mr A Squibbs. Gabe knocked on the latter, and a deep, booming voice asked them to come in. The atmosphere felt very austere, and Gloria was trying not to laugh. 'It is like something out of a Dicken's novel,' she whispered to Gabe.

'I agree, what shall we expect on the other side of the door, I wonder,' he whispered back.

As they entered the room, a thick cloud of pipe tobacco smoke hung heavily in the air, and in the slant of sunlight that shone through the window, dust particles danced around. Mr Squibbs sat behind an enormous mahogany desk in a leather chair, he was about sixty-years old with a white beard and moustache. His attire consisted of a black three-piece suit, and it looked as if he had never bought a new one since this one had been fashioned in about 1910. Gloria bit her lip and composed herself, setting a sombre expression on her face.

'Ah, yes, good morning to you all, sit down, I think there are sufficient chairs to accommodate you,' he said.

There were five rickety-looking dining chairs set out in front of his desk on which they all dutifully sat down.

Mr Squibbs explained that he had received a small package from a Miss Letitia Carbonneau who lived in Quebec, she was apparently Miss Mabel Jessop's housekeeper. The package had contained the last will and testament of Miss Jessop, along with a letter from Miss Carbonneau addressed to us here at the office. It explained that she had taken care of Miss Jessop for the last few years after her mind began to wander and was eventually unable to take care of herself. She often spoke about her English nephews, and on numerous occasions, shown her a photograph of four handsome boys standing with her sister Lilian at London Zoo. She had made Letitia promise that after her death, she must contact Squibbs, Champeney and Mordecai, as they had always been the family solicitor when they lived in Somerset and make certain that her nephews were well taken care of. He showed them the photograph, and Gloria let out a small gasp when she recognised it.

'I took that photograph when Aunt Lilian and I took you all to the zoo to see the baby elephant that had just been born. Over the years, Mabel must have looked at the photograph and forgotten that her sister was actually your step-grandmother after she married Marcus, not your mother at all. I feel certain that must be where the misunderstanding has set in.'

'If that be the case, I will require proof of your identity, did you bring your birth certificates?' Mr Squibbs asked.

The brothers reached into their pockets and withdrew the documents, which they handed over to the solicitor, Dwight and Julian had fortunately remembered their change of name deeds. He scrutinised each one carefully, matching up each of their names with the letter in his possession from Miss Carbonneau, once he was satisfied, he returned them to their rightful owners.

'They all appear to be in order, therefore, I am now in a position to read out Miss Jessop's last will and testament.'

He opened an envelope, pulled out a sheet of paper, cleared his throat, and read it out. Once all the legal terminology had been dealt with, Mr Squibbs concluded his dialogue by announcing that the sum of Mabel's estate was to be divided equally between each of the brothers and informed them that the total sum amounted to £8401 12s 3d.

The seated party were astounded, it was far more than anybody had anticipated, and they found it incredible that a woman they had never met would leave them such an amount. Mr Squibbs concluded all the relevant business, legal papers were signed, banking details were given, and they left the office in a somewhat bemused manner.

'Did that really happen?' Gloria asked.

'I think so,' Dwight said, to which his brothers nodded in

agreement. 'It was so unexpected, but all legal and correct, we are each now about £2000 better off.'

'First thing we ought to do is take Mama out for lunch, if it were not for her, we would not be in this fortunate position,' Gabe said with a big grin on his face.

They all linked arms and headed off along High Street, where they found a pleasant restaurant to eat and discussed the morning's events. Gabe had already decided to put his share of the money in a trust for Ruby to receive when she reached twenty-one years of age. David agreed that he too would put his share away for Robby and Jeremy, Julian had no idea what to do with his other than invest it at the bank.

'What about you, Dwight, darling, will you do the same for Milton and Stephen?' Gloria asked.

Dwight looked a little uncomfortable and flushed slightly before he spoke. 'Actually, now that we are all here together, I might as well tell you of my plans which the receipt of this money, alongside Aunt Fleur's, will let take place.'

'This is all rather mysterious, darling, what plans?' Gloria asked.

'Well…. since I returned after the war, I have not really been able to settle, there is so much more to see in the world with different opportunities, and Rebecca and I want the best for our boys. Elias has a friend at the Courier Mail in Brisbane who would take me on willingly as advertising manager, they are crying out for people to emigrate to Australia. There is so much space and land, one can live in a house by the sea rather than in flats with everyone on top of each other…..' He caught the look on his mother's face, and a feeling of guilt rose inside him.

'I know it is the other side of the world, Mama, but Rebecca and I have talked it through, and it is what we want. There is much to plan, and it will take quite some time to put everything in place, it could be a few months before we leave.'

Gloria was very taken aback, she heard the words but could not take them in, the other voices around her sounded distant in her ears. Julian heartily agreed with his brother, having seen numerous different countries himself over recent years. David was all in favour of living with space and fresh air around you, and Gabe looked a little sheepish as if he had already been aware of Dwight's plans.

Nothing they said could take away the awful feeling Gloria had that if Dwight took his family to Australia, she might never see them again, and at this moment, the thought was too much for her to bear. She put on a brave face, and although the mood of the lunch table was more subdued following Dwight's revelation, she would have ample opportunity to talk to him when they returned to London. Therefore, they all finished their lunch and headed off to the train station.

It was very late when they arrived at Euston, and Gabe walked slowly home with Gloria to their flats, she spoke to her son as they walked. 'I am suspecting that you knew about your brother's plans, why did you not tell me, Gabe?'

'Even though I knew, I never thought he would go through with it, but this inheritance has made it financially possible for him now. You still have me, David and Julian, and nothing is stopping you visiting Australia, ships do go there regularly, you know, just think what an adventure it would be,' Gabe said.

'I know, darling, it was just a bit of a shock, that is all, I have just got you all back home safe after the war, and now Dwight will be off again, but if a new life in Australia is what he desires, then it is not for me to stand in his way. But for now, I am exhausted and would like a good night's sleep, I think this has all been quite enough of an adventure for one day,' she replied.

They reached Endsleigh Court, and Gabe saw his mother to her door, he kissed her and wished her goodnight.

'Goodnight, darling, I will see you tomorrow,' Gloria said.

Five months later, Gloria stood on the docks of Southampton port waving wildly to Dwight, Rebecca, Milton and Stephen, tears were streaming down her face as the *SS Esperance Bay* slowly pulled out of the harbour. Gabe put his arm around her shoulders, and she leaned against him.

'Do you think I will ever see them again?' she sobbed.

When they could no longer see the gigantic ship on the horizon, Gabe turned his mother around and walked her to the hire car, he opened the door of the blue Triumph Mayflower, and she sat down in the passenger seat looking utterly bereft. She was clutching the present Dwight had given to her just before he boarded the ship with his family for the month-long journey. It was a beautiful red leather writing case, with a pad of Basildon Bond airmail paper and envelopes inside, he had also bought her a silver Parker fountain pen with the promise that they would write to each other monthly.

Gabe was about to speak and tried to say something which might console her, but Gloria raised her hand and said, 'Please, darling, no, there is nothing you can say, leave me a while, I will be alright soon.'

He drove to the train station in silence, glancing sideways at his mother every now and then, she stared out of the window for the entire journey. He could sense her distress and also the immense effort she was making to compose herself. By the time they had parked up the car and boarded the train, she had powdered her nose, re-applied her lipstick and gave Gabe a small smile across the table. He took her hand and said, 'It will be alright, Mama, by all accounts they will have a marvellous life, we must be happy for them, I will miss him too, I was closest to Dwight than the others you know, working at the paper was our life for many years, I will find it impossible to replace him.'

Mercifully in Gloria's life, there was never much time to feel sorry for oneself, there was always a diversion around the corner, and it was on Julian's latest return from New York that summer with a fiancée at his side that pulled Gloria out of the doldrums. Her name was Lara Jablanczy….

'We met at the hotel in New York where Julian stayed before his return flight to England on each journey, I was the receptionist. We became very friendly and went for dinner a few times, and before we knew it, we had fallen in love.'

Lara spoke with a strong eastern European accent, and it transpired that her husband had been shot and killed in 1946 on the border between Hungary and Austria whilst they, and many others, were attempting to flee the east as the iron curtain descended. After months of tremendous hardship, Lara and her friends arrived in England as refugees and were able to start a new life. Lara had always dreamt of going to New York and saved up enough money for her passage, it was everything she had imagined it would be and meeting Julian made it perfect.

They were talking over dinner, Julian wanted it to be a special evening and, moreover, for his mother to approve of Lara in view of his disastrous first marriage. Across the table, Gloria was able to study Lara, the woman was in her late twenties, a few years younger than Julian, and very beautiful. Her long dark brown hair was swept up in a French twist accentuating her large dark brown, almost black eyes. She had all the appearance of a Romanian gypsy woman, and for a brief moment, Gloria remembered Madam Burton and smiled inwardly to herself at how foolish all of that seemed now.

Lara was wearing a black satin swing dress, and she looked at Julian adoringly, the only flaw in her complexion was a scar on her forehead about an inch long, the cause of which Gloria thought it best not to know. Lara had already found work on reception at the Savoy Hotel, her experience from working in New York stood her in good stead, and she settled in immediately.

The dinner passed most agreeably, and it was gone midnight when Julian hailed a taxi to take Gloria home. He insisted the driver drop her at the entrance to the flats and paid for the fare. He kissed his mother's cheek and gave her a hug, whispering in her ear, 'I hope you like her, Mama, I love her very much.'

'Yes, darling, I do, marry her and be happy,' Gloria replied.

They married the following July at St Pancras church, all the family came to the wedding, except for Dwight, of course. Sadly, Lara had no family of her own, but her friend Betty was maid of honour and Ruby bridesmaid. She had been thrilled when Lara asked her, nineteen-year-old Ruby was very taken with her new Aunt. Indeed, she was quite in awe of her glamorous looks and sense of style, and they often went shopping together. Ruby had grown into a confident young woman and achieved her ambition, she was now personal secretary to the Kensington Post editor and enjoyed life immensely.

There was a small reception at the Savoy, thanks to Lara's manager, and after spending the night in the bridal suite, the newly married couple flew to southern Spain for a honeymoon in the sun. Lara returned pregnant and gave birth to a beautiful baby girl in April 1952. They named her Christina Linda Huxley, she was a delightful bundle of dark hair and complexion, just like her parents, and Gloria was absolutely thrilled to have another granddaughter.

EPILOGUE

As one would expect, Gloria lived the last years of her life to the full. Riccardo retired from the National Health Service in 1958, and he proposed to Gloria the day after his retirement, confessing he had loved her from the first time they met. Although Nathan was the only man Gloria had truly loved, wholly and passionately, she loved Riccardo as a dear friend and companion and agreed to marry him.

Despite both being in their early seventies, life became a whirlwind of travelling and seeing the world, and Riccardo had the perfect surprise up his sleeve. For their honeymoon, he arranged a trip to Australia to visit Dwight, whom Gloria had not seen for eight years. They boarded the *Rockhampton Star* to Brisbane for the month-long passage and marvelled at the countries and places they visited at the various stop off ports along the way, all captured on Gloria's new Kodak cine movie camera, of course.

Dwight, Rebecca, thirteen-year-old Milton and eleven-year-old Stephen greeted them at Brisbane port, waving wildly from the dock as the brand new Blue Star line passenger ship pulled in.

Tears of joy streamed down Gloria's face as she squeezed her son tightly, eventually breaking away to greet Rebecca in much the same manner. Milton and Stephen watched in awe of their grandmother, who had disembarked wearing black slacks, a leopard fur coat and a beret. She looked fabulous.

Dwight and his family lived in a magnificent Colonial-style

house in the suburbs of Brisbane, with a porch overlooking the beautifully manicured garden. Gloria spent hours sitting there with her family, talking and learning about their life in Australia. The boys had flourished in the beautiful climate, they were tall and strong from swimming and sports and sun-tanned from the outdoor life they led. Dwight was extremely successful and well respected at the Brisbane Courier Mail and very content with the life he had made for his family.

Gloria and Riccardo stayed for two months, and when it was time to return to England, as much as she knew she would probably never see the family again in her lifetime, the parting was a happy one. She could easily see that Dwight's decision to emigrate had been the right one for them.

On their return to England, Gloria and Riccardo planned their next adventures, deciding that life was now far too short to spend the rest of their time in London.

They flew to New York together and took a European tour, including Italy, as Riccardo expressed a desire to see Rome once more before he died. He showed Gloria his old ancestral home in Tuscany, now a shell of the immense villa it had once been when the Giordano family were wealthy and held title.

'Yes, I confess my father was a count, although the family fortune has long been lost and our home fallen into disrepair, I still hold the title of Conte, but it is of no significance now,' he told Gloria.

'I always took you for a nobleman, my dearest Riccardo, you make me a very happy contessa,' she laughed and kissed his cheek.

The years passed, and in 1966 after a lifetime of good health, Gloria began to feel unwell, her heart was starting to fail, and there was very little Riccardo, or anyone could do other than keep her company and ensure she was comfortable. She never had the heart to sell her sister's house in Ramsgate, and when she became ill, Riccardo had made sure they moved there permanently for the cleaner air, much to Gloria's indignation. Her love for London had never diminished, and despite her protests, Riccardo insisted.

It was a lovely, warm, sunny day in July, the sun filtering through the bedroom window, the soft breeze gently blowing the lace curtain as Gloria lay sleeping. Riccardo, Gabe and David were seated around the bed, whispering amongst themselves when her eyes opened slowly, and she blinked in the sunlight.

'Are you there, my darlings?' she asked in a weak voice. 'Come closer and sit with me.'

At eighty-one years of age, her beautiful emerald green eyes were fading, but she managed to smile at her husband and eldest sons and spoke quietly.

'Take care of each other, my darlings, and the family, it is your turn now, I am so tired.'

Riccardo stood up and listened to her heart with his stethoscope, it was beating very slowly.

'Rest, Mama, and save your strength,' Gabe said worriedly.

'I knew Madame Burton was wrong, I did find true happiness.... in all of you. Everything will be alright, please, do not worry, I have had a wonderful life,' Gloria whispered and held out her hand towards them.

They each wrapped one of their hands around it and watched as her eyes gradually closed, and she gently passed away.

THE END

ACKNOWLEDGEMENTS

A special thank you to Steve Wells for the front cover illustration.

And a huge, special thank you to my husband, Richard, for his encouragement and patience over the months of writing Gloria, and for just being him...

Other books by Emmaline Severn

RICHARD THOMAS PARKER – As a family descendant, Emmaline writes a true account of the events leading up to the hanging of Richard Thomas Parker, the last man to be publicly hanged in Nottingham, on 10th August 1864, for the murder of his mother at Fiskerton, Nottinghamshire.

"STEADY AS SHE GOES"
The poignant wartime memories of a WWII navy 'medic'

Told as a touching conversation between father and daughter in his latter years, this short story recounts his memories of that time.

Also published by the author with the **Field Detectives** under the name **Catherine Pincott-Allen**

A FURTHER ACCOUNT OF THE HACKER FAMILY - This book is a focused research project on Colonel Francis Hacker's genealogy, primarily his direct ancestors and descendants during the 17th to early 18th century. It helps dispel some of the myths and legends surrounding their family tree. It also touches on the historical facts relating to Francis's involvement in the execution of King Charles I in 1649, which ultimately led to Francis's own execution on 19 October 1660.

9 781738 556823